PELICAN BOOKS

A HISTORY OF MODERN JAPAN

Richard Storry was born in Doncaster in 1913. He was educated at Hill House, Doncaster, Repton, and Merton College, Oxford, where he was awarded a Postmastership in History. On leaving Oxford he went to Japan, early in 1937, as lecturer at the Government College of Commerce in Otaru, a seaport on the northern island of Hokkaido. Returning to England in 1940 he served during the Second World War as an army officer in the Middle East, Singapore, India, and Burma. In 1949, as a Research Scholar of the Australian National University, he was attached to the Australian Diplomatic Mission in Tokyo. As a Research Fellow of the National University he spent a further eighteen months in Japan, in 1953–4 and returned there on many occasions.

Richard Storry was Emeritus Professor of Japanese Studies at the University of Oxford and Emeritus Fellow of St Antony's College, Oxford. He is the author of *The Double Patriots: A Study of Japanese Nationalism*, published in 1957, co-author, with F. W. Deakin, of *The Case of Richard Sorge*, published in 1966, and author of *The Way of the Samurai* (1978) and *Japan and The Decline of the West in Asia 1894–1943* (1979). He also edited *Mirror, Sword and Jewel* by Kurt Singer (1972). Richard Storry died in 1982.

A HISTORY
OF MODERN JAPAN

———

Richard Storry

PENGUIN BOOKS

PENGUIN BOOKS

Published by the Penguin Group
27 Wrights Lane, London w8 5TZ, England
Viking Penguin Inc., 40 West 23rd Street, New York, New York 10010, USA
Penguin Books Australia Ltd, Ringwood, Victoria, Australia
Penguin Books Canada Ltd, 2801 John Street, Markham, Ontario, Canada L3R 1B4
Penguin Books (NZ) Ltd, 182–190 Wairau Road, Auckland 10, New Zealand

Penguin Books Ltd, Registered Offices: Harmondsworth, Middlesex, England

First published 1960
Reprinted with revisions 1961
Reprinted 1963, 1965, 1967
Reprinted with revisions 1968
Reprinted 1969, 1970
Reprinted with revisions 1972
Reprinted 1973, 1975
Reprinted with revisions 1976
Reprinted 1978, 1979
Reprinted with revisions 1982
Reprinted 1983, 1984, 1985, 1987, 1988

Made and printed in Great Britain by
Hazell Watson & Viney Limited
Member of BPCC plc
Aylesbury, Bucks, England
Set in Monotype Baskerville

For Isamu

CONTENTS

PREFATORY NOTE

The author wishes to record his gratitude to the late Sir Vere Redman, who was the first to suggest that he should write this History, and to Warden Deakin and the Fellows of St Antony's College, Oxford, for their support and encouragement while it was being written.

INTRODUCTION

No European, surely, can ever feel that he is qualified to write an entirely adequate history of an Eastern country. Certainly for a Western historian Japan presents peculiar difficulties. For although the social and political changes in Japan during the past hundred years have been both drastic and widespread, nevertheless the Japanese nation has been spared, so far, the ultimate upheaval of a violent revolution. Thus in spite of everything a certain basic continuity with past traditions, some of them very ancient, has been preserved. In Japan, as in Great Britain, old and new exist together, are indeed intertwined: but so are East and West. In fact it is becoming increasingly less easy to separate the specifically Eastern and Western components of Japanese life and thought. Anybody who travels to Japan by way of Asia must feel on arrival that he has entered a semi-Western environment. Yet the longer he remains in the country, the more clearly he will perceive that Western ideas and techniques, now generally accepted and applied, sometimes undergo a subtle but definite change when transplanted to Japan. This was much more true, of course, in the first quarter of this century, and earlier, than it is today. It could be claimed, indeed, that the younger generation – those who were born at least a decade after the Pacific War – greatly resemble their contemporaries in Europe and America. In course of time the similarities between Japan and the West may outweigh the differences.

The factor, then, that lends great interest to the history of modern Japan, and makes the writing of it a peculiarly challenging task, is the Japanese response to intrusion by the Western world. For this response was a highly nervous, vivid compound of love and hate. The same might be said, no doubt, of India or China. But Japan was the first country in Asia to be industrialized and therefore the first in Asia to use the weapons of the West against the West. The Western world, feeling through the agency of Japan the first modern intrusion by the East, responded with emotions not fundamentally different from those experienced by the Japanese. This powerful interaction, much of it so recent as to make a detached view of it all the harder to grasp, has shaped Japanese history over the last ten or eleven decades.

It is this period that forms the main substance of the following pages, although the first three chapters will deal with earlier centuries, starting from the shadowy beginnings of Japanese history.

Let us begin, however, by narrowing the focus down to a single, fictional, Japanese family today.

It is a winter's evening in Tokyo. In a four-roomed house in one of the western suburbs a family sit after supper enjoying the glow from an electric foot-warmer, known as a *kotatsu*, sunk in the centre of the floor. Over the shallow square pit that contains the heater is a low table. Over the table is a large quilt, perhaps twice as large as the table. Round the table, sitting on cushions on the floor with their stockinged feet hanging into the pit and with the quilt covering their knees, sit four people of different ages. They are old Mrs Saito, her son, her daughter-in-law, and favourite grandchild, a young man in his twenty-first year. This young man, Saito Mamoru, * is lecturing his elders on the aims and ideals of the Chinese Communist Party – a theme on which he considers himself to be an expert, for he is one of the most active members of the Chinese Friendship Association at his university in Tokyo.

Old Mrs Saito, now approaching eighty, can scarcely follow him – he uses the jargon of the Left intelligentsia and his speech is prickly with English and German words – but she senses that his remarks are both dangerous and wicked, and she becomes increasingly restive and disapproving. His father, Saito Terao, is more sympathetic, but as he dislikes seeing the old lady provoked he will soon take her side and tell his son to stop talking. This will be the cue for his mother, Saito Shizue, to act as peacemaker, to get up and fetch some

* Following the accepted custom in Japan, surnames are given before personal names.

bean cakes, or to suggest that they watch television. This is the crisis of the evening. The young man, Mamoru, will lose his temper and shout at his mother; whereupon his sister, sitting just outside the circle, will look up in irritation – she has been deep in a magazine devoted to pop music – and complain of the distracting noise. Everybody's face becomes suddenly red with embarrassment or anger. Grandmother says she will go to bed. Her daughter-in-law speculates aloud on the feelings of the neighbours. In the end, as on so many other evenings, Mamoru will apologize for his bad manners, but not for his opinions, and a rough kind of harmony will be restored in this overcrowded house until the next row. The Saitos are in some ways a typical urban Japanese family.

On the whole they are fortunate. Mr Saito, being now fifty-five, must retire this year from his managerial post in a large company; but he will be retained as a part-time consultant, and he has some savings. Things are not, of course, what they were before the war, when his parents had been able to employ a servant, a country girl who was happy to receive the equivalent of £3 a month and her keep, with holidays twice a month and three days every New Year. Food, for the salaried man, was cheap in those days; and public transport was not invariably overcrowded.

Still, life had been much worse at the end of the war and in the first two years following the surrender. After the incendiary bombs had burnt the house in Tokyo, with all its contents, to a heap of ashes and charred timber, his parents lived for weeks in an air-raid tunnel. Eventually, through the kindness of relatives, they found a plot of suburban land to rent; and on this they built, with borrowed money, the home in which Mr Saito now lives. When first built it consisted of one room only. It was the strain of this undertaking, as much as general debility from malnutrition, that killed Mr Saito's father in the winter of 1947. It was soon after the old man's death that Mr Saito joined the firm that was to engage his wholehearted loyalty for the next three decades. This company, once the Korean War was under way, began to make very large profits; and when the Korean War boom ended in 1953, the year of Mr Saito's marriage, the firm blossomed into a much larger organization, somewhat in debt to the banks, but not over-worried on that score. Before the war the president of the company had been at the same college as the managing director of one of these banks and was related by marriage with two directors of another.

The troubles of the family, as Mr Saito would be the first to admit, are spiritual rather than material. Mr Saito, if asked to explain, would put it this way.

During the Pacific War there was something to die for. He never had much use for the old army. He had feared and disliked the military instructors of his school days, and his recollections of regular army officers were, on the whole, disagreeable. He had served throughout the Pacific War in central and south China. He had not risen above the rank of Superior Private, and he recalled, with some bitterness, the bullies who had commanded his platoon and company. There were exceptions, of course. His battalion commander had been an admirable man, stern but not unjust, an inspired and inspiring officer. The regimental commander had been like god, as though sharing some of the holiness of the Sovereign whom he so devoutly represented and served. Nevertheless, as Mr Saito might reflect, that regimental commander, astride his horse reviewing his battalions in the dust outside some walled Chinese city, was as narrow-minded as the run of Japanese army officers, who, after all, had led the country into a disastrous war against the United States and Great Britain. Why fight both at the same time? Better to have concentrated on Britain first. Everybody knew that America was too strong. No; the old army was too like the old police force. You might respect them. Often you feared them. But below respect and fear there was, for an intelligent man, a very secret contempt.

And yet, this having been said, there was a certain spirit about the old days. All that talk about Japan's mission, about the emperor's unique position in the world, about the matchless virtues of the national morale – all that talk had a residual glory, for a Japanese, that no post-war disillusionment, however severe, could entirely shatter. It was a matter of ethics. Since the people knew that they were the twigs and branches of a mighty tree, whose trunk was the imperial family, it was natural for them to be honest and punctilious in their dealings with each other and in their mutual relationships within the family. Hardships could be endured in such a cause as the emperor's. And no corps of officers or police could stand between the love of the individual for his god-descended ruler.

Nowadays all that kind of thing had disappeared. Everybody was free, or claimed the right to be free. Schoolchildren knew little, sometimes nothing, of their country's history; and if they were aware that there was an emperor living in Tokyo they had no idea of his divine descent. Educational reforms under the Occupation and left-wing teachers had overthrown the old, narrow, severe, but still (in Mr Saito's phrase) 'spiritual' school system in Japan. There was no moral instruction at school. No wonder then that, as they grew up, children were so rude to their elders, so selfish, so infected with Communist ideas. Things had come to a pretty pass when an eldest son could insult his own father to his face, or a daughter announce openly her intention to marry a man of her own choice, without reference to the plans made for her by the older members of her family.

Such thoughts disturb the soul of Mr Saito as he lies beside his wife on a thin mattress on the floor of the room in which, an hour before, the family had been wrangling.

In the next room the old woman turns her head uneasily on the old-fashioned wooden pillow to which she has been accustomed all her life. It is not the pillow that keeps her awake. Looking back on her youth she can remember no emotional friction as persistent as that which disturbs the family today. She blames her daughter-in-law for most of the trouble. When she thinks of the way she had to obey her own mother-in-law, old Mrs Saito cannot refrain from sighing at the easy life of younger married women in modern times.

Old Mrs Saito no longer trembles at the recollection of that mother-in-law of sixty years ago. For through self-discipline she came in the end to be dutiful in heart as well as manner. Her mother-in-law had been born when Japan was still feudal, with a Shogun in Yedo and the land divided among the *daimyo*. The emperor dwelt in Kyoto, secluded and holy. Her mother-in-law's immediate forbears were provincial *samurai*, two-sworded warriors who walked before their *daimyo* as he was conveyed by palanquin on the long annual journey to Yedo. Although she had no first-hand memory of that world, she had seemed mentally very close to it. She had been raised, of course, in an environment increasingly dominated by such importations as banks, post offices, railways, telephones, and cameras, but she never appeared to be quite at home with them. She never wearied of telling her daughter-in-law the story of the Emperor Meiji's funeral in 1912, of how she had sat that summer night near the Outer Moat, pressing her forehead against the cold pavement as the cortège passed, with its whine of flutes and creaking of ox-wagon wheels.

Old Mrs Saito well remembers the February night in 1936, when her mother-in-law died. There was deep snow on the ground. It took ages to find a doctor. Thank goodness, thinks Mrs Saito as sleep closes upon her, the old lady never lived to endure the air raids nine years later.

Young Saito Mamoru in the third room, in bed with his brother, listens with impatience to his grandmother's snores, loud through the paper screens. There is no virtue in these old people. They hate the new Japan. My father fawns on the Americans but in his heart he is repelled by the very thought of them. Yet he would sooner have them controlling Japan than see our country socialist. He would sooner have me a drunkard, sooner see me fritter away my life at pinball, than know that I have sympathies with the Communist Party. Why don't I leave home? But I can neither go nor stay. After all, it is terrible to be a Japanese.

Unable to sleep, Saito Mamoru switches on the electric light, hanging low above his mattress, and begins reading in

a left-Socialist magazine an account by one of his own professors of a recent visit to Peking. Probably he will never know
that at middle school his father, too, had 'dangerous thoughts'
and would read far into the night while the others slept. The
books then were translations of Wells, Shaw, and Sorel.

In the Saito household there is a reflection of the tensions
that afflict Japanese families today – the mutual opposition
of half-discredited tradition and inconoclastic experiment.
Saito Mamoru and his sister, although they are hardly aware
of it, are products of the American Occupation, Japan's
fourth and latest cultural invasion, though not, surely, her
last. The other three have left their traces in the Saito home.

Near the Shinto 'God-shelf', a small shrine on the wall
above the sleeping figures of Mr and Mrs Saito, there is a
miniature Buddhist temple, a reminder of the first cultural
invasion of Japan in historical times, that of Buddhism from
China in the sixth century A.D. In the cramped little kitchen
there are the remains of a sponge-cake, a gift from one of
Mr Saito's business friends. This type of cake, known as
kasutera, was introduced to Japan by the Portuguese in the
sixteenth century, together with Christianity. The latter the
Japanese were to reject for more than two centuries; but
they kept the cake. This second cultural invasion, which included some rudimentary but useful scientific knowledge
acquired mainly from the Dutch, was not substantial, compared with the first and third, but it produced its own
important reaction.

The third invasion, also from the West, began in the
middle of the nineteenth century, soon after Japan was
opened, at the point of the gun, to foreign commerce. It
lasted with varying degrees of intensity until the outbreak of
the Pacific War. Its manifestations in the Saito house are
too numerous to be listed; they include, it might be said,
every article of Western use in the home – from the strip
lighting to the shoes and gumboots standing in the front
porch, from the coathangers in the cupboard to the boy's
bicycle pump near the kitchen door. The family now have a
flush lavatory, refrigerator, washing machine, and fly

screens on the windows, so it can be said that the fourth, American, invasion has made a material alteration to the house. And, as we have seen, its non-material effects have been considerable.

Inextricably mingled with these adaptations and borrowings from abroad are the traditional appurtenances of Japanese life: the straw *tatami* matting covering the floor; the deep bath and wooden containers used in the bathroom; the rice container with its flat wooden server, like a sculptor's palette knife; the rope sandals in the lavatory; the *geta*, or clogs, by the front door; the quilts and sleeping garments; Mrs Saito's set of ceremonial tea utensils; the *kakemono*, the hanging scroll, in the recess of the main room; the *sake* (rice wine) bottles and cups; the teapot in the kitchen; and many other objects of humble and daily use. Most of them, it is true, derive from China or from Chinese influence. But they have become uniquely and traditionally Japanese.

The Shinto *kamidana*, the 'God-shelf', and the tiny Buddhist temple enshrine the spirits of the family ancestors; and even Mamoru sometimes prays briefly before them in the morning, though his prayer may be for a Communist Japan. When the old lady prays she is talking to her parents-in-law, to her mother-in-law especially, and to her husband, the indirect victim of war-time semi-starvation. But the *lares et penates* of the house include a wider company, a host of ancestors – warriors, merchants, farmers. Above and behind these are the greatest gods of all, the emperors, stretching back in line from the present ruler through Taisho and Meiji to the Sun Goddess. It is a proud, powerful, oppressive tradition, the finally inescapable legacy of long racial homogeneity, of rigid formalism and limited but incomparable art shattered time and again by the outrageous violence of man and nature. Such is the aura, intangible but omnipresent, imposed upon the Japanese by their history.

It can be argued that Commodore Perry, when he forced the gates of Japan in 1854, performed a prime disservice not only to Japan but also to the world. Pearl Harbour, one might claim, was the logical, indeed inevitable, delayed rejoinder to an unwanted intrusion by the West. The validity of this claim rests upon the nature of the Japanese race. Japan has been called, at different periods in modern times, the Britain and the Germany of the Far East. The Japanese have been described variously as quaint, brutal, sensitive, callous, refined, coarse, loyal, fickle, lovers of beauty, and creators of ugliness. Influences from China, Korea, Europe, and America have contributed their share to this contradictory amalgam. So that it is hard at times to isolate specifically native elements. Nevertheless the impact of something peculiarly Japanese, in art and war and commerce, has been a formidable phenomenon of the past eighty years. We have only to reflect upon such matters as *hara-kiri*, the tea ceremony, the Kamikaze planes, or the delicacies of Japanese painting. There may be stranger nations than Japan. But none, surely, in recent history has been so praised and so reviled, so much discussed, so little understood.

Chapter 1

THE EARLY CENTURIES

[1]

IN the bright autumn sunshine of a day in November 1940 some fifty thousand Japanese, all specially invited, were gathered before a pavilion erected on the plaza, or great open space, in front of the Imperial Palace in the heart of Tokyo. In the pavilion, facing the multitude, were the emperor and empress together with members of their family. The occasion was one of peculiar dynastic and national importance. For it was the commemoration of the 2,600th anniversary of the founding of the empire, in 660 B.C., by Jimmu Tenno, the first emperor and direct ancestor of the twentieth-century ruling house.

Japanese scholars who had made some study of the matter were well aware that there was not the slightest valid historical evidence for the tradition that the empire was founded in 660 B.C. But until the end of the Pacific War a critical approach to the national myths was apt to lead the unwary into the crime of *lèse-majesté*; and more than one teacher in the academic world had lost his livelihood for questioning the accuracy of the ancient legends. For these were presented as essential spiritual truths, if not as literal historical fact, to all Japanese children in the first years of their primary education.

However, in Japan now as much as anywhere, it is recognized that the origins of the Japanese people have not been traced to the satisfaction of scholars. There is general agreement only on the proposition that the very early ancestors of the Japanese were immigrants from the Asian continent, from China, Manchuria, and Korea. Some have argued persuasively that there is a strong oceanic or Malay strain in the

Japanese race; but until further evidence can be discovered this theory must be regarded as no more than tentative.

It is clear, at any rate, that before the arrival of what must have been successive waves of immigrants Japan was inhabited by a race which now survives in dwindling numbers in the norther island of Hokkaido. This is the Ainu. Pure Ainu – and there are very few of them today – show many points of difference from the Japanese. Their physiognomy, for example, is not only hirsute but also markedly non-Mongolian. Their large, round, sad eyes suggest a Caucasian origin. They have never had a written language; and their religion is a form of animism, in which the bear has a special cult of its own. Up to very recent times their way of life has been that of the hunter and fisherman. In their heyday they were great warriors. Certainly they gave the Japanese a good deal of trouble, and it was many centuries before they were effectively subdued. The derivation of many Japanese place names, including that of Mount Fuji, can be found in the Ainu language; and it is probable that certain Ainu superstitions became incorporated in ancient Shinto beliefs. By the end of the twentieth century the Ainu, as an identifiable race, are unlikely to exist. But we should not forget that they were almost certainly the original inhabitants of the Japanese islands, that they played their anonymous but important part in the history of Japanese religious and social development.

The people from the continent of Asia, who in the distant and so far unidentifiable past drove the Ainu from portions of south-west Japan, regarded themselves as descended from higher or superhuman beings whom we may call 'gods'; although the Japanese word, *kami* – often translated as 'god' – has a wide range of meaning, embracing anything superior or powerful as well as divine. An elaborate mythology, depending for centuries on oral tradition, grew up around these ancestral deities. So far as we know it was not until the eighth century A.D. that this mythology was recorded, fully, in writing; and it is now accepted by Japanese as well as Western historians that the two great chronicles, the *Kojiki* and *Nihon Shoki*, covering the early myths were compiled in order to consolidate the position and enhance the prestige of the ruling imperial house.

To relate here in detail the story told in the *Kojiki* and *Nihon Shoki* might be tedious for the general reader, especially when it is remembered that the old myths play little part in the education of the younger generation of modern Japanese. But just as the Arthurian legends have a place, however undefined, in the heritage of the British people, so the ancient myths of Japan have their place today in the hearts of the Japanese. Moreover, these myths were of course a very potent factor in the development of Japanese militarism and in the thought and behaviour of a race that for a brief period dominated a third of Asia. One cannot guess how many, among those fifty thousand on the palace plaza in 1940, admitted in their hearts the dubious veracity of the event they were commemorating. But it is safe to say that few in that place and at that time could have allowed scepticism to mar their appreciation of what was unquestionably an impressive occasion. In any historical account of Japan, then, it is unjustifiable to ignore the legends in the *Kojiki* and *Nihon Shoki*.

It is recorded that when heaven and earth began various deities came into being in the 'Plain of High Heaven'. Among them were a certain god and goddess known as Izanagi and Izanami. These two together gave birth to the islands of Japan. Izanami died; and then Izanagi alone gave birth in a very unorthodox manner – while washing his eyes and nose – to three illustrious deities, of the Sun, Moon, and Storm. Only the first and third concern us. The deity of the Sun was the goddess Amaterasu Omikami. Her brother, the god of the Storm, was the violent and always impetuous Susanowo-no-Mikoto. Izanagi appointed his daughter Amaterasu ruler over the 'Plain of High Heaven', and her brother Susanowo was granted dominion over the 'Sea Plain'. But he refused to obey this command, and he committed a number of acts offensive to his sister, Amaterasu. For example, he broke down the divisions between her rice fields. Amaterasu became so alarmed that she shut herself up in a cave, and the world was plunged into darkness. Whereupon the deities of Heaven assembled outside the cave. They erected a sacred tree. In its upper branches they placed a jewel and in the middle branches a mirror. Then one of the goddesses performed a ribald and indecent dance, causing her audience to roar with laughter. This merriment aroused the curiosity of Amaterasu, who peeped out of the cave. She saw her reflection in the mirror; and this enticed her further out. One of the god drew her out completely and forbade her to return to the cave. Light once more filled the world.

As punishment for his treatment of his sister, Susanowo was expelled by the gods of Heaven. He descended to the province of Izumo in western Japan. After many adventures, and after siring a great progeny of gods and goddesses, Susanowo finally went down into the 'Land of Darkness'. Among his adventures was an encounter with a monster, which he killed. In one of its eight tails he found a large sword. He presented it to Amaterasu. This sword came to be associated with the jewel and mirror, mentioned in the previous paragraph, as part of the imperial regalia.

So far as there is a coherent chronological sequence in the early myths, Susanowo and his offspring can be regarded as representing the first Japanese to dwell in the islands. Their abode, it will be noted, was the province of Izumo, in what is now Shimane Prefecture, on the coast of south-western Honshu facing the Sea of Japan. But they were not the ancestors of the imperial family.

It was the grandson of the Sun-goddess Amaterasu, a god named Ninigi-no-Mikoto, who was commanded to rule the 'Central Land of Reed Plains' (Japan). The submission of the inhabitants of Izumo having been obtained in advance, Ninigi, equipped with the jewel, mirror, and sword and accompanied by other deities, descended upon Mount Takachiho in Kyushu. His great-grandson was the first earthly emperor, always known by his posthumous title, Jimmu Tenno. He became emperor by virtue of his successful expedition to the province of Yamato in central Japan, the area to the south of modern Kyoto. It was in this region that he established his capital after considerable fighting and as the climax of a journey from Kyushu which, according to tradition, lasted several years. The establishment of the capital took the form of the building of a palace in which Jimmu Tenno celebrated his conquest by ceremonies in honour of his ancestress, the deity Amaterasu. It was this event that took place, according to tradition, in 660 B.C.; and it was this event that was commemorated so augustly in Tokyo in A.D. 1940.

The story has been given here in its barest outline. As told in the ancient chronicles it is diffuse, and embellished with many details of an extraordinary yet often earthy nature. And sober history, of course, does not start with Jimmu Tenno.

What is to be learned from the mythology of the race? The symbolism suggested by the account of the Storm-god Susanowo's relations with the Sun-goddess Amaterasu is apparent, as is the significance of Amaterasu's retirement to the cave and her enticement out of it. Here we have the clash between sunshine and storm – the destructive storm that breaks down the divisions between the rice fields. When the storm seems to triumph utterly the sun recedes, and it is winter. Will the sun ever return in strength? To simple people depending on the growing of crops the question is the most fundamental they can ask. A very natural answer – and one given in many parts of the world even today – is that it is only by ceremonies, amounting to ritual enticements, that the sun can be restored and the coming of spring ensured.

The primary deities, then, were personifications of nature; and, as we should expect, the worship of the sun occupied the central place in a religion of this kind. After the introduction of Buddhism this religion, in essence a crude polytheism, became known as Shinto ('the way of the gods'). The name is of Chinese origin, but the faith has always been regarded as indigenous to Japan; although it has been claimed on rather shadowy evidence that the sources of early Shinto are to be found in northern Asia.

The mythology suggests that there were perhaps two main streams of migration from Asia to Japan. One made its way to Izumo, the modern Shimane Prefecture, the other to the island of Kyushu. Both regions are fairly close to Korea, and between them and Korea there are one or two island stepping-stones. It would seem that the descendants of the Kyushu immigrants moved east up the Inland Sea, subduing the original inhabitants and eventually securing the allegiance, however loose, of the Japanese in Izumo. The leading clan of the successful Kyushu folk rather naturally claimed descent from the paramount deity, Amaterasu, the Sun-goddess.

Where are we to place the chronological beginning of the Japanese ruling house? According to the traditional version, found mainly in the *Nihon Shoki*, the first seventeen emperors, including Jimmu Tenno, had an average age of a hundred. Accepting as correct the order of sequence of the early emperors, as related in the chronicles, we may not be grossly wrong if we place Jimmu Tenno somewhere about the beginning of the Christian era. But it is not until we reach the end of the fifth century A.D. that we are on firm historical ground.

During the first four hundred years of the Christian era the descendants of Jimmu Tenno gradually extended their hegemony over most of western Japan, including Kyushu and the island of Shikoku. But they did not confine themselves to these regions. In the middle of the fourth century an empress named Jingu organized, and, it is said, took command of, a military expedition to Korea. This was probably the culmination of a series of raids on Korea by the Japanese. The expedition resulted in the establishment of a Japanese colony on the tip of the Korean peninsula. Thenceforward the Japanese for a period of over two hundred years played an important part in the internal politics of southern Korea.

For the Japanese, the Korean connexion was to have tremendous consequences. Of these the most striking was undoubtedly the introduction of the Chinese script. The Japanese language is now so intimately associated with the use of this script that it is easy to overlook the really formidable technical difficulties that were involved in establishing this association. In their spoken forms Chinese and Japanese differ profoundly. Pure Japanese is a deliciously poly-syllabic tongue. Chinese is monosyllabic. The syntax of the one language has nothing in common with the other. For this reason, no doubt, the use of Chinese ideographs spread only slowly in Japan. It is probable that the Chinese script was known to some people in Japan as early as the first century A.D., but the official adoption of the script is usually dated from the beginning of the fifth century, and a great many years were to pass before it became known beyond a narrow circle of scribes attached to the ruling imperial family.

There were many other significant importations from or, like the Chinese script, through Korea. Entire communities of Koreans came to settle in Japan; and they included skilled artisans, such as workers in metals and experts in the culture of silkworms. By the middle of the sixth century there were more than 100,000 Koreans, and Chinese from Manchuria, domiciled in Japan. For the most part they were much better educated – either in the literary sense or in their knowledge of artistic or technical skills – than the Japanese among whom they lived and with whom in course of time they were to be assimilated. Their contribution to the cultural development of Japan can hardly be overestimated. Their qualitative importance can be gauged from the fact that by the opening of the eighth century more than one-third of the noble families of Japan claimed continental descent, Korean or Chinese.

Receiving so much from Korea and, through Korea, from China, the Japanese were hardly able or ready to exclude from their shores a continental religion that was soon to compete with the indigenous faith, though the two would, in the end, complement each other. The religion was Buddhism, and its arrival in Japan can be dated from about the middle of the sixth century.

Buddhism never supplanted Shinto. After Buddhism was firmly established and widely disseminated most Japanese were both Buddhists and Shintoists, as they are today. In time those who felt the need of some philosophical justification for such dualism – and the Japanese are, on the whole, too empirical by nature to be fond of searching for first principles – were able to claim that, after all, the Shinto deities were *bodhisattvas* and that therefore the two religions were fundamentally identical.

However, there was at first a good deal of opposition to Buddhism which, so it was feared, might endanger the worship of the national gods. In the sixth century there had arisen that rivalry of powerful clans surrounding the emperor which, as we shall see, is a recurring theme throughout nearly all Japanese history. Largely for secular reasons connected with the struggle for power, one great clan, the Soga, gave their support to Buddhism and, after some setbacks, won the day. Nevertheless the advance of Buddhism would have been checked had not the imperial family, after some wavering, decided to support the Soga clan. Buddhism was further promoted, on an extensive scale, at the end of the sixth century by the ruler, Shotoku Taishi (the Crown Prince Shotoku, the nominal ruler being his aunt, the Empress Suiko). Shotoku Taishi, a man of true intellectual distinction, was possibly one of the first native-born Japanese to have some real comprehension of the moral and philosophical nature of Buddhism.

Even today it could be said that the appeal of Shinto is aesthetic or emotional rather than moral. Its specifically ethical content is, and always has been, rather meagre. Rites, rather than ethical conduct, have been of central importance in the observance of Shinto; and at the heart of these rites that of purification is probably the oldest. Shinto apologists argue, correctly, that the rites imply certain standards of morality. Yet round Shinto there has never grown up a body of ethics, or of metaphysics, comparable with what is readily associated with other great religions of the world. It is Buddhism that in Japan has satisfied the not very persistent instinct for theological and philosophical speculation; and it was Shotoku Taishi, at the turn of the sixth and seventh centuries, who was the first to enrich Japanese life with the sophisticated thought and art of the Buddhist universe. Indeed not only Buddhist but also Confucian influence is to be detected in what the Japanese call the 'Constitution of 17 Articles' – it was, rather, a set of ethical maxims – promulgated by Prince Shotoku in A.D. 604. 'The management of State affairs', Shotoku is alleged to have stated, 'cannot be achieved unless it is based on knowledge, and the sources of knowledge are Confucianism, Buddhism, and Shinto.'*

[II]

At about the time of Prince Shotoku's death, China, after many years of internal strife, entered upon a period of peculiar splendour and elegance. This followed upon the establishment of the brilliant T'ang dynasty (A.D. 618–906). The T'ang empire, spreading from the Yellow Sea to the shores of the Caspian, was the marvel of Asia. It was natural for the ruling clans of Japan to be deeply impressed by the magnificence of this civilization. Although the sea passage was not easy, parties of Japanese, some of them official embassies, made their way direct to China, to the T'ang capital at Ch'ang-an. These parties included a number of scholars who stayed in China, sometimes for several years, to study various aspects, both religious and political, of T'ang culture. Here we can perceive that characteristic of the Japanese that has been active whenever they have been brought into contact with a civilization differing from their own; namely a quite indefatigable curiosity, a passion to learn, and an aptitude for choosing, borrowing, adapting, and 'japanizing' foreign ideas and techniques.

After Shotoku's death, in 621, the Soga clan consolidated and increased their power and showed unmistakable signs of preparing to usurp the imperial throne. However, in 645 they were overthrown, in a violent *coup d'état*, by Nakatomino-Kamatari, better recognized by his later name, Fujiwara Kamatari. He is considered by the Japanese to be one of the

* It must be said that most Japanese scholars now doubt whether the 'Constitution of 17 Articles' was in fact composed by Shotoku himself. They suggest that it was written many years after his death, as a tribute to him.

great figures in their history. This is because he was the
author of a system of ambitious administrative reforms designed to create in Japan a reproduction of the T'ang empire.
Fujiwara Kamatari was a Chinese enthusiast and he instituted his reform programme immediately after the overthrow of the Soga. A very elaborate and complex central
government was set up; and on paper, at least, every level of
administration down to the smallest subdivision was changed
to comply with the system existing in China. Seventh-
century Japan was still a rather loose confederation of
clans – the mountainous topography of the country made it
so – and although the prestige of the ruling house was high,
being founded on a generally accepted native religious
tradition, its effective power as a government was by no
means robust. The rise of the Soga family showed that an
ambitious clan could not only seize the reins of power but
also threaten the imperial house. Therefore, to build up the
imperial government and incidentally to buttress his own
power, Fujiwara Kamatari adopted the centralized Chinese
model of administration. It was not in fact ideally suited to
Japanese conditions; and in course of time it broke down.
Eventually the power of various clans demolished, in reality
if not in name, much of the Japanese version of the T'ang
system. Nevertheless, for a very long period – for about four
hundred years – the system, though often revised, worked
after a fashion. Throughout most of that period real power
was in the hands of the descendants of Fujiwara Kamatari.
Outside the imperial line the Fujiwara family is perhaps the
most distinguished in Japanese history.

One of the aspects of T'ang influence that left a permanent
mark on Japanese life was the decision, early in the eighth
century, to build a capital city in emulation of Ch'ang-an.
This was Nara, home of the imperial court for less than eighty
years. Yet during that comparatively brief period great
Buddhist temples and, it must be assumed, many palaces and
residences were built at Nara. Some of the temples have survived, the best examples of T'ang architecture to be seen at
the present day; and there exists still in Nara a unique

storehouse, known as the Shoso-in, containing a remarkable collection of furniture, ornaments, and personal belongings used by the imperial family in the eighth century.

The culture, primarily Buddhist in inspiration, that flowered in Nara was further developed at the later and permanent capital, founded in 794, of Heian-kyo, to be known in course of time as Miyako or Kyoto. This ci'y represented a second and more ambitious attempt to construct a Japanese reproduction of Ch'ang-an. Here, as the years went by, metropolitan culture took on a distinctively Japanese flavour. Indeed by the middle of the ninth century the Japanese felt that they had little to learn from contemporary China. By that time the T'ang empire was in disorder, and China was not to be in the hands of a firmly established imperial dynasty until that of the Sung, founded in 960. In fact from early in the ninth century Japan entered a period of relative isolation, for not only did connexions with China become tenuous, but also relations with Korea had long ceased to be intimate, following the abandonment of the colony in Korea in the seventh century.

In Japanese history the famous Heian period is generally reckoned to have begun in 794, the year of the establishment of the court at Heiankyo (Kyoto), and to have ended in 1185, the year in which a military government was consolidated under Minamoto Yoritomo. However, the rise of the military houses – epitomized by the triumph of the Minamoto family – was apparent many years before 1185. It is in the ninth, tenth, and early eleventh centuries that are to be seen the best examples of Heian life and culture. It was a culture confined to a limited, hereditary circle, a culture that paid meticulous attention to the formal, the ceremonious, and the elegantly expressed in life and art. (Its quality may be apprehended by reading 'The Tale of Genji', Arthur Waley's noble translation of *Genji Monogatari*, the work composed by the court lady, Murasaki Shikibu, in the first quarter of the eleventh century.) It was a culture supremely concerned with style. And this, in many paintings, poems, *belles lettres*, and works of carving and architecture, reached perfection.

The Fujiwara, the real rulers of Japan throughout most of the Heian period, were on the whole humane as well as aesthetic. Banishment rather than death was the reward they gave their rivals and opponents. And if they failed to extend the benefits of their sophisticated civilization to the people at large, it is undeniable that they passed on a tradition of profound respect for learning and the arts that acted as a softening, humanizing influence on the military clans who eventually seized power and retained it up to, and indeed beyond, the nineteenth century. It would not be going too far to say that the artistic instinct, perhaps the most engaging and enduring quality of the Japanese people, is the fruit of a plant nurtured, in hot-house conditions, for more than three hundred years by the Fujiwara.

In the Heian period there was an important change in the political position of the monarchy. The real power of the emperors declined and fell into the hands of the Fujiwara, who governed first as regents (*sessho*) and then as civil dictators (*kampaku*). Through intermarriage the Fujiwara contrived to gain direct control of the imperial line. Having married off a Fujiwara heiress to a youthful emperor it was usually possible to induce him to abdicate – imperial duties were very tedious, being sacerdotal as well as secular – in favour of his son, as soon as the latter was old enough to sit still throughout a palace ceremony. The leading member of the Fujiwara family at the capital would then secure for himself the appointment of regent. In course of time it became the practice for the regent to retain direction of affairs, not as regent but as civil dictator (*kampaku*), if the emperor did not abdicate after reaching manhood. The height of the Fujiwara ascendancy was the hundred years from 967 to 1068. Of the Fujiwara of this age Michinaga was the most notable. He held supreme power for over thirty years, while eight sovereigns, mere figureheads, occupied the throne, the average age of abdication being thirty-one.

It is as well to emphasize at this stage that the political impotence of their emperors throughout much of their history was less shocking to the Japanese than one might, at first sight, suppose. What was shocking and, in Japanese eyes, unforgivable was direct usurpation of the throne. In this matter traditional Japanese ideas differed sharply from Chinese. The old Chinese concept of sovereignty held that the monarch enjoyed 'the mandate of Heaven', but only so long as he was virtuous. If he lacked virtue he might be overthrown. In Chinese history, then, there was often well-accepted philosophical justification for a successful rebellion. Thus China was ruled by several dynasties. But in Japan, though there have been countless instances of civil strife and warfare, there has been only one imperial dynasty. There have been instances of attempted usurpation, and some Japanese sovereigns have met violent deaths; but such examples are sufficiently rare to prove the rule that for at least fifteen hundred years there has been a taboo on conspiracies to abolish the hereditary right – to provide the sovereign – of the ancient imperial house. Mythology, stressing the descent from the sun goddess, made the holder of the throne sacrosanct. Being sacrosanct he was considered immaculate. But to be really immaculate he had to be, politically speaking, emasculated. For to exercise power involves action that may or may not win approval. Passivity alone avoids all criticism. Thus the monarchy was, and is, regarded as being 'above the clouds' – in other words above the storm and stress of daily government. This dualism, a persistent feature in the history of Japan, was acceptable to the Japanese. It is true, as we shall see, that towards the close of the Tokugawa shogunate there was a movement, propagated in the first place by scholars, to 'restore' to the emperor the powers which, it was held, had been wrongly taken from him by the administration of the *shogun*. This movement, however, was in fact dealing in terms that were ideal rather than practical. For since the modernization of Japan in the nineteenth century the sovereigns, whatever their powers have been in theory, have acted only on the advice of ministers and officials.

Towards the end of the Heian period the emperors, either on the throne or in retirement, were able to win back power, or some of it, from the ubiquitous Fujiwara. But they lost it again, this time to one of the great military families, the Taira.

These military families, who came to form a special class, based their power on two solid props – the tenure of tax-free estates and the employment of retainers and tenants skilled in the arts of war.

In theory, since the reforms of the seventh century all land belonged to the central imperial government, who allotted it for cultivation to clansmen and peasants. The latter were supposed to pay taxes, in produce or labour, to the government on the land which they used. In practice there had grown up throughout the country a network of tax-free estates. The first holders of such property appear to have been the Buddhist temples. During the Nara period, the heyday of Buddhist influence in Japan, provincial temples, branches of a mother house in the capital, became centres of local administration. Initially, tax-free land was confined to virgin land brought into cultivation; but it ceased, in time, to be so limited. The imperial court made grants of tax-free land to the provincial temples, as well as to such institutions as the famous Todaiji Temple in Nara. The economic wealth of the temples naturally increased the worldliness of their inmates; and it was not many years before the more important abbots began to form military units to protect temple estates. These military units soon became permanent garrisons.

In a mountainous country local territorial ties are always powerful. It was very difficult for the government to exercise continuous direct control over areas distant from the capital. Members of the court aristocracy were made governors of provinces; but more often than not they stayed in the capital, enjoying its sophisticated delights, while the real control of the provinces remained in, or passed into, the hands of the most vigorous clan chieftains in the areas concerned. Again, the prolific Fujiwara family shed some of its members in the provinces. They were given, or acquired, tax-free estates and over the years they became divorced from court society and indistinguishable, very often, from local clansmen.

In this way – and it was a process of centuries – there arose the phenomenon of Japanese feudalism. Towards the end of the Heian period the generality of peasants paid their taxes, in kind or service, not to the government but to provincial landowners or their agents. The process was of course deplored by the imperial administration, and from time to time steps were taken, with little success, to check or reverse it. But local power rested with those who could muster the greatest number of armed men. At first these may have been relatively few – possibly one or two thousand. Perhaps the early temple garrisons were amongst the largest. But, in considering the origins of the military class, we should not forget the part played by the necessity of maintaining forces first to resist, and then to suppress, the Ainu. In the eighth century, for example, the government ordered the establishment of provincial forces in the north-east, to act as a kind of standing territorial army. It was organized on a hereditary basis. It foreshadowed what was to become the privileged warrior class.

The court aristocracy – and in the Heian period the term was almost synonymous with the house of Fujiwara – found it increasingly useful to call in the military clans to preserve order in the capital, which was often disturbed by the armed followers of Buddhist temples and Shinto shrines who brawled at the very gates of the Imperial Palace. But the decisive factor in opening the way to military control of the government was the outbreak, in the twelfth century, of a struggle within the Fujiwara family. Quarrelling with each other over political appointments, competing factions of the Fujiwara enlisted the armed support of certain military houses. Among these two were outstanding – the Minamoto and the Taira. The former had amassed great estates in the east of Japan, in what is called the Kanto, near the modern Tokyo. The Taira, though also at one time formidable in the east, based their strength for the most part on the provinces bordering the Inland Sea. The dissensions of the Fujiwara, who were courtiers rather than fighting men, led to two bloody civil disturbances. When these were over, the Fujiwara discovered that power had fallen into the hands of their supposed subordinates, the military houses of Minamoto and Taira.

[III]

It was the Taira who were the first to lay their clutches on the imperial court and government. Taira Kiyomori and his supporters were the teeth and claws of a court faction that entirely overthrew its rivals. The latter were beheaded, committed suicide, or were sent into exile. It was the first occasion for over three hundred years that political opponents were punished with death – a clear indication that the military man was now in power. By intrigue, intermarriage, and the threat or use of force Taira Kiyomori closed his grip upon the central government, taking many important offices into his own hands. The glory of the Fujiwara now faded for ever.

The ascendency of the Taira under Kiyomori lasted some twenty-five years up to his death in 1181. He was a very human tyrant, impulsively generous as well as cruel and iconoclastic. The contrast between the bellicose paladin of a military house, such as Taira Kiyomori, and the refined, faintly effeminate Kyoto courtier can be overstressed. But it has existed, to some degree, even to the present day. It should be observed, none the less, that military families in close touch with the palace always tended to become, in their turn, civilized – or, as some have alleged, corrupted – by the art and manners that pervaded the very atmosphere of Kyoto. This was to happen notably to the Ashikaga, as will be mentioned in its place a little later. There were signs that even Taira Kiyomori was affected by the softening influences of the court.

Partly for this reason the head of the Minamoto family, after seizing power from the Taira, established the centre of his administration not in the imperial capital but at Kamakura, on the sea coast south-west of modern Tokyo. The overthrow and destruction of the house of Taira, finally accomplished by the Minamoto at a great sea battle in the Shimonoseki Straits in 1185, is part of the romantic age of Japanese chivalry, in the sense that it became the ever-popular theme of story-tellers and a favourite subject for theatrical drama. Japanese tradition from this age presents us with punctilious, implacable figures riding in coloured armour with bow and sword through bamboo and pine. This is the real début of the *samurai;* and it is during this period that we have the first recorded instance of that painful form of suicide, the *hara-kiri.*

The leader of the Minamoto, though not their commander in the field at the overthrow of the Taira, was Yoritomo.* He set up at Kamakura a system of national administration known as the *Bakufu,* which means, literally, 'camp office'. It was an implicit demonstration of the fact that the government was now in the hands of the military class. In 1192 Minamoto Yoritomo received from the emperor, a boy of thirteen, the title, *Sei-i tai-shogun.* This means 'barbarian-subduing great general'. The title had been given to others in earlier times, but only for specific military purposes and for a limited period. From the time of Yoritomo onwards it became associated with a permanent office. In this sense Yoritomo was the first *shogun,* or 'generalissimo'. In theory at least the government established by Yoritomo at Kamakura did not replace the imperial administration in Kyoto. The Kamakura *Bakufu* was designed primarily to regulate the affairs of the military men who owed allegiance to the Minamoto family. But it was soon evident that the *Bakufu* was a much more effective administrative, and judicial, system than that provided by the nominal government.

The Kamakura *Bakufu* lasted for about 150 years. During those years the dualism apparent in Kyoto was reproduced at Kamakura. Yoritomo's heirs lacked his force of character, and power in the *Bakufu* soon passed to the Hojo family – Yoritomo's widow, a commanding and able personality in her own right, was a Hojo. The Hojo ruled as regents (*shikken*)

---

* The architect of victory was Yoritomo's younger brother Yoshitsune, a very famous figure in Japanese history about whom all manner of legends grew up. Yoritomo distrusted him and eventually he was killed by Yoritomo's supporters. But a myth developed, and was propagated by military enthusiasts even in modern times, that Yoshitsune escaped to the continent and became none other than Genghis Khan. As a heroic character Yoshitsune is always associated with his devoted follower, Benkei, a stout-hearted monk of outsize stature and great physical strength who has been called 'a Japanese Friar Tuck'.

for the *shogun*. Thus thirteenth-century Japan presented a structure of government inconceivably complicated to any-one observing it from outside. For example, a situation arose where the emperor was a puppet manipulated by a retired emperor and his courtiers, the Fujiwara. They themselves, forming the nominal government, were under the orders of the agents in the capital of the government of the Kamakura *shogun*, who in his turn was a puppet of a Hojo regent. Yet because many of the Hojo regents were men of great ability this astonishing system worked. For its effective operation it depended on a network of personal loyalties held together and kept in repair by force of character and tireless capacity at the top. Largely because of this dependence on personal factors it was fated to break down.

But before this happened the country was faced with a critical external threat to its very existence as an independ-ent state. In 1274 and again in 1281 the Mongol Emperor Kublai Khan sent great armadas against Japan. In the second invasion the Mongols are said to have massed a force of 150,000 men. They had reason to feel confident, for their empire covered vast areas of the Eurasian terrain from southern Russia to Korea.

The first assault, in 1274, was less serious than the second. But it was a very formidable threat. The armada began by attacking two islands, Tsushima and Iki, that lie between Kyushu and Korea. The small garrisons on these islands fought to the death – a tradition observed in 1945 on other islands guarding the approaches to Japan. The Mongols then made a landing in Kyushu and a stubborn battle took place. However, a severe storm threatened the ships as they lay off-shore; and the Mongol force embarked and withdrew. The elements were to intervene even more effectively on the side of Japan in 1281. On this occasion, after landing in Kyushu, the Mongols fought, in the small bridgehead they had seized, a campaign that lasted without interruption for fifty-three days. Then on 14 August 1281 a typhoon descended upon the Mongol fleet and virtually wiped it out. This typhoon the Japanese had every right to regard as providential. In shrines and temples throughout the land prayers had been offered for deliverance from the invaders. The typhoon, then, was called 'The Divine Wind', the Japanese name for which is *kamikaze*.

The Buddhist clergy and Shinto officials gained much face as a result of the discomfiture of the Mongols. They attributed the appearance of the *kamikaze* to the vigour and sincerity of their prayers. The fighting men, on the other hand, faced bitter disappointment, for there were no enemy estates to be confiscated and distributed among the victors. Moreover, as the war and all its preparations, together with the need of vigilance against a possible third assault, had impoverished the country, it was difficult for the *Bakufu* to reward the fighting men in any way. This brought it into disrepute; and indeed the regime of the Hojo lasted for only a generation after the Mongol invasions. In 1331 the Hojo deposed the Emperor, Go-Daigo, a man of ability who had been making plans, quietly, to secure the overthrow of the *Bakufu*. Go-Daigo was exiled; but two years later he contrived to emerge, with support from several important warriors. There were defections from the Hojo camp to his banner; and one of his commanders attacked Kamakura and overran it. Whereupon the last Hojo regent, together with his immediate family and about eight hundred retainers, committed *hara-kiri*.

The Kamakura period is remembered, not only because it witnessed the consolidation of the power of the military houses, but also because during this time there were lively movements in religion and art. Three great Buddhist sects, Jodo-Shinshu, Nichiren, and Zen, arose. The first two were popular sects, founded by remarkable men – Nichiren, for example, reminds one of Martin Luther – who gave to Buddhist doctrine a particularly Japanese twist; in the one case it was made simpler, more pragmatical, and, in the other, somewhat nationalist. Zen was not a creed for the common people, but rather for the warrior, aristocrat, and scholar. It depends on neither texts nor ritual, and is therefore peculiarly difficult to explain; and indeed in a few lines explanation is

doubtless impossible. Zen offers salvation through enlightenment through an ineffable apprehension of the meaning of
the universe – or, as we might put it, through grace – which
may be sudden but can hardly be obtained without severe
self-discipline and meditation. From the first, Zen, which
came to Japan from China, had a special appeal for the
fighting man; and the association between the warrior class
and the Zen sect continued up to and through the Pacific
War. It fortified the two supreme ideals of the *samurai* –
fidelity and an indifference to physical hardships.

Zen Buddhism had a substantial influence on the art of
the Kamakura period; for Zen stressed the need to achieve
unity with nature. Thus landscape painting flourished. So
did portrait painting and the painting of historical scenes on
scrolls; and their distinguishing mark is a certain splendid
vitality. From this period, too, dates the famous *Dai Butsu* –
the huge statue of Amida in bronze to be seen today at
Kamakura. Finally, in these years the arts of the swordsmith
and of the armourer reached a level of perfection that con-
noisseurs have described as incomparable.

Not for long was the Emperor Go-Daigo able to enjoy the
fruits of his success against the Hojo. One of his supporters,
Ashikaga Takauji of the house of Minamoto, who had
already switched sides once, turned against him, set up
another member of the imperial line on the throne and had
himself appointed *shogun*. For a time there were two courts;
and there was civil war between them. In the end the rivals
of Go-Daigo were victorious. On becoming *shogun* Ashikaga
Takauji established his government in Kyoto, in a district
known as Muromachi. Thus the period of the Ashikaga
shogunate, lasting from 1339 to 1573, is known as the Muromachi age. It was marred by almost continuous violence,
amounting to full-scale civil war over a great many years.
The causes of these struggles need not be enlarged on here,
for they have little relevance to later history. The later
Muromachi period is known as the 'age of the overthrow of
the higher by the lower'. Conditions were so chaotic – such
was the breakdown of law and order – that only the fittest

could survive. Great houses were overthrown by mere bandit chiefs. Old names disappeared, and new names, new territorial lords, sprang into fame; for many of the established military families had become enervated by long association with the *shogun*'s court in Kyoto.

In sharp contrast to the disorder, violence, and poverty common in the provinces, the Ashikaga *shogun* lived in great luxury, seduced by the traditional atmosphere of the imperial capital. The taste of the Muromachi age at its best was hardly less refined than that of the Heian era. Two *shogun* of the age, Yoshimitsu (1358–1408) and Yoshimasa (1445–90), gave themselves over to aestheticism and the patronage of the arts. Under their stimulus not only painting but also landscape gardening, classical drama, and such arts as the tea ceremony and flower arrangement reached standards of excellence that are still revered.

The imperial court, on the other hand, was often in dire straits financially. So much so that one emperor was reduced to selling specimens of his calligraphy on the streets of Kyoto. The survival of the imperial court was indeed due merely to the ancient tradition that, come what may, there must always be an emperor of the old imperial line.

Despite the political confusion and social upheavals of the time, trade and commerce made significant progress during the fifteenth and sixteenth centuries. The Japanese began to make their mark as seafarers, both as traders and pirates. The latter, in the days of the Ashikaga, were the scourge of the China coast from Shantung to the Pearl River. But Japanese went overseas as traders also. Contact with China became close and important – the art of the Muromachi age owes much to Chinese influence – and as trade increased, so there grew up in Japan various important harbour communities. One of these, the town of Sakai which was the port of Osaka, became a kind of free city, like those of the Hanseatic League, ruled by local merchants. By the beginning of the fourteenth century money had largely replaced rice as the chief medium for exchange; and in the fifteenth century imports of copper cash from China increased this trend. In exchange for these and other imports the Japanese exported manufactured goods, such as folding fans, screens, and swords. In this trade feudal lords, and Buddhist abbots, played an important part. The breakdown of central government turned many provincial magnates into virtually independent rulers. Those who possessed good harbours soon perceived the utility of using them for foreign trade.

Such was Japan, a land of political chaos but economic growth, when some Portuguese, on their way by junk to Macao, were driven ashore by a contrary wind on a small island off the coast of Kyushu. So far as we know they were the first Europeans ever to set foot in Japan. The precise year when this occurred is not known; but it was either 1542 or 1543. In 1549 there arrived at Kagoshima, in Kyushu, the first, and also the most distinguished, Christian missionary to visit Japan. This was the Spanish Jesuit, Francis Xavier. But Christianity was not the only appurtenance of the West introduced to Japan by the Portuguese. The merchants and sea captains from Macao brought with them and sold to the Japanese something that was valued more highly than the Christian faith. This was the smooth-bore musket.

Chapter 2

FIRST CONTACT WITH THE WEST

[I]

THE Japanese soon learned how to make muskets of their own, and the art of the gunsmith spread rapidly throughout the country. The new weapon was of particular utility to Oda Nobunaga, a *daimyo** of central Japan, who contrived to subjugate his neighbours in a series of victories that made him by 1578 the leading figure in the land. In his battles he was the first to make full use of the fire power of the musket. He was favoured by the fact that the territories early under his control were those especially famous for the excellence of their gunsmiths; and he was able to equip a large proportion of his foot soldiers with muskets.

In many respects Oda Nobunaga resembled Taira Kiyomori, from whom indeed he was indirectly descended. Fearless, irreligious, boisterous, and autocratic, he was a master of military strategy; and in his rise to fame he had a measure of good luck, for two of his most dangerous rivals were too busy fighting each other to offer a serious challenge to his power. He had the gift of choosing loyal allies and subordinates, though he was to meet his death at the hands of one of them, whom he had offended, so it is said, by the roughness of his manner. The name of Nobunaga is always associated with those of Toyotomi Hideyoshi and Tokugawa Ieyasu. They began their careers under his shadow, and between them they carried on the work Nobunaga set his hand to – namely the unification of the country under a single, powerful authority. Hideyoshi was his vassal, Ieyasu his devoted ally.

* *Daimyo* (lit. 'great name') is the term used by the Japanese to describe a territorial lord of the feudal period.

These three – Oda Nobunaga (1534–82), Toyotomi Hideyoshi (1536–98), and Tokugawa Ieyasu (1542–1616) – each
in his own way contributed to the pacification of Japan after
a century of civil strife. It has been said that Nobunaga
quarried the stones, Hideyoshi shaped them, and Ieyasu set
them into place. But their characters, and methods, differed.
The quality of each is suggested by a well-known Japanese
story. The three men, it is said, were faced with a bird that
refused to sing. Nobunaga's reaction was impulsive. 'I'll kill
it,' he said, 'if it doesn't sing.' Then Hideyoshi is supposed
to have said: 'I'll force it to sing for me.' But Ieyasu said:
'I shall wait until it does sing.'

Nobunaga's ascendancy was fairly brief, for at the age of
forty-nine he was killed in a surprise attack on him by one of
his supporters, who in turn was quickly defeated by Hideyoshi. Had Nobunaga lived he might have unified the entire
country under his rule. As it was his authority did not extend to the north or to the extreme west; but in place of the
political chaos of central Japan – of about half the provinces
of the country – he imposed a single, firm rule. He could
not be *shogun*, for by this time it was an accepted tradition
that only members of the Minamoto house could hold this
office, and Nobunaga was a Taira. However, the existing
Ashikaga *shogun* in Kyoto was powerless, his functions being
little more than decorative, although they lacked the sacerdotal aura that surrounded the equally nominal powers of
the emperor. *Shogun* and emperor alike were in reality,
though not in name, entirely subservient to Nobunaga's
will. Still, he treated the imperial house with respect, while
consolidating his position as the undoubted *primus inter pares*
among the *daimyo*.

At Azuchi, on a strand by Lake Biwa, Nobunaga built a
wooden castle upon a stone base, the finest structure of its
kind yet seen in Japan; and he is remembered, too, for his
construction of a fleet of six vessels larger than any built in
Japan up to that time. He dealt a very severe blow to the
Buddhist sects as a dangerous military and political force.
No superstition held him back from attacking and destroy-

ing the Buddhist strongholds on Hieizan near Kyoto – the fighting monks had been unwise enough to ally themselves with his enemies – and no considerations of humanity prevented his ordering the slaughter of the women and children who survived among the ashes of the burnt-out monasteries and temples.

It may be that it was his dislike of the Buddhist sects that disposed Nobunaga to look kindly upon the Jesuit missionaries, the successors of Francis Xavier. He was indeed cordial towards them, showing them many favours, including the grant of land at Azuchi for a Christian seminary. He was of course entirely without faith in any religion: an aspect of the matter well understood by the Jesuits. For the Vice-Provincial of the Order in Japan wrote of Nobunaga in his annual report: 'This man seems to have been chosen by God to open and prepare the way for our holy faith, without understanding what he is doing.' For his part Nobunaga seems to have been impressed by the personal qualities of the Jesuits whom he met. They were, after all, as Loyola described them, the 'cavalry' of the Church Militant, chosen for their tact and intellectual powers as well as for their character. Nobunaga praised the missionaries in high terms. 'These are the men whom I like,' he said: 'upright, sincere, and who tell me solid things.' It is not surprising, then, that contemporary Jesuit accounts speak very highly of Nobunaga. Thanks to the reports that were sent to Lisbon and Rome during this period he was the first Japanese to enjoy a reputation in Europe. One of these reports suggests that Nobunaga planned to proceed to the conquest of China after completing the subjugation of 'the sixty-six kingdoms of Japan'. But these tasks had to be attempted by his successor, Hideyoshi.

Toyotomi Hideyoshi is in certain respects the most attractive of the three outstanding warrior rulers of this time. Less cruel than Nobunaga, less cautious than Ieyasu, Hideyoshi had a love of the extravagant, of the prodigious, that is more than a little engaging; and his career has the particular fascination that attaches to the rise of a *parvenu*. For he rose from nothing, his father having been a peasant foot soldier.

He combined diplomacy with force, winning friends among those towards whom Nobunaga had shown only implacable hostility. It can be said, of course, that in the labour of unifying Japan much of the pioneer work had been done for him by Nobunaga. Thus Hideyoshi could afford to be more constructive than his predecessor. Despite his small stature – he was almost a dwarf – and his personal ugliness, this man, described by the historian Murdoch as 'a base-born monkey-faced adventurer', could impress his rivals with his charm as well as his strength. Nevertheless it is as a strategist in war as well as an energetic administrator that he is remembered – though it must be admitted that his Korean adventure, unless it is regarded purely as a device to rid Japan of thousands of restless warriors, was an act of folly, indicative of gross megalomania. For the great invasion of Korea in 1592 was intended to open up the way to the Japanese conquest of China.

In the ten years between the death of Nobunaga in 1582 and the first expedition to Korea – there was a second in 1597 – Hideyoshi succeeded in bringing to heel a turbulent pack of feudatories in all parts of Japan. First he inflicted a resounding defeat upon a senior *daimyo* who, with one of Nobunaga's two surviving sons, had been rash enough to challenge him. His next campaign was directed against Ieyasu. The other son of Nobunaga had appealed to Ieyasu for support in opposing the upstart Hideyoshi, and Ieyasu, who had at one time put to death his own wife and eldest son on suspicion of plotting against Nobunaga, complied out of loyalty to the memory of his late ally. A curiously static kind of warfare ensued between Hideyoshi and Ieyasu, both of whom fortified themselves behind strong breastworks. After several months the parties agreed to be friends, and thenceforward Hideyoshi and Ieyasu worked together in harmony, with the latter very much the junior partner in the alliance. Having come to terms with Ieyasu, Hideyoshi turned his attention to a bellicose monastery of the Shingon sect of Buddhism. But having defeated them, he treated the monks with greater clemency than Nobunaga had shown towards the occupants of Hieizan. He crucified a few of their leaders and then spared the rest, many of whom later found service under Ieyasu. His next step was to deal with opponents in Shikoku, after which he proceeded, having secured an alliance with some *daimyo* in the north, to the suppression of centres of resistance in the island of Kyushu in the extreme south-west, accomplishing this task with a huge force of no less than a quarter of a million men. Shimazu of Satsuma, whose power in Kyushu had been that of a strong and virtually independent monarch, was forced to pay homage to Hideyoshi, who then treated him with generosity. The pacification of Japan was completed by the capture, with the cooperation of Ieyasu, of the fortress of Odawara, south-west of the modern Tokyo, and the submission thereafter of the principal *daimyo* in the north of the country. This was in 1590. The whole country was at peace for the first time for over a hundred years It is no wonder that the period from the later part of the fifteenth century to the close of the sixteenth is known in Japanese history as *Sengoku Jidai*, or 'the age of the country at war'.

Hideyoshi's campaigns, of which the barest outline has been given, were completed within the compass of only eight years; during which he had time to set up an efficient system of central administration, to reform the coinage, to institute a national land survey, and to oversee the construction of a fortress far stronger than Nobunaga's at Azuchi – the castle at Osaka, a labour of building that occupied more than three years with many thousands working at it day and night. For the grounds were a mile wide and the walls nearly seven yards thick. And in this period he built also a luxurious residence at Kyoto known as the Juraku Mansion.

Much might be written to illustrate the cleverness with which Hideyoshi rearranged the map of feudal Japan, allotting fiefs in such manner that potentially dangerous *daimyo* were checkmated by reliable supporters of his own. He consolidated his grip on the warrior class with a mixture of firmness and diplomacy, neither of which were at any time predictable. A foreign missionary, writing as early as 1586, tells us:

He [Hideyoshi] is so feared and obeyed that with no less ease than a father of a family disposes of the persons of his household he rules the principal kings and lords of Japan; changing them at every moment, and stripping them of their original fiefs, he sends them into different parts, so as to allow none of them to strike root deep.

He obtained from the emperor the title, commonly held by a Fujiwara, of *kampaku* (civil dictator) and he would have liked to be *shogun;* but this he could not be, save by adoption into the Ashikaga or some other branch of the Minamoto house. But Hideyoshi took pains to act in the emperor's name, holding the emperor's commission, so that those who opposed him were, technically, rebels. In Japan, where the outward form of things counted for a great deal, this was of some importance. As a demonstration of his intimacy with the emperor, Hideyoshi invited the young sovereign, Go-Yozei, to spend five days at the Juraku Mansion amid elaborate ceremonies and fêtes. On the second day of the visit Hideyoshi assembled the principle *daimyo* and made them swear allegiance to the emperor and to His Majesty's chief minister, the *kampaku.*

The motives behind Hideyoshi's great expedition to Korea are not fully known. But plain ambition, the itch to leave a deathless name for himself as a conqueror, played its part. There is a well-known tale of a visit that Hideyoshi paid to the shrine of Minamoto Yoritomo near Kamakura, when he is alleged to have addressed an image of Yoritomo in some such words as these: 'Only you and I have been able to take all the power under heaven. But you were of illustrious stock and not, like me, descended from peasants. But after conquering all the empire I mean to conquer China. What do you think of that?' And in a very friendly talk with Jesuit missionaries at Osaka he boasted that he would invade and subdue the Chinese empire and would then make the Chinese adopt the Christian religion.

China presented a kind of challenge, a temptation even, to a successful predatory adventurer such as Hideyoshi. The Chinese, in their immeasurable pride, despised the 'dwarfs' across the Yellow Sea, regarding them, as they regarded all alien races, as truly barbarian. It was forgotten neither in China nor in Japan that the third Ashikaga *shogun*, the aesthetic Yoshimitsu, had consented to describe himself as 'subject of the Ming' and had sent valuable gifts to the Chinese ruler, who accepted them as tribute. A desire to come to grips with the 'conceited' Chinese, to teach them a lesson, could be aroused very easily among the warriors of sixteenth-century Japan. For many decades fighting men from the maritime provinces of western Japan had taken part in piratical attacks up and down the China coast. The idea, then, of a full-dress invasion was one that would make an appeal to the Japanese fighting spirit. Moreover, from Hideyoshi's point of view, an overseas expedition was an admirable way of occupying the energies and depleting the numbers of those who might well disturb the peace at home or even threaten, in some unlooked-for combination, his own supremacy.

The king of Korea, loyal to his suzerain the Ming emperor, turned down Hideyoshi's demand for the right of passage for Japanese troops through Korea; whereupon an expeditionary force was landed in several divisions on the peninsula. The invading army from Japan numbered some two hundred thousand. Its columns advanced with a speed that must command respect, for their progress was by no means unopposed. The first division, under a Christian warrior named Konishi, crossed the Straits of Tsushima on 24 May 1592. After storming Pusan it fought its way north and was in Seoul on 12 June. Fortified by other divisions the advance was continued to the Imjin river and then to Pyong-yang; and at the same time a division under Kato Kiyomasa, an aggressive Nichiren Buddhist and Konishi's prominent rival, pushed to the northeast, reaching the Tumen on the frontier of the country.

There now occurred something that was to be repeated 360 years later. The Chinese intervened. At first their numbers were too small to have any effect upon the issue. This error was amended, however, when a substantial host of Chinese crossed the frozen Yalu in mid-winter, at the end of January 1593. The Japanese were soon in difficulties. They started to retreat down the length of the peninsula.

Already their problems had been much aggravated by the remarkable successes achieved by the Koreans at sea. Here a brilliant part was played by the Korean admiral, Yi Sun-sin, whose name deserves to be better known in the West. Yi Sun-sin, a commander of genius, must be ranked in the highest class, with De Ruyter, Nelson, and Togo. His success was due in large measure to the use he made of one vessel in his fleet, the so-called *Kwi-son*, or 'tortoise-boat', which appears to have been his own invention. This was a large galley with its rowers and fighting men protected by a curved roof that covered all the deck. Some authorities say that this roof or shell – for the ship closely resembles a large tortoise or turtle – was made of curved iron plates, others that it was made of wood in which were implanted formidable iron spikes. At any rate it provided an effective defence against fire arrows and musket balls. No Japanese ship could compete with it. It was able to inflict heavy losses on the Japanese by ramming their vessels and so sinking them. One vivid example of Yi's tactics should be quoted. The admiral fell in with a Japanese fleet that hoped to make its way up the coast to assist Konishi's force north of Seoul. He turned and fled. As he had hoped, the Japanese broke their line and pursued him vigorously. Suddenly Yi ordered the rowers of his 'tortoise-boat' to reverse oars. What had been the stern became the prow; darting backwards it rammed the first ship of the pursuing fleet and sank it. Yi then dealt with the other Japanese ships in the same fashion, and it is said that over seventy of them were sent to the bottom.

Almost exactly twelve months after the first landing the Japanese began to evacuate Korea, leaving one division in occupation of parts of the southern coast. Hideyoshi himself never crossed to Korea to take command of his army in the field, although this was his original intention. It may be that it was his notorious devotion to his aged mother that kept him at home. But he planned the strategy of the campaign and directed it at a distance, rather like MacArthur in 1950 – indeed in temperament these two are not wholly dissimilar. In prolonged negotiations with Chinese envoys in

Japan, negotiations in which the Koreans were ignored by both sides, Hideyoshi's anger was aroused by a patronizing letter from the Chinese emperor investing him with the title King of Japan. There followed a second Japanese invasion of Korea, accompanied by much bloody fighting in which on the whole the Japanese had the best of it. However, a truce was being discussed when Hideyoshi died in September 1598; and not long afterwards the expeditionary force was withdrawn from Korea. In an interception of part of the evacuation fleet the illustrious Yi had the ill fortune to be mortally wounded by a musket ball.

Hideyoshi's continental adventure, like the Korean War of the twentieth century, imposed appalling misery upon the common people of Korea. Apart from the cruelties inflicted on the populace by the invading armies, the campaign brought famine and disease to most of the country south of the Han river. This overseas expedition can scarcely be regarded as anything but an unmitigated calamity. The leading *daimyo* taking part did not, as it turned out, lose many of their number in the six years' struggle; but among their retainers the losses were severe. What is indisputable is that the Korean expedition left a legacy of hatred and contempt that has endured into this century.

How did the commonalty of Japan – the ancestors of our representative family, the Saitos – fare in this period? It was during the ascendancy of Hideyoshi that the line was drawn more firmly between the *samurai* class and the peasantry. Because he himself had emerged from the peasantry Hideyoshi was, no doubt on that account, all the more determined to rebuild the structure of class that had broken down to some extent during the civil strife of the fifteenth and sixteenth centuries. He issued and enforced decrees proclaiming that nobody under an obligation to a superior could leave his employment without his overlord's permission, that no *samurai* could become a townsman, and that all peasants should surrender their weapons to the government. This last measure, known as 'the Sword Hunt', was enforced under the cunning pretext that the confiscated weapons were to be melted down for use as nails in the construction of a hall for a great statue of Buddha to be erected by Hideyoshi in Kyoto. The common people, then, were deprived of the means of self-defence and of social advancement. As to their livelihood a comprehensive statement is hardly possible. Conditions varied throughout the country. But it may be accepted that the life of the peasantry was extremely rigorous, often miserable; for they were subject to the caprices not only of their feudal lords but also of nature itself in a land in which annual typhoons, to say nothing of earthquakes and volcanic eruptions, brought recurrent disaster. All that can be said is that in the territories directly administered by Hideyoshi the hardships of the peasantry were a little less acute than those prevailing elsewhere, since Hideyoshi, in the impositions he made to meet the cost of his grandiose works of building and of his extravagant entertainments, usually turned to the fiefs of other great territorial lords. Historians agree that in Hideyoshi's day Japan enjoyed unwonted prosperity. But the benefits were enjoyed directly, of course, by only a small percentage of the total population.

The cultural life of the oligarchy, however, showed great activity. Hideyoshi's example promoted a craze for the ostentatious. The Japanese refer to the Nobunaga-Hideyoshi period as Azuchi-Momoyama, after Nobunaga's castle and the palace at Fushimi, near Kyoto, which Hideyoshi built in 1594, only a few years after he began the construction of the Juraku Mansion. The Momoyama period is famous in the history of Japanese art; for if it reflects a faintly cloying opulence it was the age, none the less, of Sen Rikyu, the greatest of the tea-masters, and the more sumptuous displays of fine living – such as Hideyoshi's mass tea ceremony at Kyoto – had only an ephemeral influence on contemporary taste.

[11]

This society, dominated by a warrior caste that combined savage ferocity on the battlefield with an elegant and pleasing niceness in the home, regarded with inquisitive attention the

few strangers from southern Europe now settled, as priests or
merchants, in its midst. And on the whole it treated them
very well. As merchants the Portuguese were welcomed, and
as missionaries they were at least tolerated – in spite of some
opposition from the Buddhist hierarchy – for the *daimyo* of
south-western Japan perceived at the outset that the Portuguese merchants and sea-captains treated the Jesuit fathers
with great respect. So the encouragement given to the
missionaries by certain of the Kyushu *daimyo* stemmed very
largely, in the first place at any rate, from a mercenary
motive. But mutual good-will was soon established. In a
famous letter to Europe, written only three months after his
arrival in Kagoshima, Francis Xavier declared:

> The people whom we have met so far are the best who have yet
> been discovered, and it seems to me that we shall never find
> among heathens another race to equal the Japanese. They are
> people of very good manners, good in general, and not malicious;
> they are men of honour to a marvel, and prize honour above all
> else in the world.*

The honeymoon lasted for a good many years. As we have
seen, Nobunaga showed great favour to the foreign priests;
and so sanguine were they that they began to have hopes of
converting the whole of Japan to Christianity. For at first
Hideyoshi, too, seemed very friendly towards them. The
total number of Japanese converts has often been exaggerated; but the most reliable estimate gives us a figure, as a
maximum, of about 300,000 out of a population of something
between 15 and 20 million. While some scholars have claimed
that this shows that Christianity made only a small impact
upon the Japanese, others have argued that, on the contrary,
in view of the small number of foreign and native missionaries working in Japan at any one time – rarely more than a
hundred – the figure is a remarkable testimony to the progress
of an alien religion in a highly civilized pagan country.
What is at least certain is that for about fifty years Christians
had an influence, particularly in Kyushu, out of proportion

* Translated by Professor Boxer: C. R. Boxer, *The Christian Century in
Japan.* London (Cambridge University Press), 1951, p. 37.

to their numbers. Several *daimyo* were converted, and one or two of them propagated the faith in their domains, bearing down on the hostile or recalcitrant with a zeal comparable with, but on the whole less savage than, that shown by Catholics in parts of Europe at that time. Some of Hideyoshi's generals in Korea, who were converts like Konishi, had the cross displayed upon their banners; and if in their conduct of warfare they were not noticeably more humane than other Japanese fighting men, they were not exceptional among Christians of that age. In considering such matters we should recall the nature of the Spanish struggle in the Low Countries and the New World, or the character of the Thirty Years War that was to rage up and down central Europe.

The foreign Jesuits in Japan, all of them Portuguese in their loyalties if not Portuguese by birth, were joined towards the end of the sixteenth century by Spanish friars, mainly Franciscan and Dominican, from Manila. There was no rejoicing in the Jesuit camp at the arrival of new workers in the field. On the contrary, the friars were detested as interlopers, and indeed they entered Japan in defiance of a papal brief that reserved that country for the Jesuits, although eventually Rome was induced to give official sanction to the presence in Japan of the Spanish mendicant orders. Professional jealousy was reinforced by the antipathy that existed, as it still does, between Spain and Portugal. The ill-feeling between the races was, if anything, exacerbated by the union of the two kingdoms in 1580 under Philip II of Spain. Moreover the Jesuits were dismayed by the evangelizing methods adopted by the friars, who concentrated their attention on the poor, the sick, and the outcast among the population, whereas it was always the policy of the Jesuits, taking into account the social stratification of Japan, to confine their evangelizing work to the *samurai* class. The friars professed to be shocked at what they called the worldliness of the Jesuits; they also accused the Jesuits of taking part in commercial transactions for their own profit.

There was some justification for this charge. In Hideyoshi's time the town of Nagasaki was virtually governed by the

Jesuits. The local population was overwhelmingly Christian, and the Japanese governors of the town were under the influence of the Jesuit fathers. The latter not only exercised, indirectly, considerable administrative power but also took a percentage of the profits derived from the sale of the cargoes of Portuguese vessels arriving from Macao. In fairness to the Jesuits, however, it must be said that such transactions formed their main source of income for the upkeep and extension of their churches, seminaries, and printing press. It was their knowledge of Japanese and their generally high personal character that led the Jesuit fathers at Nagasaki into the world of trade at a very early stage, for they were found to be almost indispensable, both as interpreters and as umpires, to Portuguese merchants and Japanese buyers alike.

The trade with Macao, of which the import of Chinese silk was an important constituent, was valued very highly by Hideyoshi, and by his successor, Ieyasu. The Manila trade, too, was held in great esteem. On the whole there was extraordinarily little visible xenophobia in Japan at that time.

However, on two occasions Hideyoshi showed sudden displeasure at the foreign missionaries. Just after the completion of his Kyushu campaign Hideyoshi, without warning, issued an edict condemning the missionaries and their creed, and in the same decree they were told to leave Japan in short order. At the same time Hideyoshi declared that the Macao trade could continue. This edict was not, in fact, put into force, although naturally it caused some alarm. The missionaries behaved with great discretion, and the storm blew over. But ten years later a more severe crisis faced the Christians in Japan. A Spanish galleon, outward bound from Manila for New Spain, was wrecked on the coast of Shikoku and its rich cargo was salvaged and then confiscated by the leading local inhabitants. The Spaniards appealed to Hideyoshi to intervene on their behalf. Now not long before this happened Hideyoshi had received the Jesuit Bishop of Japan with some kindness; so it appeared that his attitude towards Christianity was complacent. Yet he must have been in a touchy mood, beset as he was with many worries, for it was at this time that he got the condescending letter from the Chinese emperor that so enraged him; and his famous Momoyama palace at Fushimi had just been laid in ruins by a series of devastating earthquakes that had rocked central Japan. It was at this unpropitious moment that Hideyoshi was informed that the pilot of the galleon had boasted of the mighty power of King Philip and had admitted frankly that the Spanish empire overseas had been built largely upon the pioneering activities of the Spanish missionary friars. Hideyoshi was furious. There were plenty of people in his own *entourage*, including Buddhist priests, who had been warning him behind their fans that foreign priests could be the advance guard of foreign invasion. It now seemed to Hideyoshi that these admonitions were justified. He arrested a number of converts made by the Franciscans and sentenced to death twenty-six Christians, including six Spanish Franciscan friars. These were martyred, by the Japanese form of crucifixion, at Nagasaki early in February 1597. Hideyoshi did not strike at the Jesuits; and his death in the following year, 1598, gave the Christians in Japan a welcome respite.

Hideyoshi's heir was his small son, Hideyori. Very elaborate arrangements had been made by Hideyoshi before his death for the guardianship of this five-year-old boy. It is unnecessary to discuss them here, except to remark that in the council of guardians Tokugawa Ieyasu, who was now based upon the town of Yedo, was the most powerful. On the other hand his position was not unassailable, and it was in the nature of things that there should be a trial of strength, sooner or later, between him and the other prominent *daimyo* committed to guardianship of the boy Hideyori. The struggle was not long delayed. It was decided at Sekigahara in central Japan on 21 October 1600, when two great combinations of territorial lords, one under Ieyasu and the other under his chief rival, met in a battle that ended in full victory for Ieyasu – a victory of which he was fairly confident in advance, for he had come to a previous agreement with certain of the *daimyo* among his opponents that they would change sides at a critical point in the battle. The winners naturally received great benefits in a redistribution of fiefs, while the losers – with the exception of Shimazu of Satsuma and one other *daimyo* – suffered confiscation or great curtailment of their domains. Ieyasu now began to establish the Tokugawa system of administration that was to last for some two hundred and fifty years; and his treatment of the *daimyo* was based upon which side they had taken in the famous fight at Sekigahara. It became the tradition of the Tokugawa house to look with caution and suspicion upon those families that had been arrayed against it at Sekigahara; and the rearrangement of fiefs was such that their power was largely neutralized.

However, Ieyasu's mastery of the country could not be called complete until 1616, when he overcame the supporters of Hideyori in their great fortress at Osaka. In that year the family of Hideyoshi was entirely supplanted and that of Ieyasu firmly established. For at the end of a bitter siege – a complicated campaign, in two separate phases, in which Ieyasu as usual resorted to treacherous cunning – Hideyori and his mother and their principal retainers committed suicide, and later on Ieyasu executed the only other surviving member of the house of Hideyoshi, his little grandson Kunimatsu, then eight years of age.*

[III]

Tokugawa Ieyasu was of the house of Minamoto, being descended in a direct line from Minamoto Yoshiie, the great-grandfather of the famous Yoritomo who founded the Kamakura *Bakufu* in the twelfth century. Thus Ieyasu was eligible for the office of *shogun*. This he secured for himself in 1603. But two years later he abdicated in favour of one of his sons, Hidetada, a young man of twenty-six whose capabilities

* Ieyasu knew full well that the fortunes of his own house, the Minamoto, had in the past escaped ruin through the clemency extended by Taira Kiyomori to the two boys, Yoritomo and Yoshitsune. Conversely it was known to Ieyasu, as to every Japanese who knew his history, that by sparing the lives of his enemy's children Kiyomori brought about in the end the great defeat of the Taira clan.

were sound; and father and son worked together very harmoniously. Ieyasu fixed the seat of his nominal retirement at Sumpu (the modern Shizuoka) and Hidetada remained at Yedo (the modern Tokyo), the headquarters of the shogunal administration, of what was to be called the Tokugawa or Yedo *Bakufu*. Ieyasu, of course, continued to supervise the general government of the country, for, in the words of a Japanese historian, 'he held on with a grip of iron to what he had been and to what he had got.' If Nobunaga resembled Taira Kiyomori, there was a close similarity between Ieyasu and Minamoto Yoritomo – Hideyoshi is in a class by himself – and to some extent Ieyasu deliberately modelled his character upon that of Yoritomo. Ieyasu identified the interests of Japan with those of his family. His consistent aim was to cement the foundations, already laid by Nobunaga and Hideyoshi, of an orderly, peaceful state under a military government, well removed, like that of Kamakura, from the softening influence of Kyoto and dominated with merciless vigilance by his own family. To this end Ieyasu devoted all the resources of his cool-headed, implacable disposition. It goes without saying that he was a military commander of the highest class. Without this basic qualification he could have achieved nothing; and his experience of war extended over forty years. No doubt his greatest personal assets were his almost faultless judgement of men and his profound and unshakeable patience. Among the instructions that he is alleged to have left to his successors is an exhortation to patience that deserves quotation in full.

The strong manly ones in life are those who understand the meaning of the word Patience. Patience means restraining one's inclinations. There are seven emotions, joy, anger, anxiety, love, grief, fear, and hate, and if a man does not give way to these he can be called patient. I am not as strong as I might be, but I have long known and practised patience. And if my descendants wish to be as I am . . . they must study patience.*

* From Professor Sadler's translation of the legacy of Ieyasu in A. L. Sadler, *The Maker of Modern Japan*. London (Allen & Unwin), 1937, pp. 389–90.

In 1600, some months before the battle of Sekigahara, Ieyasu showed favour to an Englishman, Will Adams, of London, but originally of Gillingham, in Kent, the pilot of a Dutch vessel that reached Japan with only twenty-four survivors out of a crew of over a hundred. So far nobody has been able to disprove the claim that Will Adams was the first Englishman ever seen in Japan. If he was the first, he was also one of the most fortunate; for he made an excellent impression on Ieyasu when the latter summoned him to his presence, and between the two there grew up an association that was profitable to both. Ieyasu learned a good deal from Adams about conditions in northern Europe, about mathematics, navigation, and maritime lore generally; for to the end of his days Ieyasu had a typically Japanese thirst for all kinds of knowledge. He employed Adams as diplomatic agent when Dutch and English traders began coming to Japan; and early in their acquaintance he persuaded Adams to direct the construction of a ship in the European style. In return Adams was given an estate as one of Ieyasu's vassals, and, since at first he was refused permission to return to England, he married a Japanese woman and settled down as a person of substance in the country. His tomb is to be seen near Yokosuka. His niche in Japanese history is small but assured. The Jesuits did their best to harm Adams on his arrival by denouncing him and his shipmates to the Japanese as pirates. On the whole Adams returned good for evil, rendering help later on to both Portuguese and Spanish in Japan. But he opened the eyes of Ieyasu to the fact that in some countries in Europe the Iberian Catholics were looked upon as dangerous enemies of a very insidious kind.

This side of the matter was emphasized further, of course, by both the Dutch and English when they began trading with Japan, the former in 1609, the latter in 1613. Thus the religious bigotries of the West poisoned the relations between the European traders in Japan, who did not hesitate to traduce each other to the Japanese.

From this back-biting the Portuguese and Spanish priests were the main sufferers in the end. It must have come as an agreeable shock to Ieyasu to find that among European trading nations there were two that were quite content to do business without any concern for the propagation of the Christian faith. In fact Ieyasu and his contemporaries scarcely regarded the Dutch and English as Christians at all – a point of view shared, no doubt, by the Spanish and Portuguese. Hideyoshi's anti-Christian edicts were not enforced by Ieyasu, but this mildness was dictated by the wish to do no harm to the trade with Macao, the Indies, and Manila. The Dutch and then the English (who in fact traded for only ten years, from 1613 to 1623) seemed to offer a potential alternative source of foreign trade. At the same time a number of events were combining to make Ieyasu increasingly suspicious of Christianity. There was a bribery scandal touching two Japanese Christian officials; and, more serious, there was an exposure of what seemed to be a plot by certain Japanese Christians to overthrow the Tokugawa government with the aid of foreign troops. Then there was the incident of the survey of the Japanese coast by a Spanish mariner. Permission had been obtained, of course, for this survey, but when Ieyasu discussed it with Adams the latter declared that in Europe such activity would be condemned as espionage.

So in 1612 and again in the following year Ieyasu issued edicts prohibiting Christianity. But these were not enforced very strictly. A further edict, in 1614, ordered all foreign priests to gather in Nagasaki and then to leave Japan for good. The edict also ordered the demolition of all churches and the renunciation of their faith by native Christians. The edict accused the foreign priests of 'longing to disseminate an evil law . . . so that they may change the government of the country and obtain possession of the land'. And the document referred to Japan as 'the country of the Gods (*kami*) and of Buddha'. However, Ieyasu's operations against Osaka gave the Christians a short reprieve. On the other hand Osaka castle contained many Christians among its warriors, and they displayed flags bearing the cross and invocations to the saints. Furthermore there were both Jesuits and friars within the castle when it fell. Circumstances such as these did nothing to soften the hearts of Ieyasu and his son Hidetada towards the Christian community.

Ieyasu did not long survive his triumph at Osaka. He died in the summer of 1616. Hidetada proved to be more severe than his father in his attitude to the Christians; and before very long a progressively rigorous persecution was oppressing foreign missionaries and native Christians alike. Several Jesuits and friars had evaded the expulsion order of 1614, or with others, newcomers to Japan, smuggled themselves back into the country over a number of years. Both they and the Japanese Christians often showed unbelievable courage in the face of ingenious tortures designed to procure apostasy. The government was determined to root out a faith that was held to be wholly subversive; and it must be granted that after the middle of the seventeenth century Christianity, like Communism in the 1930s, was to all appearances extirpated from the land. Yet in 1865 it was discovered that in at least one locality near Nagasaki Christianity had survived in certain households as a secret faith passed on from father to son.

Japanese Christians today hold in honour not only those who died steadfast under torture but also those who fell in the defence of the castle of Hara on the Shimabara peninsula east of Nagasaki. At the end of 1637 there was a rising of the populace of Shimabara and its neighbourhood against the oppressive measures of two *daimyo*. From its early days the rebellion assumed a religious character and when the insurgents, with their wives and children, fortified themselves within the old castle of Hara they set up banners bearing Christian inscriptions, often in Portuguese. For about three months they fought valiantly against the numerically superior forces that the Yedo *Bakufu* sent against them. From the beginning they knew that their cause was, in the worldly sense, hopeless. They awaited the *Bakufu* attack, as a Japanese account has it, 'in order to gain their wishes after death'. With invocations to Jesus, Mary, and St James on their lips the besieged, numbering well over thirty thousand with their women and children, fought on until the inevitable end, which came in April 1638. Nobody was spared in the final massacre that took place when the inner citadel was overcome.* The Dutch, complying with Japanese demands, sent a vessel to bombard the beleaguered castle from the sea. This action played little or no part in hastening the castle's fall, and it would have been very difficult for the Dutch to have rejected the demand made of them, but it was a squalid episode, none the less, and it did nothing to increase their standing among other Europeans at the time.

The Shimabara revolt created a tremendous sensation, as well it might. The Portuguese were suspected, no doubt unjustly, of having had a hand in it. At all events the government in Yedo decided to put an end to all further intercourse with the Portuguese. Spanish ships and traders were already banned from Japanese shores; the English had closed their trading post in Japan in 1623, on account of mismanagement and disappointment at the low profits received, and they came no more for many years; and the Portuguese themselves, before Shimabara, were confined to a small island, Deshima, in Nagasaki harbour. In 1637, the year of the Shimabara outbreak, it was decreed that no Japanese should leave the country under pain of death, and that death would be the welcome awaiting any Japanese who, having left the country, should return.

After Shimabara all Portuguese had to leave, and it was decreed that, if any Portuguese ship came to Japan again, its crew would be executed and its cargo burnt, together with the vessel itself. In 1640 a ship did arrive from Macao, carrying no cargo but a deputation of courageous men bearing presents, in the faint hope that the *shogun* Iemitsu (Ieyasu's grandson) might relent; for the Portuguese owed the Japanese a good deal of money. All but thirteen of those on board were beheaded at Nagasaki, and the vessel was burnt. The thirteen survivors, after witnessing the execution, were sent back to Macao. Before they departed they were addressed, so it is said, by an official in these terms: 'You are witnesses

* It is recorded, however, that there was one survivor, a traitor awaiting execution in the castle dungeon.

that I even caused the clothes of those who were executed to be burned; let them (the citizens of Macao) do the same to us if they find occasion to do so; we consent to it without demur. Let them think no more of us; just as if we were no longer in the world.'

Indeed the Japanese were not to be shaken in their resolution to isolate themselves from the world. In place of the Portuguese it was now the Dutch who were confined to Deshima, in Nagasaki harbour, and the entry of Dutch ships was strictly rationed and controlled. Only the Dutch, and some Chinese, were permitted to carry on trade with Japan. The Dutch accepted severe restrictions; for the trade, such as it was, brought them a satisfactory profit. The English for their part made an effort in 1673 to resume the trading connexion that had been broken fifty years earlier. But their ship was turned away for the reason, so the Japanese declared, that Charles II was married to Catherine of Braganza, the daughter of the King of Portugal.

The closing of the country in the seventeenth century had consequences for Japan that are apparent to this day. It was pointed out in the previous chapter that in the fifteenth and sixteenth centuries Japanese traders and seafarers had made their mark in other parts of Asia. There were small communities of Japanese in Luzon, Siam, and elsewhere near the Equator. Only the action of an authoritarian government harshly and consistently applied was able to put in reverse what would seem on the face of it to be the natural expansion southwards of an energetic maritime race. A Japanese conquest of the Philippines, for example, would have been well within their capacity during the seventeenth century; and in the eighteenth they might well have anticipated Great Britain in the navigation of Australian waters. Certainly the story of European colonization in south-east Asia and, perhaps, in Australia and New Zealand would have taken a very different course if the Tokugawa government had not forced the Japanese to turn in upon themselves. It is certainly true that the Japanese chose to cut themselves off from the West at the very moment when the tide of the Renaissance was in full flood over most of Europe. The trickle of scientific knowledge that reached the country through the Dutch at Deshima, though its importance must not be underrated, was of course wholly insufficient to keep Japan abreast of the movement of thought in contemporary Europe; and it so happened that the European race, the Portuguese, with whom the Japanese had the longest contact up to 1639 was perhaps the one least likely to pass on to them the revolutionary discoveries in astronomy and the natural sciences, and indeed in the experimental method generally, that laid the foundations of modern Western technology. Apart from a number of new words that were incorporated in the Japanese language, the only important permanent legacies of the Portuguese were the musket – and tobacco.

[IV]

It was not fear of foreign conquest that led the Tokugawa government to close Japan, but rather a lack of confidence in its own position *vis-à-vis* dissatisfied elements in the state, notably the *tozama daimyo* and the *ronin*. These terms require some explanation.

Observing the principle established by Ieyasu, his son Hidetada and his grandson, Iemitsu, divided the territorial lords into three broad categories. First, there were those who were members of the Tokugawa family, sons of Ieyasu and their heirs. Secondly, there were those who were regarded as reliable vassals, who had fought on the side of Ieyasu at Sekigahara in 1600. These became known as *fudai* ('hereditary') *daimyo*. These two categories were established in fiefs dominating the real heart of Japan, from Mito, north-east of Yedo, to Wakayama, south-west of Kyoto. Certain *fudai* lords were to be found, also, in domains well beyond central Japan, so placed that they acted as a check upon the third broad category of feudal lord, the *tozama* ('outer') *daimyo*. The *tozama daimyo* were those who submitted to Ieyasu only after the Battle of Sekigahara. They presented a problem to the Tokugawa government, for among them were some of the richest of the great lords, and a combination of them, if allowed to gather their forces, could offer a serious challenge to the shogunate. As we shall see, it was in fact an alliance of *tozama daimyo* of the south-west that eventually brought about the overthrow of the Tokugawa house in the nineteenth century. One of the nightmares of the Yedo *Bakufu* in its first fifty years was the prospect of one or more of these 'outer' lords obtaining help in weapons and, perhaps, even manpower from abroad. By closing the country and by prohibiting Japanese from leaving Japan the *Bakufu* effectively cut off sources of foreign supply from the *daimyo*, for it placed under its own direct control the Dutch and Chinese trade at Nagasaki.

In the re-allotment of fiefs after Sekigahara a great many warriors were left without an overlord. Some became farmers, others took service under new masters, but large numbers became what were known as *ronin*, literally 'wave men', namely masterless warriors. Throughout the Tokugawa period the *ronin* were a distinctive element in society, and we shall meet them again, for they projected into the twentieth century a tradition embraced by many adventurers, notably on the Asian continent. The *ronin*, in history and legend, appears in many guises: as a gallant freelance, jealous of his honour; as a brawling swashbuckler ready for any deed of violence; as a bully; as a social nuisance. It was this class of men that formed the majority of the hard-fighting garrison of Osaka castle; and many of the farmers defending the fortress on Shimabara had been *ronin* in their day. There was always a danger – or so the government, in its almost morbid fear, believed – that the *ronin* in the south-west might invoke foreign help in some rising against the Tokugawa hegemony. So this was a further valid reason, in the government's view, for closing the country.

The Tokugawa shogunate erected a complicated but very effective structure of control to forestall any possibility of internal revolt. Among the measures it took was the establishment of a permanent hostage system. Every *daimyo* was compelled to reside alternately in his fief and in the shogunal capital at Yedo, and when he was in his fief he had to leave behind him in Yedo his wife and family. All travellers entering and leaving Yedo were scrutinized very strictly at barriers on the roads leading into the city, the guards being under orders to be particularly watchful for 'guns going in and women going out'; for a *daimyo* contemplating rebellion would be sure to make some effort to get his family away to safety and, at the same time, to pass arms into the city to his sympathizers there. No marriages between *daimyo* families could take place except by permission of the *shogun*. Severe restrictions were placed on the building of new castles, and indeed on the repair of old ones. The regular journeys to and from Yedo, to say nothing of the expenses involved in attendance at the *shogun's* court and in the upkeep of a Yedo residence, imposed a constant burden, in time as well as finance, on the territorial lords. For the early Tokugawa *shogun* – like Louis XIV – were clever enough to perceive that the more time you make a man spend on ceremonial affairs the less he has for activities of his own. Thus in Yedo the *daimyo* had to call on the *shogun* on at least three days a month, and in addition they were summoned to take part in many formal and, in a utilitarian sense, meaningless functions at court. They were also loaded from time to time with 'embarrassing favours' that could not be refused – such as contributing to the extension of the great castle at Yedo or to the very costly upkeep of the mausoleum shrine of Ieyasu at Nikko. By such means the shogunate intended to prevent any one *daimyo* from amassing or retaining excessive wealth. No *daimyo* was allowed to make a direct approach to the emperor's court at Kyoto, a city under the control of a high *Bakufu* official; and no *daimyo* was allowed to pass through Kyoto on his way to and from Yedo. Finally, the Tokugawa government set up and perfected a secret police system that was, it must be admitted, a model of its kind; so much so that one Japanese scholar has characterized the Tokugawa regime as the prototype of the absolute police state. Although the *daimyo*, more especially the 'outer' lords, were granted virtual autonomy within their territories, they were watched by the *Bakufu*, through its network of agents, with nervous, unwearying vigilance.

In its own domains the shogunate prescribed for the common people, as well as the warrior class, meticulous rules affecting most phases of their daily lives – their dwelling places, their dress, and the principles governing their social intercourse. These rules became the model for the great *daimyo* in the administration of their fiefs. They themselves observed in general the rules of conduct and etiquette laid down in shogunal regulations for the military houses.

The philosophical foundations that underlay the structure of Tokugawa rule are discussed in the next chapter. All that needs to be said here is that during the first few decades of its existence the Yedo *Bakufu*, by example and persuasion, went far towards enforcing an ideological orthodoxy admirably calculated to preserve the great aim of Ieyasu, namely the permanent supremacy of the house of Tokugawa in a rigidly hierarchical, peaceful, but warrior-dominated society; a society uncontaminated by the outside world; a society in which lack of order was synonymous with all that was evil. And the Japanese lived in peace – except for local peasant risings – with themselves, and with the world, for two and a half centuries – a record that most nations, reviewing their own history over a similar period, must surely envy.

Chapter 3

INTRUSION BY THE WEST

═══════════

[1]

EVEN today there lingers in Europe and America an engaging mental picture of Japan as a land of ubiquitous kimonos, of geishas posing beneath pagodas, of 'paper houses', of square-sailed junks becalmed in the Inland Sea. This vision of the 'real' Japan is comparable with the idea of Great Britain – sometimes presented by optimistic travel agencies overseas – as a country where all Scotsmen wear the kilt and bucolic Englishmen are dressed in hunting pink or smocks.

This illusory picture of modern Japan derives indirectly from the shock of delighted astonishment felt by aesthetically alive Europeans and Americans when they 'discovered' Japan during the nineteenth century. In this discovery the wood-block prints of Hiroshige, Hokusai, Utamaro, and many others played a leading part. In Great Britain the craze for 'Japaneserie' was at its height during the last twenty years of the nineteenth century – *The Mikado* was one symbol of the craze – but it was prolonged by the Anglo-Japanese Alliance until well into the First World War.

What enchanted those who knew Japan only from the wood-block prints, from the works of such writers as Loti or Lafcadio Hearn, or from a globe-trotter's tour from Kobe to Yokohama (with side excursions to Nara and Nikko) was the survival – perceptible in country districts up to the Pacific War – of certain elements of the self-contained society that had matured under the Tokugawa shogunate. That society was indeed in many respects most pleasing to the eye. Being wholly strange to the West it retains a peculiar fascination for us.

Consider, for example, the roads, and one road in particular – the Tokaido (Eastern Sea Road) connecting Yedo (the modern Tokyo) with Kyoto. Five principal highways started from Nihonbashi in Yedo. Two of these, the Tokaido and the Nakasendo (Central Mountain Road) led to the 'home provinces' round Kyoto. The other three went to Nikko, to north-east Japan, and to an area north-west of Mount Fuji. But the Tokaido was the most famous; for it was the busiest. Perhaps only Kim's Grand Trunk Road could rival, for colour and interest, the Tokaido during the last hundred years or so of the Tokugawa shogunate. For up and down the Tokaido there passed the great processions of the western *daimyo* on their way to and from the Tokugawa court at Yedo, the *daimyo* himself carried in a palanquin in the heart of the procession, before which the vulgar had to make profound obeisance on their knees, their heads touching the ground. The retinue of armed men, especially for one of the important 'outside' lords, might be very large and was invariably preceded by retainers who on meeting or passing others would call out the name of their lord and summon those of lower rank to make the appropriate genuflexion. The *samurai* retainers wore two swords, and in common with all men save priests and outcasts, had their back hair drawn forward in a queue over the centre of their shaven skulls. Once a year the *Opperhoofd*, or director, of the Dutch factory at Deshima passed along the Tokaido – he was treated, and after the mid eighteenth century, respected like an 'outside' *daimyo* – on his regular spring visit to the *shogun*'s court, the Negroes and Indonesians among his servants providing a spectacle very strange to the Japanese along the road. In terms of speed the most impressive travellers were the official express messengers who rode or ran in pairs, one bearing a lacquer box containing government documents or money and the other a lantern marked 'Official Business'. A relay system enabled urgent messages to cover the distance between Yedo and Osaka in two and a half days, the usual time being a little over one week. Then there were, of course, frequent pilgrims travelling singly or in groups on their way to visit famous temples and shrines, merchants' carriers, troupes of actors, purveyors of quack remedies, and, from time to time, an imperial envoy from Kyoto journeying with his suite to Yedo Castle.

Yet travel was not easy, in spite of the well spaced resting-places – the famous fifty-three stations of the Tokaido – along the road and the many inns and tea-houses that catered for those making a journey. At intervals there were barriers. All travellers had to pass through these between sunrise and sun-set. It was at these barriers that the officials and spies of the *Bakufu* were especially active and thorough in their persis-tent curiosity about everyone who was using the road; and the usual penalty for making a detour, to avoid a barrier, was death. Furthermore, not many rivers were bridged, although some could be crossed on bridges of boats tied together. At one river, the Oigawa, even the use of boats was prohibited. The ban was imposed for strategic reasons, the policy of the shogunate being to maintain a static society. Thus at the Oigawa everybody and everything had to be forded across, the more important travellers crossing on the shoulders of porters.

These porters were local villagers who were compelled to supply this service, part of the system of *corvée* in force along all the main highways; for each village, during three months of the spring and three of the autumn, had to provide a quota of men and horses for official traffic. This form of compulsory service was a very irksome burden upon the always hard-pressed, overtaxed peasantry and it led in a few cases to armed uprisings.

Owing to the paucity of bridges and to the narrow moun-tain passes that had to be crossed, there was very little wheel traffic on the main roads. Produce in bulk was generally moved by sea; and its usual destination was Osaka, the dis-tributive headquarters of the country. In the days of the Ashi-kaga *shogun* this city was already famous as a merchandising centre; and until this century it remained pre-eminent, though Yedo came to be a rival. Even today Osaka can claim to be in some respects the commercial capital of Japan. In the Tokugawa period, at least after the middle of the eighteenth century, there were, so it is said, as many as twenty thousand boats of one kind or another working between Osaka and Yedo.

For in spite of the Tokugawa determination to preserve a static hierarchical society, very important changes, mostly undesired by the shogunate, were taking place within this society. Their origin was the spread of money in a country that was organized from above on the basis of a rice economy. The official standard of wealth was rice. The status of a *daimyo* was expressed in terms of the assessed rice crop in his domain. The *samurai* class as a whole received its income, from *shogun* or *daimyo*, in bales of rice. And rice at the beginning of the Tokugawa age was the principal means of exchange. But during the long years of internal peace, and with the growth of such cities as Osaka and Yedo (having a population of over half a million by the early eighteenth century), the use of such cumbersome material as rice as a means of exchange gave way to money.

Silver and copper coins had been in very limited circulation for several hundred years, but it was not until the fifteenth century that they began to resemble, if faintly, what we understand as a currency. However, foreign trade in the sixteenth and early seventeenth centuries promoted greater circulation of coins, since the main export from Japan in the vessels of the Portuguese, Spanish, Dutch, and English was gold and silver. This naturally encouraged the development of mining, and the minting of coins. The convenience and use of these were complementary; and as the seventeenth century progressed, more and more of the *samurai* class traded their rice for cash with merchants in Osaka, who soon developed into a very rich, though still socially inferior, community. As Yedo grew, becoming the headquarters of a very large population of non-productive warriors, so the merchant class there multiplied in numbers and in wealth.

On the other hand the *samurai* class steadily lost economic power. For it was the boast of the *samurai* that he was indifferent to money, or, rather, to the details of acquiring and holding money.*He looked down on the merchants, for they were, after all, the lowest of the four broad social classes in the land – warriors, peasants, artisans, and merchants, in that order.

By the early years of the eighteenth century the warriors of Japan, *daimyo* and retainers alike, were in debt to the merchant class. This class, now enriched, contrived to develop for itself in the cities of Yedo and Osaka a manner of life that was vigorous and sophisticated at the same time. It is reflected in most of the colour prints depicting Yedo life, in the novels of Saikaku, and in the plays of Chikamatsu; for it was in this period that the Kabuki theatre, in spite of intermittent restrictions placed upon it by a disapproving *Bakufu*, flourished as a bourgeois form of art. From time to time the government would try to prune the affluence of the city merchant class. There would be cancellations of *samurai* debts, or the outright confiscation of the property of some over-ostentatious rice broker; and earnestly-phrased injunctions were issued time and again from Yedo Castle against extravagance in dress and behaviour among the merchant class.

Yet these measures had little effect; and while in the countryside, especially after 1700, the conditions of all but a few usurers and rich farmers grew more rigorous – the rural *samurai* class often living in a state of defiant but uncomfortable indebtedness – there prevailed in cities such as Yedo a robust, pleasure-seeking life, predominantly bourgeois in tone. Still, the merchants were unable, and were indeed perhaps unwilling, as merchants, to acquire the social prestige that usually accompanies economic power. To some extent their position may be compared with that of the wealthier Armenian subjects of the Ottoman empire; but the parallel cannot be pushed too far. For the lot of the Japanese merchant under the later Tokugawa *shogun* was, in reality, a good

* Fukuzawa Yukichi (1835–1901), the famous founder of Keio University, tells us in his autobiography how he was taken away, by his *samurai* father, from his teacher because the latter was giving instruction in elementary arithmetic. Fukuzawa's father said that it was 'abominable that innocent children should be taught to use numbers – the instrument of merchants'.

deal happier. In practice the Japanese class structure was rather less formidably rigid than would appear at first sight. Social mobility, it is true, was very slight; but it was not entirely non-existent. From time to time wealthy and ambitious merchants achieved *samurai* rank through adoption or marriage. Conversely, impoverished warriors were glad, sometimes, to enter the merchant class. There is no doubt, too, that financial power enabled individual merchants to wriggle themselves into important political positions within certain fiefs. One Japanese of the Tokugawa period has recorded – it may be with a touch of exaggeration – that the anger of the rich merchants of Osaka could strike terror into the hearts of the *daimyo*. In course of time some of the more powerful brokers and money-lenders became in effect bankers to the great feudatories. The house of Mitsui, for example, was famous in this field long before it built up its supremacy as a huge capitalist combine in modern Westernized Japan.

The rise and efflorescence of this capitalist class was not really compatible with the continued existence of a feudal society; and indeed, by comparison with early Tokugawa Japan, the country in the late eighteenth and early nineteenth centuries can hardly be described as truly feudal except in a rather formal sense. It may be said that under the *Bakufu* Japan remained scientifically, industrially, and politically backward. But commercially there took place on a small scale in Japan, during the seventeenth and eighteenth centuries, the same development that was seen in contemporary England, France, and Holland – namely the growth of mercantilism. In other words in Tokugawa Japan the city was the monopolistic 'mother country' and the surrounding countryside was the Japanese substitute for the overseas colony. There was of course no industrial revolution, but handicraft manufacturing was diverse and well developed, often catering for a national market; and there was considerable mining both of metals and coal. There was a good deal of regional specialization, much encouraged by enterprising *daimyo*. One area, for example, would concentrate upon the manufacture

of porcelain, another on silk, and so on. On the whole, however, these handicrafts were the products of part-time, household industry, supplementing the extremely meagre livelihood of rice-growing peasants. Most of the capital that was
accumulated piled up in the hands of the numerically small
merchant class – the traders and the money-lenders.

Generally speaking the peasants, the broad base supporting this society, suffered abominably. There is no space here
to discuss the unfortunate economic effects on the peasants,
and on the lower, country *samurai* class as well, of the often
feverish fluctuations in the price of rice that followed upon
the speculations of the Osaka brokers, or to dilate upon the
harshness of the system of taxation to which the peasants
were subjected. Rice remained the standard of value, though
in many transactions it was largely supplanted by money as
the means of exchange, and both the shogunal government
and the *daimyo* paid lip service to the importance of a happy
and healthy peasantry; but in general their behaviour towards this, the most numerous class in the country, would
make one believe that they were determined to extract from
the peasant every last ounce of his produce over and above
what was just sufficient to keep him working in his fields.
Oppression was handed on downwards. A *daimyo* nagged to
settle some of his debts would halve the stipends of his retainers; and they in turn would try to compensate themselves
by exactions on the peasantry working on their lord's domain.
As if this were not enough, the eighteenth and early nineteenth centuries were marked by periods of ruinous famine.
After one of these the population fell by over a million. An
indication of the state of affairs in the countryside can be
found in the widespread custom of *mabiki*, a word that in its
literal sense means 'thinning out' (as with young rice plants)
but which meant, in the context of Tokugawa Japan, the
practice of infanticide. The typical farmhouse could not
afford to feed more than a certain number of mouths; and
unwanted babies were very often exposed to the elements.
Thus we find that, while there was a steady increase in the
population of the country during the seventeenth century,

thereafter it remained constant at something rather over 29 million, actually falling after a great famine in the 1830s. For a country the size of Japan, virtually deprived of all foreign trade and dependent upon a single stable crop, this was a very large population.

By repute the Japanese countryman is regarded as submissive and long-suffering. Certainly the Confucian tradition of obedience to superiors did not predispose the farming community to question the authority of the *samurai* class. Nevertheless if things seem intolerable the Japanese peasant has been known to revolt in a manner reminiscent of the Jacquerie; and in the latter years of the Tokugawa shogunate, and also in the first decade (1867–77) of the Meiji period, there were a great many peasant uprisings in various parts of the country. Some left-wing Japanese scholars have claimed for these disturbances a political revolutionary character, but this seems far-fetched. With very few exceptions the risings were motivated exclusively by local economic grievances. There was no evident desire to change the existing order of society or system of government.

These peasant disturbances can hardly be cited as a sign of the impending break-up of the Tokugawa government, but they can be regarded, certainly, as indicative of its failure to match political stability with sound economic administration. By the early nineteenth century the façade of the shogunate, firm though it seemed, hid from view a very creaking governmental structure that was ready to collapse if it were subjected to a really challenging blow. This could come from two directions. A foreign nation, or group of nations, might threaten the shogunate; or it might be the object of attack from an alliance of the 'outside' lords. What in fact happened, in the 1860s, was a combination of these two separate threats, together with a third, rather unexpected challenge, from the imperial court at Kyoto. But before we come to consider these developments, a word must be said, fairly briefly, about the *shogun* themselves and the currents of thought that on the one hand strengthened and, on the other, undermined their political supremacy in Japan.

[II]

There is in fact very little that need be remarked, in this book, about the *shogun* from Hidetada, Ieyasu's son, to Keiki, the last of the fifteen *shogun* of the Tokugawa line, who died in the twentieth century. There were a few able men among them, but broadly speaking they leaned heavily on the advice of counsellors, often permitting the latter to exercise the real control of public affairs. Perhaps the most interesting, because the most gifted and eccentric, of these *shogun* was Tsunayoshi, who reigned in Yedo from 1680 to 1709. A scholar, a patron of the arts, very much in control of the government, generous to the emperor and the Kyoto nobles, Tsunayoshi is best remembered for his excessive concern for the welfare of Japanese animal life, more especially dogs.

Prompted by certain monks and by his mother, a devout Buddhist, Tsunayoshi felt that his failure to beget an heir – his only son died young – was a punishment for acts of cruelty committed by his ancestors, and that these might be expiated by a national policy of kindness to animals, especially dogs. For he was born in what was known, according to the traditional zodiac, as the 'Year of the Dog'. So he decreed that all animals, and dogs above all, must be treated with the greatest courtesy and consideration.

This policy was enforced for some twenty years in a manner most tiresome to the people at large. Those who caused the death of animals, of birds even, had to answer for it; and punishments included exile, imprisonment, and death. Stray dogs, for example, had to be cared for. Tsunayoshi gave land in Yedo for this purpose. To the carefully maintained kennels that were built on this land dogs were conveyed on occasions in palanquins, escorted in honour as though they were minor *daimyo*. The death of an animal, particularly the death of a dog, had to be reported to the authorities, who made searching inquiries as to how and why the animal had died. It is not surprising that the creator of this canine paradise was know in Yedo as the 'Dog *Shogun*'.

Although like his forbears and successors he kept telling the Japanese to live thriftily, Tsunayoshi, especially in the last years of his reign, abandoned himself to extravagance. During his rule there occurred what was called the 'Genroku Age', a fairly short period at the end of the seventeenth century. During this age the urban civilization of Yedo and Osaka was unusually brilliant; and correspondingly there was, so everybody said, a decline in the old *samurai* virtues of hardihood, loyalty, and martial excellence. All the more striking, then, was the episode, which took place at this time, of the revenge of the 'Forty-seven *Ronin*'.

This is perhaps the most famous melodrama in Japanese history and is still re-enacted on the Kabuki stage and on the cinema and television screen. The full story, even when stripped of the fictional accretions that have grown up round it, is long and complicated. But its gist can be told simply and in a few sentences.

A *daimyo* named Asano wounded, in the *shogun*'s castle at Yedo, another lord named Kira who had grossly insulted him. For this act Asano was condemned to commit formal suicide, which he did. A number of his retainers decided to avenge his death, which had taken place, of course, as a result of the offensiveness of Kira. The loyal retainers were now men without an overlord – hence the title of *Ronin* – and under the leadership of one of their number, a chief retainer called Oishi, they made ready, with extreme care, a plan to attack and kill Kira, the villain of the piece. The execution of the plan was not easy, as Kira was very much on his guard. But at last, early one snowy morning in winter, Oishi and his fol- lowers – there were in fact forty-six of them in all – stormed Kira's house in Yedo and killed him. They took his head to the temple where their dead lord Asano had been laid to rest, and having presented Kira's head to Asano's tombstone they gave themselves up to the authorities. For a long time the shogunal government could not decide what action to take. Oishi and his men had caused a breach of the peace and there- fore deserved to be punished. But they had shown themselves, in a rather lax and pleasure-loving age, to be paragons of private morality; for Confucian ethics laid down that no man should allow the unjust death of a father or of an immediate feudal superior to go unavenged. The *shogun*, Tsunayoshi, felt that on the whole Oishi and his followers ought to be pardoned. This indeed was the opinion of most of the population of Yedo, high and low alike. But the view of certain influential scholars was that a sentence of honourable suicide would meet both requirements of public law and order and the real wishes of the loyal retainers themselves, who must surely desire, having achieved their aim, to join their avenged lord in the next world. This argument impressed the *shogun*. So Oishi's band committed *hari-kiri*; and their tombs, adjacent to that of Asano in the temple of the Sengakuji in Tokyo, are still respectfully visited by many thousands every year.

Oishi, the leader of the famous *ronin* band, was praised then and in succeeding generations as exemplifying the ideal of Bushido, or 'the way of the *bushi* (warrior)'. Thanks to the Pacific War this word, Bushido, has become widely known outside the confines of the Far East, and for a great many people, both European and Asian (including a large number of modern Japanese), it is charged with associations of a very unpleasant nature. During the Pacific War it was often claimed by the West that Bushido was in fact a fairly recent invention, a concept worked out and developed by Japanese nationalists in the nineteenth century at the earliest. This is not entirely true. For although Bushido, as a specific term, was not popularized until about the 1890s, both the word and the concept were known at least 300 years earlier. Indeed, in so far as Bushido means a Spartan devotion by a warrior class to the arts of war, a readiness for self-sacrifice, and loyalty to a martial superior, it existed as an ideal in the twelfth century, and its origins can be traced back several hundred years before that.

But it was during the Tokugawa shogunate that the ethic of loyalty, as a vital constituent of Bushido, achieved a semi-religious status. This was because the *shogun* of the Tokugawa line, though often sincere patrons of Buddhist institutions,

made Confucianism – or, more strictly, later Chinese rein-
terpretations and elaborations of Confucianism – into the
orthodox ideology of the state. To this branch of Chinese
philosophy, Neo-Confucianism, the shogunal government
lent its entire authority, going so far as to invest one line of
scholars in this subject with the hereditary title of 'Lords of
Learning'. Neither Buddhism nor Shinto – and at this time
the two faiths were, institutionally, often interrelated – were
set aside. Buddhism was usually regarded by the authorities
as a praiseworthy religion, especially for the lower classes;
and the Confucian scholars favoured by the shogunate declared that in essentials Shinto and Confucianism were identical. Still, Confucian ethics, with their emphasis on the duties
of inferiors to superiors and on the supreme importance of
harmony within a rank-conscious society, were ideally suited
to the permanent interests of the Tokugawa house. This alone
is sufficient to account for the ideological policy, if we may
use such a term, of the shogunate. After all, the concept of
loyalty must have seemed invaluable as an effective check
upon any anti-Tokugawa tendencies among the military
class. But this view, in the very long run, was quite mistaken.

It was the policy of the Tokugawa *shogun*, beginning with
their founder Ieyasu, to encourage learning – by which they
meant the study of the Chinese sages – and in the seventeenth
century, as Japan settled down to long years of peace, it was
no longer considered quite enough for a self-respecting
samurai to perfect himself in the military arts while neglecting
the cultivation of his intellect. There was a notable promotion
of learning, and of a number of schools for *samurai* youth, in
the late seventeenth and early eighteenth centuries; and
among the teachers, of whom some are still famous in Japan,
there arose conflicting schools of thought corresponding to
various branches of Chinese philosophy. These do not concern us here. What is important is the fact that out of this
intellectual activity there developed, slowly over the years, a
kind of chain reaction very injurious to the prestige of the
shogunate.

The official encouragement of learning led finally to the

appearance of a group of scholars who were to question the fundamental basis of the shogunate as an institution. For as these scholars examined the concept of loyalty, a corner-stone of the Neo-Confucianism so firmly endorsed by the *Bakufu*, they began to think that after all perhaps the Japanese owed loyalty not so much to the Tokugawa *shogun* in Yedo as to the rather neglected line of emperors, who lived in tolerable comfort but without any power in Kyoto. The next step – and the whole process was spread over a great many decades – was to begin suspecting that the *shogun* were in fact usurpers. The final stage in this chain reaction was to believe that the *shogun* ought to make way for a restoration of the emperor to his rightful position as real sovereign of the country. This belief, of course, was not dangerous until the weakness of the shogunate was demonstrated in the middle of the nineteenth century, following the intrusion by Europeans and Americans upon Japanese soil. But long before Commodore Perry sailed into the Bay of Yedo in 1853 there had occurred a revival of traditional nationalist feeling, associated with a renewed interest in the *Kojiki* and *Nihon Shoki** and with the appearance of a number of Shinto sects. By the early nineteenth century there was already a school of thought inimical to the shogunate and therefore often persecuted by it, a school of thought aggressively nationalist in tone and thus implacably hostile to those who stressed the excellence of the Chinese sages. The Sinophiles indeed were looked upon as disloyal; for the nationalists pointed out that Mencius had said that rebellion against an unvirtuous emperor could often be justified. This could have no application to Japan. Everybody knew, said the nationalists, that the emperors of Japan enjoyed the lasting virtues bestowed by their divine descent.

Thus among the educated classes in Japan there was already, by the 1850s, a mental climate prepared for a return of the emperors to the centre of the stage. There was also – though this was much less apparent – a half-conscious readiness among a few people to abandon the national policy of exclusion.

* See pages 24–8.

The Tokugawa rulers had made the first breach in the dyke they had erected against the outer world when in 1716 Yoshimune, the eighth *shogun*, relaxed the ban on the importation and study of works in Western languages – which in practice meant books written in Dutch – entering the country through the Deshima settlement at Nagasaki. With commendable perseverance translations were made of some of these works, the Japanese being especially interested in books on medicine and military science. In course of time there grew up a small but influential group of Japanese specialists in the Dutch language and culture, and through them some knowledge of European sciences, as well as of events in the world at large, percolated to the government in Yedo. But the ban on Christianity was not relaxed. On the contrary, any mention of this religion or of its evangelists was enough to ensure the confiscation and probable destruction of any book from overseas. Curiosity about the outside world has always been a Japanese trait – the Chinese, on the other hand, for centuries regarded knowledge of countries beyond China as superfluous – and this has produced in the Japanese reaction to foreigners and foreign countries both admiration and dislike. In Tokugawa days, particularly towards the end, these emotions were complicated by fear, as there arose on the northern horizon the vague threat suggested by Russian penetration of eastern Siberia, northern Sakhalin, Kamchatka, and the Kuriles. This implicit menace, though it was perhaps exaggerated by the *Bakufu*, coupled with the economic weakness of the country, inspired some Japanese from the end of the eighteenth century to advocate the opening of the land to foreign trade, the building of a mercantile marine, and a search for markets and colonies overseas.

It was clear, at any rate, that foreign ships – Russian, British, and American – were appearing much more often in Japanese waters. They usually asked for supplies; sometimes, but not always, these were given them, and they were pressed to sail away again as quickly as possible. For months a Russian vessel lay off Nagasaki, in a vain endeavour to induce the Japanese to accept an official envoy. When, rebuffed, the

Russians sailed away they were asked to send no more ships to Japan. This was in 1805, six months before Trafalgar. But as the colonization of Siberia proceeded, it became by the middle of the century a matter of some importance to the Russians that they should be able to obtain supplies from Japan for eastern Siberia and for their Alaskan colony. Similarly the British were bound to turn their attention to securing the opening of at least some of the harbours in Japan for their use – though not, it was thought, necessarily for their profit, since it was the opinion of many English merchants that Japan would have little to sell and could thus buy few of the products of Manchester and Birmingham.* The defeat of China in the Opium War, in 1842, and the subsequent cession of Hong Kong was followed by a prolonged British naval survey of the Ryukyu Islands, which were under the suzerainty of the *daimyo* of Satsuma, and in 1846 a British missionary was allowed to settle in Okinawa.

It looked as though either Russia or Great Britain would be the first to compel the shogunal government to open its doors. The betting, we might say, was on the Russians. For in October 1852, there set off from Europe on the long voyage to the Far East the Russian Admiral Putyatin, empowered to persuade the Japanese to sign a commercial treaty. However, when the four vessels of Putyatin's expedition approached Nagasaki in August 1853, an American squadron under Commodore Matthew Perry had already presented what amounted to an ultimatum to the shogunate.

Perry had delivered a letter from President Fillmore, requesting the opening of trade relations, and he had warned the Japanese that he would be back again in Yedo Bay the following year to receive their answer. And he told them that

---

* Nevertheless there were of course those who thought that a mutually profitable trade could be developed with Japan. And it was widely believed that it was positively immoral, as well as contrary to all ideas of progress, for the Japanese to continue to shut themselves off from the world. This was the age in England, we must remember, of confident and aggressive Victorian capitalist expansion, symbolized by the Great Exhibition of 1851.

on his second visit he would arrive with a much larger squadron.

[III]

Four factors combined to stimulate American interest in Japan. These were the development of trade with China through Canton, the growth of the American whaling industry in the Pacific, the opening-up of California, symbolized by the Gold Rush of 1849, and the progress of steam navigation. The Great Circle Route, the shortest to China from the Pacific Coast of America, took vessels very close to, and often in sight of, the shores of Japan. But sailors looked at the distant coastline with some apprehension. It was known that for any seamen who happened to be stranded in Japan – and this was apt to occur to shipwrecked whaling crews from time to time – the treatment was unfriendly and disagreeable, although in general by no means intentionally cruel. The foreigners were minutely interrogated and then transported in closed palanquins –by reason of their size excruciatingly uncomfortable for other than Japanese passengers – all the way to Nagasaki, there to await eventual repatriation through the Dutch at Deshima.

Thus one of the purposes of Perry's expedition was to obtain a promise from the Japanese of future good treatment of any shipwrecked Americans. But although much play was made of this then, and in subsequent histories dealing with American–Japanese relations, it may be doubted whether the treatment of American nationals in Japan played more than a minor part in the motives behind Commodore Perry's visit to Japan in the summer of 1853. Of much more importance was, for example, the need to secure supplies, including coal, for American ships sailing to and from Canton. There was too, the expectation that a useful trade could be driven with the closed country, an expectation sharpened by the prospect of competition from Great Britain. Certain businessmen exerted considerable pressure in Washington towards the authorization of a naval expedition to force open the closed door across the Pacific. Nobody was more active than a

certain Aaron Haight Palmer, an energetic New York commission agent profoundly interested in the steamship trade
with the Orient. Similar pressure on Congress came from
churches, missionary boards, diplomats, and naval officers.
Indeed the very development of transcontinental communications across the United States from the Middle West to
the Pacific was closely related, in the eyes of many exuber-
ant people at the time, with the vision of America becoming, as part of her 'manifest destiny', the commercial
leader in both China and Japan.

Commodore Perry, a blunt but astute autocrat of nearly
sixty, set off for the Orient with an advantage denied to most
military and naval leaders of modern times. He was allowed
to write his own instructions; and these terminated with a
very useful escape clause: '[the commodore] should feel assured that any departure from usage, or any error of judgement he may commit will be viewed with indulgence.' Since
then, among Americans at any rate, perhaps only General
MacArthur has had such a free hand. Indeed between Perry
and MacArthur there are certain evident parallels; and these
were not, it may be said in passing, unperceived by the latter.

Perry's unbending firmness towards the Japanese was
largely motivated by his knowledge of what had happened
seven years earlier, when another American naval officer,
Commodore Biddle, had tried to negotiate with the Japanese
and had been repulsed. On that occasion Biddle had been
bound by instructions from Washington to act cautiously;
and accordingly he had been very conciliatory in his approach. This had been interpreted by the Japanese as weakness, with results unfavourable to American prestige.* So
Perry on his first visit simply handed over the President's

* Biddle allowed himself to be jostled by a Japanese seaman and did
nothing to secure the punishment of the offender, merely contenting himself with an apology. A year later when a stranded American sailor
threatened his Japanese guards with vengeance from American warships
they told him they had no fears on that score, as a common soldier had
knocked down an American commander a year before and no notice had
been taken. Rumours of this affair even reached Okinawa within a year
or two.

letter to Japanese representatives on shore, having first refused to deal with the minor officials who were sent to him,
and declared that he would return for an answer next year.
Then, before departing, he sailed, in defiance of the Japanese,
further up the Bay of Yedo to within sight of the suburbs of
the city.

The 'Black Ships', as they were known, created a tremendous sensation on shore. There were, on this first visit in July
1853, four of them – two driven by steam. Most of the Japanese had never seen or imagined such ships. But the government in Yedo was not taken by surprise by this unwelcome
visit. Plenty of warnings of a general nature had been received, through the Dutch, that some such expedition was on
its way. Furthermore, information about Perry's squadron
had reached Yedo from Okinawa, through Satsuma; for
Perry was in the Ryukyus before coming to Japan, and it was
in fact his full intention that advance news of his impending
arrival should reach the Japanese authorities.

Perry's expedition, and of course Admiral Putyatin's of the
same year, faced the shogunate with a most unpleasant
dilemma. Quite apart from the laughable disparity between
the military power of Japan and that of the great Western
nations now pressing upon her, a disparity that would ensure
the complete defeat of Japan if she chose to go to war, it was
perfectly easy for a hostile fleet to impose starvation upon the
inhabitants of Yedo, for the great bulk of the food supplies
for the city came in from the north and west by sea. Interference with this traffic and with Japanese fishing vessels
would have an effect on Yedo that would be both rapid and
catastrophic. Serious resistance, then, was scarcely feasible.
This hard fact was appreciated by the shogunal government,
notably by its leading figure, a clear-sighted counsellor
named Abe Masahiro. Foreign pressure might be, must be,
opposed step by step, in a rearguard action. But in the end
the *Bakufu* would have to give way, unless it was prepared to
contemplate the utter ruin and defeat of the country – including the ruin of the Tokugawa house – to be followed perhaps
by a colonial or semi-colonial status under one or more of the

Western nations – an unthinkable prospect, though it was to be faced by Japan less than a century later, in August 1945. On the other hand, to open the country was almost equally dangerous, at least to the position of the shogunate. For who among the *samurai* class would continue to respect a 'Barbarian Suppressing Great General' (*Sei-i tai-shogun*)* who denied his title by an open surrender to foreign threats? Already financially weak, the shogunal autocracy was in no shape to survive any notorious loss of face. In any case the days of direct personal rule by the *shogun* were over, Ieyoshi – the twelfth *shogun* of the Tokugawa line – leaving all government to his counsellors. He took office in 1837, and his death in 1853, only a month after Perry's first visit, though it meant little from a practical point of view, was a further complication for the government. The later *shogun*, indeed, exercised no more real power than the emperor. The prestige of the latter, on the contary, was increasing. We have referred to the revival of emperor-centred nationalism in early-nineteenth-century Japan, and there is no doubt that well before Perry's appearance the court at Kyoto was gradually strengthening its position. One indication of this renaissance had been the establishment, rather unwisely sanctioned by the *Bakufu*, of a college in Kyoto for the education of the ancient court nobility.† At this college the sons of the nobility, and many nobles themselves under the age of forty, received a training that gave them a knowledge and confidence sufficient to take an active interest in public affairs. The result was that in the confused struggle to overthrow the *Bakufu* in the 1860s the old court nobility – the so-called *Kuge* – had a certain positive role to play. Later on in more modern times, as we shall see, at least two heirs of the Fujiwara, Prince Saionji and Prince Konoye, achieved outstanding positions in political life.

Thus at the very moment when the shogunate was faced with its most critical and embarrassing external problem its

* See page 39.
† This college became eventually the *Gakushuin*, or 'Peers' School'. It still exists in Tokyo.

position within Japan was unstable, while that of its rivals, the Kyoto Court and the 'outside' lords, was becoming increasingly firm.

It was a sure sign of weakness that the *Bakufu*, after Perry's departure in 1853, should have taken the unprecedented step of seeking the advice of the *daimyo* as to the answer that should be made to President Fillmore's letter. Abe Masahiro, the chief counsellor and hence the real ruler of the country, had a translation of the President's letter sent to all the *daimyo*, high government officials, and leading Confucian scholars. In a covering communication Abe Masahiro included a sentence that also suggests that he was hoping to have replies favouring compliance with American demands (protection of stranded sailors, mutual trade, provision of coal and other supplies at one or more Japanese port). For Abe wrote: 'It is requested . . . that you will express your opinions freely on the matter even though they may be contrary to established policy.'

The replies were confused. There were those that contained a warning that any concessions now would only open the way to further demands (a sound prophecy, as it turned out) and therefore the established policy of exclusion should be adhered to. This argument was expressed with particular force by the powerful Lord of Mito, a member of the Tokugawa house. He told the government that the foreigners would end by swallowing up Japan. 'If we fail to drive them off now,' he said, 'we shall never have another chance.' And there were many *daimyo* and others who took this line, either from sincere conviction or from a wish to add to the embarrassment of the shogunate. But others advised that the country be opened, at least for the time being. Their view was that Japan should study and master the mechanical techniques of the foreigners in order to turn the tables on them in later years.

It must be remembered that the Russian expedition under Admiral Putyatin, which had arrived in Nagasaki in August 1853, remained for three months until, faced with the calculated procrastinating tactics of the Japanese, it sailed away, only to reappear in the same harbour early in January 1854. The presence of the Russian squadron had an important bearing, though the Americans were the last to admit it, on the effectiveness of Perry's mission.

So the decision reached by Abe Masahiro and the government was understandable. In a decree the *Bakufu* declared:

Everyone has pointed out that we are without a navy and that our coasts are undefended. Meanwhile the Americans will be here again next year. Our policy shall be to evade any definite answer to their request, while at the same time maintaining a peaceful demeanour. It may be, however, that they will have recourse to violence. For that contingency we must be prepared lest the country suffer disgrace. Therefore every possible effort will be made to prepare means of defence.

There was much activity in Yedo Bay, and along the coastline, in the construction of further gun batteries, the drilling of men, and so on. Outwardly it looked as though the *Bakufu* would take a fairly strong line when Perry returned, for it even made a public announcement of the emperor's wish to have the foreigners driven off. But behind this brave show Abe Masahiro and his colleagues were resigned, it cannot be doubted, to the probability of having to accept the American demands.

Perry duly returned with seven ships in February 1854. Meanwhile, as we have seen, Putyatin, with four Russian ships, was back in Nagasaki. Perry remained firm in his attitude to the Japanese, not hesitating to utter threats at appropriate moments in the negotiations, which indeed were not long drawn-out.* Finally, on 31 March 1854, at a little fishing village called Yokohama, a treaty was signed. This agreement, known as the Treaty of Kanagawa, opened the ports of Hakodate and Shimoda to American ships for supplies and for trade, subject to local regulations. Shipwrecked mariners

* To his own government Commodore Perry proposed the annexation of Okinawa in the event of the Japanese turning down the demands he had to make; for Okinawa, as he pointed out, would make a good base for military operations against Japan.

were to receive help and protection. An American consul was to be allowed to live in Shimoda.

It will be seen that the door was not yet fully opened, only forced ajar a little way. Neither of the only two ports open to American ships was close to Yedo; and, more important, they were both remote from Kyoto. Hakodate was in Yezo (the modern Hokkaido), and Shimoda was at the southern end of the Izu peninsula, a small, enclosed harbour easily overseen and controlled from the land. Ratification of the Treaty was to follow within eighteen months of its being signed, but the clause permitting the arrival of an American consul after a further eighteen months was interpreted by the Japanese to mean that the consul would come only if both countries thought it necessary; and Japan, needless to say, thought it not at all necessary.

However, once opened, the door was soon pushed further on its hinges. Admiral Sterling of the Royal Navy entered Nagasaki, partly in search of Russian ships; for the Crimean War had begun. Admiral Putyatin had sailed north to the waters of Sakhalin several months earlier, still without having signed a treaty. Admiral Sterling, however, obtained a written agreement from the Japanese allowing British vessels to call at Nagasaki and Hakodate for supplies. This was in October 1854. During the next month, the indefatigable Putyatin with one vessel, the *Diana*, sailed into Osaka Bay. This created serious alarm among the Japanese, for Osaka was very close to the imperial capital at Kyoto. It is true that Putyatin soon sailed away to Shimoda, but the moral effect of his visit to Osaka Bay was considerable, even though the Japanese could claim that his departure for Shimoda was a triumph for themselves.

While in Shimoda Putyatin's ship *Diana* was severely damaged in a whirlpool caused by a serious earthquake that occurred at the end of 1854 – an earthquake widely interpreted as a sign of the wrath of the gods at the concessions made by the shogunate to Commodore Perry and Admiral Sterling. Later the *Diana* sank. Putyatin and the Russians were now at the mercy of the Japanese; who, it must be said

treated then with great kindness.* Russian-Japanese negotiations continued at Shimoda and were concluded in February 1855 with the signing of a treaty that gave the Kurile
Islands south of, and including, Etorofu to Japan and the
other islands, north of these, to Russia. Sakhalin was to remain unpartitioned between Russia and Japan. Three ports
– Nagasaki, Shimoda, and Hakodate – were opened to Russian ships. And there was a clause that was to have important
consequences. This was the provision of extra-territorial
rights, which were of course to be insisted upon by the other
powerful nations of the West in their later treaty arrangements with Japan during this period.

Before the end of 1855 the *Bakufu* had signed yet another
agreement with a foreign power, this time the Netherlands†;
and in 1856 Townsend Harris arrived in Shimoda to take up
his duties as diplomatic representative of the United States.

A stubborn, shrewd, doggedly courageous, and, at the same
time, fairly sensitive man, Townsend Harris has an important

* Putyatin wrote: 'Neither can I leave unsaid the readiness of the
Japanese to give us all assistance and to supply us with whatever we
needed. Officials who had immediately been sent by the government
sympathized with our plight, hurriedly constructed houses to shelter us
from the rigorous winter season, and tried by all means to alleviate our
situation.' From the Report of Adjutant-General Putyatin to the Grand
Duke Lord High Admiral translated by Dr G. A. Lensen in his *Russia's
Japan Expedition, 1852–5*. Tallahassee (University of Florida Press), 1955,
p. 97.

† After Perry left Japan for the first time, the *Bakufu* commissioned the
Dutch to procure vessels in Holland for Japanese use. These could not be
found, owing to the demand for shipping created by the Crimean War.
But the Dutch sent a steamship, the *Soembing*, to Nagasaki with orders to
the officers to instruct the Japanese in marine architecture, navigating,
and gunnery. Later, in 1855, she was presented to the *Bakufu* by the king
of the Netherlands. Renamed *Kanko-maru* she was the first steam vessel
possessed by Japan, and she was used by the shogunal government as a
training ship in Yedo Bay. The good feeling engendered by the visit of
this ship – which led, among other things, to the establishment of ship-
building yards under Dutch guidance – had the effect of greatly easing
the restrictions imposed on the Dutch by the 'Deshima system'. In this
much more friendly atmosphere the Dutch were able to reach a treaty
settlement with the Japanese.

place in the history of this time. With considerable skill he played on Japanese fears of British intrusion – Great Britain was now the dominant power in Eastern waters – and he overcame obstruction and prevarication to such purpose that in June 1857 he signed a convention with local officials giving extra-territorial rights to American citizens in Japan, as well as the right of permanent residence to Americans not only in Shimoda but also in Hakodate. Harris noted, with gratification, that 'missionaries may actually come and reside in Japan'. His next move was to insist on being received in audience by the *shogun* in Yedo. This proposal was resisted with great determination, but in the end Harris got his way. In December 1857 he was ushered past members of the Great Council, kneeling with their heads bowed to the fine white mats, into the presence of Tokugawa Iesada, the extremely delicate thirteenth *shogun*. After Harris had made his short speech presenting his credentials, Iesada replied in words interpreted to Harris as follows:

Pleased with the letter sent with the Ambassador from a far distant country, and likewise pleased with his discourse. Intercourse shall be continued for ever.

The occasion indeed marked the real end of the long period of virtual isolation from the world; but it was only the beginning of a many-sided invasion by the West that was to have consequences beyond the wildest fears or dreams of any who lived in Yedo on that day.

Chapter 4

MODERNIZATION

[1]

FROM the close of 1857, there ensued a ten-year period of great tension and confusion. During that decade foreign diplomats and merchants established a somewhat uneasy residence in Japan. The Japanese seemed unable to decide whether they admired or detested the strangers, some of whom, it must be said, were grossly acquisitive and deserved to be called barbarians. It was in large measure directly due to this alien intrusion that the shogunate lost such prestige that it crumbled before an armed challenge by an alliance of feudatories from western Japan united under the chrysanthemum banner of the imperial house.

Among historians there have been, successively, two main schools of opinion on what really caused the downfall of the shogunate. The first, which held the field for a great many years, believed that the Tokugawa system of government might have continued essentially unchanged had it not been for the forcible opening of the closed door by the United States and other countries; for this school of opinion claimed that it was only the coming of the foreigners that undermined the authority of the Tokugawa government, and so ruined it. This view, however, has been superseded by another, which emphasizes the undoubted fact that the whole regime had been under indirect attack from many quarters inside Japan long before Perry arrived. The slow but irresistible pressure of internal economic change, notably the growth of a merchant capitalist class, was eroding the foundations of the *Bakufu*, and therefore – so the argument runs – Western aggression, exemplified by the Perry expedition, merely provided the final impetus towards a collapse that was inevitable

in any case. But this later school of thought has tended perhaps to go too far in underrating the impact on Japan of successful Western pressure in the 1850s. For among the *samurai*
class the sense of shock induced by the advent of the foreigners
was catastrophic. It is inconceivable that the shogunate
would have collapsed had it been able to resist the demands
made by the United States, Russia, Great Britain, and other
nations of the West. Its failure to put up a successful resistance
was of course inevitable, but it was none the less fatal to its
power, weakened as this was by other forces.

The imperial house itself would have been in some danger
– as it was in 1945 – if it had been at the centre of political administration in the 1850s. However, fortunately for its prestige, the Throne was shielded from harsh realities by the
institution of the shogunate, which had to bear the entire
burden of pressure and criticism from both within and
outside Japan.

Gradually, during the ten years that followed the American Minister's reception by the *shogun* in 1857, the centre of
political gravity shifted from Yedo to the ancient capital,
Kyoto. It should not be seen, of course, as in any sense a
tale of rivalry between the persons of emperor and *shogun*.
The Emperor Komei, the 121st of his line, who reigned from
1846 to 1867, was, it is true, rather less of a figurehead than
many of his predecessors, but he could hardly act outside the
limits of his ceremonial functions without the advice of those
surrounding him; and the ultimate triumph of the imperial
cause was due, in the main, to the political cunning, foresight,
and resolution of certain very able young men from the
western clans of Satsuma, Choshu, Tosa, and Hizen working
together with a number of Kyoto nobles and Osaka merchant
families. On the side of the shogunate, between Perry's first
visit in 1853 and the end of 1867, there were three Tokugawa
rulers. Keiki, the last of them, had a decided personality and
a will of his own; but when we consider the *Bakufu* in its
twilight we must think in terms not of *shogun* – for the most
part harmless nonentities – but of a succession of leading counsellors in Yedo Castle exercising power in the *shogun*'s name.

One of these, Abe Masahiro, we encountered in the last chapter. He died in 1857. Thereafter the most important counsellor was Ii Naosuke, lord of Hikone; and for a brief period his position seemed unassailable. In 1858, in defiance of the wishes of the Throne, he authorized, in the name of the *shogun*, the Japanese signature to treaties with the United States, Russia, Great Britain, and France. These treaties, and those to be concluded with other Western nations, contained in the main three conditions. Yedo and certain ports were opened to foreigners. A very low scale of import duties was imposed upon Japan. Nationals of the eighteen countries with which such treaties were signed were exempt from the jurisdiction of Japanese courts of law. Right up until the last years of the nineteenth century the revision of these so-called 'unequal treaties' was the prime aim of successive governments in Japan; and indeed the whole question of treaty revision was the dominant factor in Japanese foreign policy throughout the second half of the century.

There was shrill and widespread opposition to the concessions by Ii Naosuke to foreign pressure. The opposition was symbolized by the slogan, 'Revere the Emperor; expel the Barbarians!' Ii Naosuke dealt very harshly with his opponents, and he became perhaps the best-hated man in the land; and one snowy morning, early in 1860, he was done to death, as his palanquin drew near the *shogun*'s fortress at Yedo. The exact spot where this noted assassination occurred is readily identifiable today; for the approach to the Sakurada Gate of Yedo Castle (the present Imperial Palace), with its background of moat and tree-crowned wall, remains unchanged, although down the hill where once the palanquins of the great lords were conveyed in state to the Castle there now passes a less engaging procession, of cars, buses, and trams.

Even after the death of Ii, slain by nationalist fanatics from Mito, the *Bakufu* contrived to put up a fairly impressive rearguard action; for in most fiefs, even in those that were to turn against it, the house of Tokugawa had some supporters. However, the decline in its fortunes became clear to everyone in

1862 when the rule, instituted in the seventeenth century, compelling the *daimyo* to spend every alternate year in Yedo was greatly relaxed and the family hostage system abolished.*

A contemporary Japanese observer wrote, in terms of picturesque hyperbole:

And so the prestige of the Tokugawa family, which had endured for three hundred years, which had really been more brilliant than Kamakura in the age of Yoritomo on a moonlight night when the stars are shining, which, for more than two hundred and seventy years, had forced the *Daimyo* to come breathlessly to take their turn of duty in Yedo and had day and night eighty thousand vassals at its beck and call, fell to ruin in the space of one morning.

But what really sealed the fate of the *Bakufu* was its failure to deal effectively in 1866 with military opposition from the Choshu clan, at the western extremity of the main Japanese island of Honshu. The Choshu forces, led by young commanders of exceptional ability, were drilled, armed, and, to some extent, clothed after the European pattern. More revolutionary, however, was the fact that these forces were not confined to members of the traditional warrior class but accepted small townsmen and peasants as volunteers. The military competence shown by the Choshu commanders was to secure for their clan after the collapse of the shogunate a dominant role in the organization of a Westernized imperial army. Indeed for more than fifty years, until after the First World War, the highest appointments in the Japanese army were held as a rule by members of the Choshu clan or their henchmen.

Previous to their successful defiance of the shogunate the Choshu authorities had challenged the maritime nations of the West. In 1862 an edict had been issued by the Emperor Komei to the *shogun* instructing him to set about the expulsion of the foreigners in the summer of the following year. The foreign envoys were duly notified of this edict, but the topsy-turvy nature of Japanese affairs at the time is well indicated by the way the notification was made. For the ministers and consuls were given verbal assurances by the *shogun*'s government that no action would be taken to put

* See pages 67–8.

the edict into force. However, there were plenty of fanatics who were determined to drive out the 'barbarians'. There had been, in fact, several atrocious murders of individual foreigners in Yokohama and Yedo – the British Legation was attacked by night on two occasions – and in September 1862 an Englishman named Richardson was hacked down from his horse and killed on the Tokaido by Satsuma retainers accompanying their lord on the long journey home from a formal visit to Yedo.

In June 1863, on the date fixed by the Throne for the expulsion of the foreigners, Choshu shore batteries on the Shimonoseki Straits, the north-western gateway to the Inland Sea, started to fire on American, French, and Dutch vessels. There was prompt retaliation by warships of France and the United States. But the warriors of Choshu continued to obstruct shipping off Shimonoseki, although that same summer they were able to see what happened to Kagoshima. This was the capital of the Satsuma clan whom the British were resolved to chastise for their failure to make amends for the murder of Richardson. Kagoshima was bombarded by a British squadron, and in consequence the greater part of the town was burned to ashes, though, as it happened, with very little loss of life. John Bright and other radicals in England strongly condemned the action. But this piece of gunboat diplomacy did not inspire the men of Satsuma with lasting resentment. On the contrary, it laid the foundations of a mutual respect that was to develop into a friendly association, lasting for many decades, between the British and Japanese navies. For in the building up and control of the Japanese navy Satsuma had a dominant part, similar to that of Choshu in the army.

There were some Choshu men, it must be admitted, who perceived the folly of trying to close the Shimonoseki Straits to alien ships. Among them were five young men who had left Japan secretly in a British vessel for Europe. Two of them, Ito Hirobumi and Inouye Kaoru, were to play a great part in the political life of their country. What they saw of London and of British mercantile and industrial might was enough to convince them that it would be impossible for the Japanese, for a great many years at least, to rid their shores of the foreigners. Ito himself had taken part in an incendiary raid on the British Legation in Yedo, and he had no great love for the 'barbarians'; but like many of his countrymen he could be very adaptable when confronted with realities. While he was in London he read in *The Times* of the stand taken by Choshu at Shimonoseki, and he hurried home hoping to persuade the clansmen to give way to the Western naval powers headed by Great Britain. He nearly succeeded, but was overborne by wilder spirits; and in September 1864 a combined British, Dutch, French, and American fleet demolished the Choshu batteries and obtained a pledge that the straits would be opened.

In their armed action against Satsuma and Choshu the foreigners were, in fact if not in name, doing the work of the shogunate; for it was the latter's duty and responsibility to exact retribution from unruly feudatories. But the task was beyond its powers. Indeed it was evident that, if the anti-Tokugawa forces were to combine, there would probably be civil war, in which the shogunate might well be defeated.

Satsuma and Choshu had for some time regarded each other with enmity, but in 1866 they reached an understanding and entered into a secret alliance, joining forces with the important clans of Tosa and Hizen, also in the west of the country. To this union some rich members of the Osaka merchant community, notably the Mitsui family, gave financial backing. Many of the court nobility at Kyoto and, it seems the Emperor Komei himself were closely associated with this anti-*Bakufu* alliance. The movement to revive the emperor's supremacy gained strength very rapidly. There were many who believed that the *shogun*, once he was induced to lay down his powers, should be given an honoured place in the new system of government. This was the policy, both sensible and generous, advocated by the leaders of the Tosa clan; and had it been followed much bloodshed might have been avoided. But Satsuma and Choshu had other ideas. The young zealots who shaped the aims of these two

clans were determined to strip the shogunal house not only
of its powers but also of its material possessions.

The British Minister of the day, Sir Harry Parkes, was a
commanding figure. Sensing that the future lay with the
western clans he made it his business to know and give
counsel to some of their real leaders, relatively young men
who swayed the will of their feudal superiors.* The whisper
grew that Great Britain favoured the unification of the
country under the emperor.

France, on the other hand, was openly sympathetic with
the shogunate. Parkes had a worthy rival in the energetic
French Minister, Léon Roches. The bitterness cherished by
Satsuma and Choshu against the shogunate was largely
aroused by the very close ties that existed between France
and the *shogun*'s government during the 1860s. It was rumoured, for example, that the shogunate signed a secret
treaty with France in 1867, when the *shogun*'s brother attended the Paris Exhibition of that year. Certainly the French
government, through Léon Roches, gave a great deal of advice, political as well as military, to the *Bakufu* in its last years.
French instructors trained the *shogun*'s forces, and the Yokosuka ironworks and docks, at the entrance of Yedo Bay, were
financed and built with French assistance. For a time the
France of Napoleon III exerted in Japan an influence sur-
passing that of any other foreign power, even Great Britain.†

In 1866 the young *shogun* Iemochi died and was succeeded, with some reluctance, by Tokugawa Keiki, his guardian.
In the following year the death occurred of the Emperor
Komei. His successor was his fifteen-year-old son, known to
posterity as the Emperor Meiji, who in a reign lasting
forty-five years was to preside with great dignity over what
might be called the Victorian Age of Japan.

* Parkes was well served by two young attachés of great ability, who
in their approach to the language and the people of Japan combined the
qualities of the scholar and of the man of action. They were Ernest Satow
(later Minister at Peking) and A. B. Mitford (later Lord Redesdale).

† Preoccupied with the Civil War and its aftermath, the United States
in the 1860s played only a minor role in Japanese affairs.

Such astonishing progress was made during the reign of the Emperior Meiji – progress justly gratifying to national pride – that it became the custom in the twentieth century for foreigners as well as Japanese to look back at the Meiji Restoration of 1867–8 as a smooth, almost bloodless, transfer of power.

It is true that the dying struggle of the *Bakufu*, and of its supporters, was not greatly prolonged. But for several months there was civil war. The *shogun*, Keiki, voluntarily surrendered his administrative powers to the youthful emperor in November 1867. This was in response to a memorandum, from the lord of Tosa, of which the operative words were:

Your Highness should restore the governing powers into the hands of the Sovereign, and so lay a foundation on which Japan may take her stand as the equal of all other countries.

However, this was not the end of the matter. Satsuma and Choshu, having moved warriors into Kyoto, planned to carry out a *coup d'état* in the form of an armed attack on the *shogun* who was residing in his Kyoto palace. So, following his 'abdication', Keiki and his supporters left the city by night for Osaka. The ex-*shogun* himself probably had no very firm intention of putting the issue to the sword. But his henchmen pressed with the greatest vigour for an attack on Kyoto and the suppression of the forces surrounding the emperor. It must be remembered that such action was not regarded by its advocates as disloyal resistance to the emperor's cause. On the contrary it was looked upon as a praiseworthy crusade to rescue the emperor from the clutches of self-seeking 'outside lords'.

So at the end of January 1868, some three weeks after the proclamation of the restoration of full powers to the emperor and barely a fortnight after Keiki's withdrawal to Osaka, the army of the ex-*shogun* advanced upon Kyoto, and at the small towns of Toba and Fushimi, between Osaka and Kyoto, there was fought a three-day battle that decided the fate of Japan. Two and a half centuries earlier, at Sekigahara, Keiki's ancestor, Tokugawa Ieyasu, had crushed his opponents, among whom the western feudatories were prominent. The latter now had their revenge. Moreover Toba-Fushimi, like Sekigahara, was won in great measure by treachery. For late on the second day of the battle part of the Tokugawa forces went over to the enemy.

Following the defeat of his army Keiki, who had remained in Osaka, took ship to Yedo. No doubt Yedo Castle could have withstood a long siege.* But Keiki gave orders for its surrender to be negotiated with the commanders of the imperial troops. Some diehard Tokugawa supporters put up a fierce resistance on the heights of Ueno in the eastern section of the city, but apart from this affray Yedo was spared the smell of bloodshed. Elsewhere certain clans, mindful of long allegiance to the heirs of Ieyasu, fought on with tenacity, the stand of the Aizu warriors at Wakamatsu in northern Japan providing an epic of heroism long remembered.† The last fires of resistance blazed in Hokkaido, at Hakodate, where an admiral of the *shogun*'s navy – later to hold high office under the emperor – held out for some months in 1869. Thus ended the supremacy of the house of Tokugawa, which provided Japan with fifteen *shogun*. The last of them, Keiki, lived on for a great many years. Not until June 1902 was he received in audience by the Emperor Meiji. Soon afterwards he was raised to the rank of prince, the highest in the nobility.

The forces that overthrew the shogunate had long been associated, in the popular mind at least, with the cry 'Expel the Barbarians!' and it might have been expected that, with their victory, anti-foreign agitation would become more strident and widespread. There was indeed an incident at Hyogo – the modern Kobe – when Hizen warriors, in pursuit of the ex-*shogun*'s army, fired on the foreign settlement; and there was a murderous assault on a boatload of French sailors near

* Medieval fortresses in Asia can be tough propositions for an attacking force, even when it is equipped with modern (pre-atomic) artillery. This was learned by the Japanese at the walls of Nanking in 1937, and by the British at Fort Dufferin in Mandalay in 1945.

† The most famous among the Aizu warriors were a group of young men known as the *Byakkotai*, or 'White Tigers'. One Japanese regiment in continual action against the British in Burma from 1942 to 1945, called itself by this title and wore 'White Tiger' badges.

Osaka. Furthermore, when Sir Harry Parkes was on his way to his first audience with the emperor in March 1868, the party was attacked by two swordsmen in the streets of Kyoto.

Nevertheless it was no part of the policy of the new men who ruled Japan to antagonize, much less drive away, the 'barbarians'. They realized that, to achieve a position of power in the world, their country would have to be modernized. With all speed it would have to catch up with the technologically advanced nations of the West. But modernization could never be accomplished without Western help and advice. The official attitude to the West was stated by the young emperor himself, in April 1868, in what was known as 'The Charter Oath':

Knowledge shall be sought for all over the world and thus shall be strengthened the foundation of the imperial polity.

A number of foreign technicians had already been employed both by the shogunate and by certain feudatories before 1868. But after that year there were many more of them – British, American, French, German, and Dutch – engaged by the Japanese government as pilots, railway and marine engineers, financial and legal advisers, agricultural experts, university and school teachers, military and naval instructors, and so on. At the same time Japanese were sent abroad – to London, Berlin, Paris, New York, and Manchester – to learn from the West.

Even before the collapse of the *Bakufu* the outward appearance of the Japanese showed some signs of the influence of the West. Many warriors, not only of the shogunate but also of Choshu and Satsuma and other clans, wore trousers instead of the *hakama* or 'skirt' that formed the lower portion of the official dress of the *samurai* class. The few who had been abroad sometimes possessed European clothes, but these were not much worn by Japanese until the 1870s, when both the carrying of swords and the traditional male hairstyle, the *chomage* or 'topknot', were abolished. The nervous, hearty gathering of foreigners who formed the merchant community of Yokohama, and later of Kobe, was

watched and studied by the Japanese with eyes that might
be hostile or envious or admiring, but which were invariably
alive with curiosity. For among the Japanese there has never
been the disdainful indifference that has often characterized
the Chinese attitude towards foreigners. The Japanese have
never been too proud to learn.

In the autumn of 1868 the emperor paid a visit of some
weeks to Yedo. It was an historic occasion, demonstrating
the formal re-emergence of the imperial house into the centre of public life; and in the following spring the court
moved permanently to Yedo – now renamed Tokyo (Eastern Capital) – and the castle of the Tokugawa *shogun*
became the Imperial Palace. As the emperor's palanquin
approached the city along the Tokaido there was drawn up
at a point on the road, near Yokohama, the regimental band
of the British infantry detachment that guarded the foreign
settlement; and to the tune of 'The British Grenadiers' the
imperial procession passed on into the modern age.

[II]

The nominal head of the new government in Tokyo was a
court noble; but the real controllers of power were men of
much junior rank, from the western clans. They formed a
remarkably efficient oligarchy. The most notable personalities in the group were, perhaps, Saigo Takamori and
Okubo Toshimichi from Satsuma, Kido Koin, Ito Hirobumi, and Inouye Kaoru from Choshu, Itagaki Taisuke
from Tosa, and Okuma Shigenobu from Hizen.

The indispensable prelude to modernization was, of course,
the abolition of feudalism and this might have proved a long,
even bloody task. Yet once having overthrown the shogunate and defeated its retainers, the triumphant western clans,
provided they preserved a united front, were in a strong
position to impose their will upon the country, for they had
no serious rivals among the other feudatories. Thus, when
Kido proposed that the lord of Choshu surrender his fief to
the emperor, and when this idea was adopted by his col-

leagues with respect to the fiefs of their own superiors in Satsuma, Tosa, and Hizen, an example was set to the other territorial lords which they could hardly ignore, much less reject.

In surrendering their fiefs the four western lords made a public demonstration of their act by addressing to the emperor a memorial, probably composed by Kido Koin. Some sentences from this document must be quoted.

There is no soil within the Empire that does not belong to the Emperor . . . and no inhabitant who is not a subject of the Emperor, though, in the Middle Ages, the Imperial power declined and the military classes rose, taking possession of the land and dividing it among themselves as the prize of their bow and spear. But now that the Imperial power is restored, how can we retain possession of land that belongs to the Emperor and govern people who are his subjects? We therefore reverently offer up all our feudal possessions . . . so that a uniform rule may prevail throughout the Empire. Thus the country will be able to rank equally with the other nations of the world.

The great changes – for which the abolition of feudalism cleared the way – that were to transform the face of Japan were indeed revolutionary; but the events of 1868–9 are properly described as a Restoration. For, as the memorial suggests, the idea of surrendering the fiefs to the emperor was based upon the intention of restoring the ancient centralized administration of Japan that had been borrowed, as we saw, from T'ang China. The last sentence of the memorial is important. It is the key to the understanding of the essential spirit of Japanese national policy from 1869 until the end of the century.

The ambition to become a great power in the world was neither unnatural nor ignoble. It seems necessary to say this; for one consequence of Japan's aggressive and bellicose expansion, from 1931 up to and including the Pacific War, has been the belief, in Japan itself as well as in the Western world, that the Japanese rise to world power – accomplished within two generations – was in some way a rather discreditable episode. But the nineteenth century was, of course, an age of confident nationalism not only for Russia,

Germany, and Italy, but also for the United States, Great
Britain, and France. It was natural for the Japanese, as the
nineteenth century advanced, to imitate the example set
them by these nations. Now Japanese imitativeness has
always alternately irritated and amused the West. But to
learn is to copy. For a backward country, technological
progress must be based of necessity upon imitation.

There is another point to be borne in mind. The Japanese
could see and take warning from what was happening in
China. That massive country, too proud and disdainful to
copy the methods of the West, was humiliated again and
again by the 'barbarians'. And a weak Japan presented a
constant temptation to those powers who were already beginning to carve out commercial empires for themselves in China
or in territories under Chinese suzerainty. No doubt Great
Britain, her hands already full with India, had for the time
being reached satiety; and America in the sixties was riven
by the Civil War and its aftermath. But it was fortunate indeed for Japan that first the Mexican fiasco and then the
menace presented by Prussia discouraged Napoleon III from
becoming deeply committed in adventures in the Far East.
Yet we should remember that the colony of Cochin China
was annexed by France in 1862, that the protectorate of
Cambodia was established in 1867, that this was followed
soon afterwards by French penetration, admittedly with little
initial success, in the region of Haiphong and Hanoi. And
there was, of course, the shadow of Russia. It was in 1860 that
China ceded to Russia the coastal area between the Amur
and the Korean frontier; and close to this frontier the Russians founded Vladivostock, which means 'Ruler of the East'.

So one can hardly blame the Japanese oligarchy for being
peculiarly sensitive about the status of their country *vis-à-vis*
the powerful nations of the West. There was, after all, some
possibility in the 1860s that Japan might slip, almost imper-
ceptibly perhaps, into a posture of semi-colonial dependence
upon one or more of the great Western powers. The British
infantry detachment at Yokohama symbolized for the Japanese a shadow that must at all costs be removed. Here one

might add that one man in his lifetime could have seen, as a child, the red-coat band saluting the emperor's palanquin on the road to Yedo and could have watched, as an octogenarian, the British Commonwealth Occupation Forces in 1946 mount guard outside the Imperial Palace in Tokyo. For the rise and fall of the Japanese empire occupied a space in time of barely seventy-five years.

Not long after the Restoration a Japanese delegation went abroad and tried in vain to secure from the Western nations some revision of the treaties which had imposed extra-territorial jurisdiction and low tariffs on Japan. The venture was premature; but the failure spurred the Japanese government to make greater efforts to hasten the modernization of the country. This proceeded at an ambitious pace throughout the seventies and eighties.

The feudal lords, after 'restoring' their territories to the emperor, had received generous compensation in government bonds, and for a brief period they were permitted to act as governors of the provinces they had once ruled. But very soon the country was divided into prefectures, to be headed by prefectural governors appointed by Tokyo.

A central, modernized system of taxation was established, together with a new system of coinage. Banks, railways, harbours, lighthouses, dockyards, telegraph offices, printing presses and newspapers, post offices, cigars and cigarettes – the entire apparatus of Western material civilization seemed to find some reproduction, some kind of echo, in Japan. Indeed the first two decades of the Emperor Meiji's reign saw a Japan to all appearances intoxicated with the strong wine of Western thought, techniques, and customs. Some prominent Japanese, such as Inouye Kaoru, even went so far as to advocate the universal and permanent adoption of European dress by both sexes, the substitution of bread for rice, and the large-scale importation of sheep to graze on those rice fields, transformed into meadows, that had not been turned over to the production of wheat, oats, and barley. Sir George Sansom refers to a popular children's song, composed in 1878, known as the 'Civilization Ball Song', in which children counted the bounces of a ball, reciting ten desirable Western objects – gas lamps, steam engines, horse-carriages, cameras, telegrams, lightning-conductors, newspapers, schools, letter-post, and steam-boats.*

In this upheaval both the *samurai* class and the peasantry endured much hardship. The peasants found that their rents remained extremely high under the new order. Indeed the condition of the peasantry actually deteriorated for several years after the abolition of feudalism; for a prime aim of the government was to encourage industrialization, but as the cost of living rose, and there was some rise in money wages for those working in industry, no benefits came the way of the hard-pressed peasants. The upshot, in some localities, was a series of disturbances, or peasant riots or uprisings which, it must be stressed, had as yet no specifically political motivation of any kind. The peasant risings of the 1870s were almost exclusively directed towards the redress of local economic grievances.

The *samurai* class suffered partly because of its sheer size numerically, amounting to well over a million and three-quarters out of a total population in 1870 of roughly thirty-four million. It is true that the modernization of Japan, in its early stages, was carried out by the *samurai* class, that the Japanese bureaucracy was staffed at first exclusively by this class, that the whole apparatus of the state was (to quote the words of one authority) 'soaked through and through with *samurai* influence'.† It is also true that it was on the whole from the *samurai* class, rather than from the existing merchant community, that the new capitalist entrepreneurs of the nineteenth century were to rise to varying degrees of affluence. But when every allowance is made for the large numbers who entered government service or took to business life successfully, there remained a large residue of ex-warriors, numbering scores of thousands, who could not

* G. B. Sansom, *The Western World and Japan.* London (The Cresset Press), 1950, p. 401.

† E. H. Norman, *Japan's Emergence as a Modern State.* New York (Institute of Pacific Relations), 1940, p. 83.

adjust themselves to the new conditions of life. They were scarcely able to live on the small pensions granted to them by the state, pensions that within a few years of the Restoration were to be compulsorily commuted into inadequate lump sums. *Samurai* grievances were exacerbated, further, by the decree forbidding anyone, other than a policeman or member of the regular armed forces, from carrying a sword. Another blow to *samurai* pride was the introduction of conscription, with its implication that any Japanese, however mean his birth, could acquire the martial virtues regarded for centuries as the attribute of a minority privileged class.

Samurai dissatisfaction expressed itself in several revolts, the most serious of which occurred in 1877 in Kyushu. This was the celebrated rebellion of Saigo Takamori about which something must be said in detail. For the whole affair, including what led up to it, illustrates clearly the turbulent nature of political and social life at the time; and, what is more, at least part of the mentality that inspired Saigo's rebellion was to reappear from time to time throughout the course of modern Japanese history up to the present day.

Saigo Takamori has been mentioned already as an outstanding member of the Satsuma clan and as one of the oligarchy which governed the country after the fall of the shogunate. The well-known bronze statue of Saigo, and his devoted dog, at Ueno in Tokyo suggests very well the nature of his personality; for physically he was a big man. And his strength of character matched his outward appearance. Men as large as this in body and spirit have not been over abundant in Japan, and for this reason they are usually remembered with affection beyond the run of their fellows. Thus Saigo is generally referred to as 'the great Saigo'. Yet he rose in rebellion against the imperial government and was officially designated as being guilty of high treason at the time.

Following the overthrow of the shogunate the oligarchy, composed, as we have seen, principally of members of the four leading western clans, worked together without serious disruption for some time; but within four years of the Restoration a serious split developed over a question of foreign

policy, namely the conduct of future relations with Korea.
The Japanese had tried to apply to Korea what might be
called the Perry treatment. A mission had been sent to that
country in an endeavour to force it to open its doors to the
new Japan. But the Koreans rebuffed the Japanese without
much ceremony, and treated later overtures with rather in-
sulting hostility – between Japan and Korea there had been
little love lost since Hideyoshi's adventure in the sixteenth
century. Saigo and an important group in the government
felt that a punitive expedition should be sent to Korea. Saigo
proposed to take personal command of the expedition, which
would not only advance Japan's national prestige and
avenge the real or fancied insults received but would also
provide occupation, and perhaps glory and profit, for dis-
gruntled, restless, and desperate members of the declassed
samurai community. For a time it looked as though Saigo
would have his way; for his main opponents in the government were abroad, on their abortive mission to secure a
revision of the treaties with the Western powers. But the
Korean issue was deferred until their return, whereupon
they maintained, successfully, that Japan should concentrate on internal reconstruction and modernization before
embarking on adventures overseas. Being deeply impressed,
from first-hand observation, by the strength of the great nations of the world and by Japan's impotence in terms of
industrial power, they perceived that Japanese intervention
in Korea would be premature; for it might well lead to com-
plications with Russia – a prospect that Saigo, dauntless but
unrealistic, accepted with equanimity but which his opponents in the government regarded as disastrous. The debate,
between Saigo and his party on the one side and the so-called
'peace' party on the other, lasted for several days and was
exceedingly bitter. In the end, having lost their battle, Saigo
and several other important members of the oligarchy withdrew from the government. In his home province, Satsuma
in Kyushu, Saigo devoted much of his time to a school he
established, in which training in the martial arts formed
perhaps the most important part of the curriculum. Although

drawn back into the government for a space he never returned permanently to Tokyo. He spent most of his time in
Satsuma watching with growing disapproval the various
government measures – such as the introduction of conscription – that seemed designed, in his eyes, to ruin for ever
the *samurai* order as the traditional pillar of Japanese society
It was indeed to be expected that in the opinion of many
former warriors the reforms of the 1870s were too drastic or
too hastily imposed. Eventually, in 1877, armed rebellion
broke out in Satsuma, with Saigo at its head.

There followed a bloody campaign lasting several months,
in which the forces of the government, commanded in reality,
though not in name, by Yamagata Aritomo of Choshu, succeeded in suppressing the rebellion, at a cost to both sides of
over thirty thousand casualties. At the end Saigo, wounded,
was beheaded on the battlefield, at his own request, by a
close friend.

Saigo's army was made up of members of the *samurai* order.
The army of the government was a new conscript force, and
its success in the field proved to everyone that the common
people, if trained and disciplined, could fight as bravely as
the old warrior class. It was an important discovery, pregnant
with consequences terrible for a large part of Asia. In the
words of Yamagata, 'the Japanese, whether of the military
class or not, originally sprang from the same blood, and, when
subjected to regular discipline, could scarcely fail to make
soldiers worthy of the renowned bravery of their ancestors'.

As a sop to *samurai* agitation the government, in 1874, had
sent a small force to Formosa to deal with aborigines who
were alleged to have ill-treated sailors from Japan and the
Ryukyu Islands. The expedition had been successful and the
matter effectively squared with the Chinese government. But
it was the suppression of Saigo's rebellion, not the Formosa
expedition, that gave Japanese leaders the confident belief
that in time an army trained on modern lines might challenge
first China and then Russia with every chance of success.

From his point of view, of course, Saigo's armed protest
was no rebellion. He was not resisting the imperial will, for

this was misdirected by 'evil advisers' whom Saigo would have driven from power had he been successful. This attitude of mind, of ancient origin in Japan, was general among all extreme nationalists and provided, to their own satisfaction, the justification of many acts of violence. In August 1945, when Japan accepted the Potsdam Declaration and surrendered, there was the most natural and lively fear that many fanatics – heirs to Saigo – would refuse to accept the emperor's command, though broadcast to the nation, on the grounds that it did not really express the imperial will but rather than of weak-spirited or treacherous ministers. It can be said that Saigo's rebellion was in one sense the last stand of the old feudal order in Japan, but in so far as it was inspired by extreme ultra-nationalist ideas it cast dark shadows forward, far into the future.

[III]

The time was drawing near for Japan to be introduced, very gradually, to that sublimated form of civil war, party politics. After the split in the oligarchy in the seventies some of its dissident members, notably Itagaki Taisuke of Tosa, conducted by means of public meetings and through the press an agitation for the establishment of representative institutions. The ideas of Mill and Rousseau were invoked to support this demand.

The notion of a political party in legitimate opposition to the government was new and alien to Japanese thought. One of the main concerns of government during the shogunate had been to watch out for and suppress the formation of any groups or factions taking an interest in public affairs. Those in authority after the Restoration found it hard to conceive of a political party that was not essentially subversive. Furthermore, in the first two decades of the Meiji period the government was so busy building up, on a pragmatic basis, the strength of the nation – the slogan of the day was *fukoku kyohei*, 'a rich country and a strong army' – that it looked upon the demand for representative institutions as almost frivolous; other things had to come first. Only firm, patriarchal rule, it was felt, could drive the backward people of Japan along the road to national greatness.

However, the so-called 'progressives', those agitating for *minken*, 'people's rights', always argued that it was this very necessity to hasten forward the modernization of Japan that made it desirable that there should be some kind of national representative assembly. Japanese liberalism, in the nineteenth century at least, was intimately associated not only with strong nationalist sentiment but also with a strident type of jingoism. For the idea of Japanese expansion grew in proportion to the spread of mass education. Compulsory education was instituted in 1872 on an ambitious scale. The educational plan called for the establishment of nearly 54,000 elementary schools – or roughly one to every 600 inhabitants – and the result fifty years later was that the Japanese became what they still are – the most highly literate people in Asia. The progress of education, together with the system of conscription, moulded the people into a nation of patriots, and it also furthered a public-spirited demand for some say, however indirect, in the government of the country. It is true that only a minority of the population was ever politically conscious in the full sense of the term. Nevertheless, education – and the word embraces the acceptance of half-comprehended Western political ideas – gave rise eventually to a real if amorphous public opinion, although as a mass phenomenon this hardly counted for much until well into the twentieth century. By that time it could be roused, as we shall see, over specific issues, such as the peace terms after the Russo-Japanese War or the price of rice in 1918. The demand for representative institutions in the early Meiji period came from a small but important section of the population, led by former members of the oligarchy and comprising scholars and writers, medium and small landowners, rice-wine brewers, and manufacturers of domestic goods in country areas. Persons such as these formed the backbone of the first political association; and there was also a fringe of eccentrics, die-hard fanatics, and an assortment of rough characters generally. These lent colour to the government's claim that this association was a dangerous body of men to be treated on occasions with great severity by the police.

This infant political association developed into a small party known as the *Jiyuto*, or 'Liberty Party' – the word 'Liberal' conveys a false impression, shot through as it is with its Western connotations; for it is fair to say that legitimate self-interest, rather than any devotion to political principles, was the motivation behind the actions of perhaps the majority of those taking a leading part in the so-called 'progressive' movement. Indeed in the climate of Japanese life it could hardly be otherwise at that time. This is not to deny the existence of any appreciation of such principles as human rights, the equality of man, freedom of speech, and so on. Such ideas were sympathetically received by a few scholars, and some lip service was paid to them by certain of the leaders of the *Jiyuto*. As one would expect, it was the younger generation, among the small politically conscious minority of the educated population, which was most attracted to concepts such as these. But the real force in Japanese politics has been the appeal exercised not by abstract principles but by very human personalities.

One of these was Okuma Shigenobu of Hizen, who in 1881 was forced to secede from the governing oligarchy of which he was perhaps the outstanding member. Having left the government he organized a political group known as the *Kaishinto*, or 'Progressive Party'. This party, unlike the *Jiyuto*, was decidedly urban in character and was closely associated with certain members of the new capitalist class, such as Iwasaki Yataro, the founder of the Mitsubishi concern. The *Kaishinto* was far less radical than the *Jiyuto*, and the two parties had little in common save the smallness of their numbers and their dislike of the government. They attacked each other with great bitterness, thus making it all the easier for the government to deal with them. Harried by rigorous police supervision and disrupted by the defection of their leaders, the two parties did not have more than a rather brief existence; but they reappeared later in another form, and under varying names they remained the two chief political parties in Japanese society up to 1940 and were the ancestors of the two Conservative parties in the post-Surrender years.

Faced with two opposition parties the government organized one of its own; and so for a time there were three political parties without a parliament – the Western pattern neatly reversed.

However, some kind of national representative assembly was on its way. In 1881 the emperor announced that this would be instituted nine years later, in 1890. This imperial edict certainly represented a concession by the oligarchy to the demand for some sort of representative government; and it was an indirect tribute to the example set by Great Britain, the United States, Germany, and France. But it was also a triumph for the Conservative members of the oligarchy, specifically Ito Hirobumi and Yamagata Aritomo of Choshu. Okuma had wanted a legislative assembly established much earlier. His advice to the emperor proposed 1883 as the date for the opening of an assembly. This was considered premature by his colleagues, who forced him to resign.

No doubt, if Okuma had been able to prevail, the Constitution would have borne the stamp of his influence, and it might have been a more liberal document than the one, framed in the main by Ito, that was adopted in 1889. It may be that Okuma would have looked to Westminster, rather than to Berlin, for his model. In the event – and not for the last time – it was Germany that exerted a baleful effect upon the course of Japanese history.

At the same time it is easy to exaggerate the debt that Ito owed the Germans when he supervised the drafting of the Constitution. Admittedly, on his visit overseas to study foreign constitutions, Ito spent much more time in Germany than in any other country. He had talks with Bismarck, who impressed him mightily. He attended a course of lectures by the authoritarian fanatic, von Gneist; and in Vienna he listened attentively to Lorenz von Stein. And no doubt Hermann Roessler, a German adviser to the Japanese Foreign Office, has his niche in history as one of the indirect sponsors

of the Meiji Constitution. But there can be little argument
that what the Germans did was to confirm Ito in the convictions he already held – namely that in the Constitution the
powers of an elected assembly should be tightly controlled
and restricted by an executive responsible, not to the assembly, but to the Sovereign Ruler of the country.

Among the measures taken in anticipation of the granting
of a Constitution was an administrative reform establishing
a cabinet system under a prime minister, in 1885, and Ito
was the first holder of this office. Three years later a Privy
Council was created, and Ito, handing over the premiership
to Kuroda Kiyotaka of Satsuma, was its first president.
There had been some demand for a constitutional convention; but the very thought of this had been anathema to Ito
and his colleagues. So from the outset the bureau, under
Ito's control, charged with drafting a constitution had been
made part of the Imperial Household Ministry. This ensured that complete secrecy surrounded the preparatory
work that was being done, and indeed enveloped the entire
venture in an aura of almost sacred dignity, raising it above
the arena of popular debate or even discussion. The duty
of the Privy Council, often meeting in the presence of the
emperor, was to put the finishing touches to the draft.

Finally, on 11 February 1889, the Emperor Meiji, now
thirty-seven years of age, in a brief but solemn ceremony at
the palace handed the first written Constitution of Japan to
the Prime Minister, Count Kuroda. The action symbolized
the important fact that the Constitution was a gracious gift
from the emperor to his subjects and not a contract, much
less a concession won from the Throne by popular demand.

The outstanding features of the Constitution may be
summarized quite briefly. The first sentence in the document states what conservative Japanese still consider to be
the essence of their country's *kokutai*, or 'national polity',
namely that Japan 'shall be reigned over and governed by a
line of Emperors unbroken for ages eternal'. The emperor is
also described as 'sacred and inviolable'; and in his com-
ments on this part of the Constitution Ito wrote that it was

unseemly that the emperor should ever be the subject of public discussion. The Constitution lays down that 'the Emperor exercises the legislative power with the consent of the Imperial Diet', and that, although he can issue imperial ordinances having the force of law, these 'are to be laid before the Imperial Diet at its next session'. The ordinances are invalid if the Diet fails to approve them.

Here then are some limitations to the prerogative. Legislative authority appears to rest, in the last resort, with the Diet; and it is of course this organ of the state that was the most striking novelty in the Meiji Constitution. It consisted of two chambers, a House of Peers and a House of Representatives. The former comprised members of the reconstituted nobility (former feudal lords and others, such as Ito himself, recently ennobled), a number of imperial nominees (holding office for life), and some representatives of the highest taxpayers. Until its demise in 1946 the House of Peers was much more powerful than the British House of Lords, to which of course it bore some slight superficial resemblance. In Ito's words the House of Peers would 'preserve an equilibrium between political parties' – for it was not thought that there would ever be a political party in the Upper House – and would, it was hoped, check what Ito described as 'the despotism of the majority' of the Lower House. By the Constitution, the powers of the House of Peers equalled those of the House of Representatives; and in practice it was able to veto legislation passed up to it by the Lower House.

The House of Representatives was an entirely elected body, but on a suffrage basis of substantial property owners who, in the first few years at any rate, amounted to little more than one per cent of the population. In practice the Diet met for three months of the year, as laid down by the Constitution, although extraordinary sessions were summoned at times of crisis. Generally speaking, however, it met for only a few hours each day when in session. It could be dissolved by the emperor on the advice of the cabinet at any time.*

* Strictly speaking, of course, the Upper House was prorogued and only the House of Representatives dissolved.

And cabinet ministers were responsible not to it but to the emperor. There was of course no rule that ministers should be members of the Diet; on the other hand it was stated in the Constitution that ministers could 'at any time take seats and speak in either House'.

An important limitation upon the powers of the Diet – and this was almost certainly borrowed from Berlin – was an article of the Constitution which stated that if the Diet did not vote on, or rejected, the Budget, 'the Government shall carry out the Budget of the preceding year'.

One chapter, or section, of the Constitution dealt with the 'rights and duties of subjects'. The people of Japan were confirmed in such rights as freedom of speech, writing, and association; their homes were guaranteed against entry or search unless with the consent of the householder, and freedom of religious belief was specifically allowed. But each of these rights was qualified, expressly, in every case by some such phrase as 'except in the cases provided for by law', or (in the matter of freedom of religious belief) 'within limits not prejudicial to peace and order and not antagonistic to their duties as subjects'. It was further stated, in a separate article, that the recognition of such rights should not affect the exercise of the emperor's powers in time of war or during a national emergency. The duties of a subject were stated to be those of paying taxes and serving in the armed forces.

On the face of it, then, this Constitution must seem to give very little away and to concentrate a great deal of power and authority in the hands of those directly advising the emperor. But it is fair at this point to recognize the force of what Ito had to say, writing some years after the Constitution was granted. 'At that time', he wrote, 'we had not yet arrived at the stage of distinguishing clearly between political opposition on the one hand, and treason to the established order of things on the other.' In the circumstances of the time, and having regard to the nature of Japanese society and the course of previous Japanese history, the Meiji Constitution represented a real, if modest, advance in the direction of parliamentary participation in government.

Had the will existed among enough public-spirited Japanese, there was nothing in the Constitution to hinder the development of certain unwritten conventions – that all cabinet ministers, for example, should be members of the Diet. And indeed, as we shall see, there was a short period, between the two world wars, when it looked as if Japan was firmly committed to a party cabinet system, although even in those promising years the service ministers were generals and admirals. The rule that the ministers of war and of the navy must be serving generals and admirals was established by imperial ordinance some time after the granting of the Constitution, of which it formed no part. This rule, immensely harmful in the long run to the national interest, played a vital part in the operation of Japanese politics, as will be shown later on; it was a principal factor in the undermining of the Diet's prestige before the Pacific War. But the blame, if any, does not lie with the Meiji Constitution.

Certainly the Constitution was framed by men of a strongly authoritarian turn of mind; and historians agree that towards the end of the eighties there developed a pronounced revival of Confucian sentiment within the governing class, in reaction to the passion for Western things and ideas. This was reflected in the famous Rescript on Education, promulgated by the emperor in 1890, which acquired, as was intended by the ministry of education, the authority of holy writ. On instructions from the ministry, which had greatly tightened its control over the state schools and had made their teachers into civil servants, a copy of the rescript, together with portraits of the emperor and his consort, was kept by every school in a secure place – in many schools this was in fact a small shrine – and was brought out on days of national commemoration to be read aloud by the college or school principal with great reverence to a respectful assembly of pupils. The rescript adjured the children and young people of Japan to observe the Confucian obligations of filial piety, obedience, and benevolence in their various relationships and to offer themselves 'courageously to the State' should emergency arise.

The rescript was no merely formal document, containing admirable but platitudinous exhortations. It was intended to be, and became, the generally accepted and deeply respected statement *ex cathedra* of the nation's fundamental ethical code for the next fifty years; and the prestige of this document in the eyes of the masses, if not in the minds of the sophisticated few, can scarcely be exaggerated.

It is very noticeable that for every concession made by a government in the Meiji period, and beyond, a corresponding safeguard was enforced. In this sense the Rescript on Education can be regarded as an insurance policy taken out by the oligarchy, largely for the benefit of their successors, against the risks that must be incurred in later years from a really liberal interpretation of the Constitution.

The Rescript on Education, and the opening of the first Imperial Diet in the same year, 1890, mark a real watershed, or half-way mark, in the long reign of the Emperor Meiji. The western clansmen – such as Ito, Yamagata, Okuma, Itagaki, and others – who had engineered the Restoration were still in the prime of life; but, whether in the government or in opposition, they had been engaged in ceaseless activity. Twenty years of tremendous changes, which they themselves had provoked or brought about, had made such men seem older perhaps than they were. At all events by the nineties they were regarded as veterans, almost as 'founding fathers' of the modern nation. On the whole the people at large were content to feel that high policy was safe in such hands.

Much headway had been made in the modernization of the country; but a great deal remained to be done before Japan could be looked upon as a strong industrial state. Above all the distasteful 'unequal' treaties were still in force. Japan, then, half-way through the Meiji era was still only half-way to its goal, complete self-respect as a fully independent power in its own right.

Chapter 5

EARLY CONSOLIDATION

[1]

THE last decade of the nineteenth century saw the beginning of Japan's industrial revolution, although this did not get into its stride until the eve of the First World War. It might have been expected that the old merchant class, long established in Osaka and Yedo, would grasp the economic leadership of the nation after the shogunate was overthrown. But with a few important exceptions, such as the Mitsui family, this class soon lost its predominant position in the new world of finance and commerce that came into being, largely under government sponsorship, after the Meiji Restoration. On the whole it was men of the *samurai* order who were the pioneers of modern business enterprise in Japan. Indeed during the early years the members of the oligarchy were themselves in a sense the leading businessmen in the country. For the first industries on the Western model were nearly all founded, promoted, or acquired by the state and were for a time state-administered.

In its determination to build up 'a rich country and a strong army' the government never considered leaving industrial development to private initiative; and in any case the amount of capital in private hands was at first very meagre. After the Restoration the government itself was hard pressed for funds. New industries could not be nourished behind a high wall of protective duties, for thanks to the treaty system Japan was restricted to a scale of low tariffs. Foreign loans would have helped. But, no doubt wisely, the government was too chary of alien interference to risk borrowing more then fairly small sums from abroad. For most of its revenue the government came to rely on taxation, the backbone of which was a newly instituted tax on land. A uniform, centrally administered land tax in cash was something novel to Japan. It meant, of course, that the peasant proprietor had to pay a fixed sum annually according to the value of his land. Naturally enough, no allowance was made by tax collectors for lean or bad harvests; and the result was that many peasants soon fell into debt to local money-lenders, charging extremely high rates of interest. As the years went by ownership of land began to pass into progressively fewer hands. More and more peasants who had owned their land became tenants, paying very high rent in kind to landlords, who of course paid the tax. It was this land tax that formed a very substantial part of the yearly revenue of the government, much of whose expenditure went to the development of strategic industries. In other words, the government made the countryside support the town; and a good deal of the political opposition to the Meiji oligarchy came from landowners and those engaged in traditional rural industries.

Although by comparison with contemporary China, or any other country of Asia, Japanese industrial progress during the nineteenth century was very striking, it hardly impressed foreigners as likely to make the nation a competitor in world markets with the great powers of the West. For example, throughout the nineteenth century, and well into the twentieth, most, if not all, of the larger vessels for both the navy and the mercantile marine were built in foreign shipyards. Up to 1914, at least, the bulk of the equipment needed by Japanese factories, mines, and railways was imported from abroad. Until the late 1870s foreigners, predominantly British, handled more than nine-tenths of all trade at the leading Japanese ports. Enjoying extra-territorial rights, the foreign merchants, observing the often seemingly maladroit struggles of a 'backward' state to pull itself up by its own occasionally ill-fitting boot-strings, could scarcely fail to have some sense of confident, and not always unjustified, superiority over the Japanese. But there were serious portents for those who chose to see them. In about thirty years, from 1868 to 1897, imports of raw materials for Japanese factories increased fivefold. More significant still, exports of finished goods over the same period rose more than twentyfold.

During those years the virtual foreign monopoly of the Japan-China steamship trade was broken by the N.Y.K. (Nippon Yusen Kaisha – the Japan Mail Line), established under government subsidy. This company grew out of a steamship concern, the Mitsubishi, under the control of the Iwasaki family, which owed its early prosperity to generous government support. Mitsubishi were to be further strengthened before the end of the century by the purchase from the government of the Nagasaki shipyards, the largest in the country. The government also sold to Mitsubishi gold and silver mines, and some undeveloped land near the Imperial Palace that was to become immensely valuable, the business district in Tokyo known at Marunouchi. These are but a few examples of the way in which this firm, Mitsubishi, began to expand into a huge business empire, becoming – together with Mitsui, Sumitomo, and Yasuda – one of the four greatest *zaibatsu*, or financial cliques, in Japan.

These *zaibatsu* were the chief beneficiaries of a policy adopted by the government some years after the Restoration. Having promoted and managed new industrial enterprises, the government handed most of them over, at almost ridiculously low rates, to a few private companies. At the same time the government retained control over key military industries. It was the few favoured private companies that became the *zaibatsu*. Since they owed so much to the government, they were bound to it by ties of obligation that Japanese have always found difficult to break; and in any case there was usually a close identity of interests between the *zaibatsu* and the political oligarchy. So on the whole the *zaibatsu* were reluctant to enter politics, in the sense of taking part in agitation against the government in the Diet, once this had been established by the Constitution of 1889. On the other hand, business rivalries among these financial cliques – between Mitsui and Mitsubishi for example – led them to be very closely associated with certain individual members of the oligarchy. Mitsui became identified with Ito and Inouye Kaoru, Mitsubishi with Matsukata. It followed that the *zaibatsu* became caught up in politics; not overtly so, perhaps, but certainly behind the scenes. It was inevitable that, after the Diet was established, the *zaibatsu* should find themselves keenly interested in various legislative measures; and this opened the way to corruption, sometimes on a large scale. This is an aspect of Japanese history that will be discussed more fully in a later chapter. For the power of the *zaibatsu*, like that of the Japanese Diet under the old Constitution, reached its zenith in the 1920s.

Undoubtedly the expansion of Japanese trade and industry during the second half of the Meiji period was due in large measure to the organizational drive and efficiency of the few powerful concerns forming the *zaibatsu*, based on a labour force that was well indoctrinated in the belief that hard work was a patriotic duty.

[II]

Progress in modernization, however, seemed too slow for the majority of Japan's political and business leaders. The establishment of an army and navy on Western lines, the development of railways, progress in industry, banking, and technical education – all this was unsatisfying to the Japanese so long as foreigners continued to enjoy extra-territorial rights under the treaties. For it meant that, in spite of everything, Japan, like China, was not regarded as belonging to the same class as the nations of the West. Many efforts were made to induce the treaty powers to give way on the important issues of extra-territoriality and Japan's tariff autonomy. Foreign governments argued that, until the entire structure of the Japanese legal system – civil and commercial as well as criminal – was revised and brought up to date, they were not prepared to leave their nationals to the mercy of Japanese courts of law. The argument implied, in other words, that the Japanese remained less than fully civilized.

So the government put its hand to a thorough revision of the national criminal and civil legal codes – this took a long time – and furthermore, in an attempt to impress and win the goodwill of the foreign envoys in Tokyo, it commissioned a British architect to design and erect a building, known as the *Rokumeikan* or 'Hall of the Baying Stag', in which social gatherings of Japanese and foreigners could be held. Here the government from time to time dispensed a good deal of sometimes lavish hospitality of the Western type. Beneath the chandeliers of the *Rokumeikan* Japanese ladies in bustles – this was in the eighties – learned the niceties of European cookery and music, or danced late in the arms of foreign 'swells'. Those who have childhood memories of the place recall it with some nostalgia. Of course it was all part of the oligarchy's campaign to prove that Japan had become a civilized modern state.

However, there were many in Tokyo and outside who were shocked by what they regarded as the government's sycophancy towards foreigners; and in 1887, when some of the details of current negotiations on treaty revision became known, there was a great outcry on the score that the government had made too many concessions. The government took stern measures against its critics, but for the time being diplomatic talks on treaty revision had to be given up. This really killed the *Rokumeikan* as a flourishing institution.

A settlement of the treaty question seemed imminent in 1889, after negotiations had been resumed. But there was much public indignation when the proposals put forward by Okuma, the Foreign Minister, were revealed, thanks to a Japanese press translation of a report in *The Times*. An extreme nationalist threw a bomb at Okuma, who survived the attack but lost a leg. Once again negotiations had to be abandoned. By 1890, however, a new criminal code was in force and a new civil code had been drafted. This strengthened the government's hand in its dealings with the foreign powers. Moreover, the government was under almost continual attack from 1890, during the sessions of the Diet, for its failure to secure revision of the treaties. It was not until 1894 that an agreement, abolishing the unequal clauses of the old treaty, was signed in London between Japan and

Great Britain. It was to come into force five years later. Similar agreements were signed fairly soon with other nations. For by the early summer of 1895 Japan's position in the world had been greatly enhanced by her successful war against China.

It will be remembered that in the early seventies the oligarchy was divided on the Korean question, that those, such as Saigo, who urged immediate armed action against Korea, were overruled. Nevertheless, Japan exerted considerable pressure on Korea and forced the country to sign a treaty giving Japan special privileges. On the other hand, China claimed suzerainty over the peninsula, as she had done for centuries. Biding their time until they felt strong enough to challenge China to a real test of arms, the Japanese strengthened their position in Korea by intrigue and other means.

In the summer of 1894 a revolt in Korea, followed by the entry of Chinese troops to assist the Korean king, gave Japan a motive for armed intervention. Short of complete Chinese evacuation of Korea war seemed unavoidable. Neither side would back down. As in 1904 and again in 1941 Japan – specifically the Japanese navy – struck the first blow before war had been declared. On 25 July 1894 the navy sank a Chinese troopship, of British registry, and captured one of the three ironclads escorting her. War was declared six days later.

During the next nine months the Japanese expelled the Chinese army from Korea, defeated a Chinese fleet off the mouth of the Yalu river, captured Port Arthur and the Liao-tung peninsula in south Manchuria, and seized the port of Wei-hai-wei on the coast of Shantung. When China asked for an armistice, the terms demanded by Japan were exceedingly severe; but they were modified when the principal Chinese envoy, the famous Li Hung-chang, was wounded by a fanatic after his arrival in Japan. Even so, the Treaty of Shimonoseki – signed on 17 April 1895 by Ito Hirobumi and Li Hung-chang – gave Japan some valuable prizes; namely, Formosa and the Pescadores, Port Arthur and the Liaotung peninsula, the promise of a very large indemnity to meet the cost of the war, and Chinese recognition of 'the complete independence and autonomy of Korea'.

Very few people in the world at large had imagined that Japan would be able to defeat, and then dictate terms to, China. Japan's triumph was dramatic and to all appearances complete. But only a week after the Treaty was signed there occurred what the Japanese were to remember bitterly as the 'Triple Intervention'. Russia, France, and Germany, through their ministers in Tokyo, 'advised' Japan to surrender the claim to the Liaotung peninsula, including of course the harbour and fortress of Port Arthur, as Japanese possession of this territory would threaten Peking and so disturb 'the peace of the Far East' – a phrase which the Japanese were to take to heart and put to good use in later years. There was no resisting such pressure. Japan had no allies; and the Russians at least were known to be in earnest, and with their fleet at Vladivostock they appeared to have the means to enforce their will.

There was massive popular indignation against the action of Russia, France, and Germany. But the Emperor Meiji told his people that they must bear the unbearable – his grandson used the same words in 1945 – and the command was obeyed. The psychological effect of the Triple Intervention lasted for decades, and may not have disappeared entirely even today. Western nations had been feared usually, and disliked very often. But on the whole they had been respected by Japan. Now they were distrusted, despised even, as hypocrites. For within five years of the Treaty of Shimonoseki Germany seized Tsingtau, France secured the lease of Kwangchow Bay, and Great Britain the lease of Wei-hai-wei and the 'New Territories' of Hong Kong, the United States annexed Hawaii, and Russia obtained control of Port Arthur and the Liaotung peninsula.

It was, of course, Russia's action that created the most perturbation in Japan. Russia had always seemed a formidable neighbour; but until the Triple Intervention, Japanese-Russian relations had been fairly stable for some time. Twenty years earlier the Russians had agreed to give the Kuriles to Japan in return for possession of all Saghalin, the large island immediately north of Hokkaido. After 1895, however, it was apparent that Russia intended to press forward in the Far East, and by the end of the century, Russian power in that part of the world was immensely strengthened by the possession of Port Arthur and the completion of the Trans-Siberian Railway. Probably the great majority of the Japanese felt that a struggle with Russia was inevitable. But among the leaders there were some, notably Ito, who believed that this might be avoided if Japan and Russia could enter into some firm agreement, or even alliance.

In spite of the humiliation suffered by the Triple Intervention, Japan's status after the war with China was vastly improved. Formosa was a valuable acquisition. The indemnity was of great economic benefit. Control of Korea now seemed much easier.

[III]

One lesson learned by the Japanese from the war was that the use of force paid good dividends. Thus the prestige of the army and navy was much enhanced. New importance of a semi-mystical nature was given to the emperor's position as Supreme Commander. It was not difficult, then, for Yamagata of Choshu, the founder of the modern army, to sponsor, as premier in 1900, an imperial ordinance stating that only generals and lieutenant-generals on the active list could be appointed Minister of War. The same rule applied to the post of Navy Minister, which could be filled only by admirals and vice-admirals on the active list. This was to mean that a cabinet could be forced out of office by the army or navy if they had strong objections to its policy. However rent by its own internal jealousies, each service tried to present a united front to the civilian world. Thus a Minister of War would never refuse to resign if the army wanted him to leave the cabinet; and no general or lieutenant-general would accept office in a new cabinet unless it was likely to fall in with the aims and wishes of the army. The significance of this limitation upon those eligible for the defence appointments in the cabinet cannot be exaggerated. It hamstrung constitutional progress almost from the start. It placed the Supreme Command – in other words the two armed services – on a level with the cabinet and gave it for practical purposes the right, not of course reciprocal, to veto cabinet decisions.

It could be claimed that at the turn of the century, and for nearly twenty years thereafter, Yamagata was the most powerful single individual in the country, although he was far from being omnipotent. Ever since the eighties the oligarchy had been confined virtually to two clans only, Satsuma and Choshu. Their supremacy is illustrated by the fact that from 1885 to 1918 every Japanese premier with two exceptions (Okuma and Saionji) came from one or other of these two clans. Indeed, until a Civil Service Examination system was set up in the late eighties the more important sections of bureaucracy were dominated by men from Satsuma and Choshu. After the Constitution came into force, the leaders of the Satsuma – Choshu oligarchy – a group numbering perhaps less than twelve persons in all – were faced with an obstreperous Lower House in the Diet. The most vocal members of the House belonged to the so-called 'people's parties' or factions, such as those headed by Itagaki and Okuma, and they were eager to embarrass the government in every possible way. For many years after 1890 successive governments were composed nearly always of officials, of members or protégés of the Satsuma–Choshu oligarchy. The parties in the Diet were determined to get power, the oligarchy to keep it. The most implacable opponent of the parties, the man who regarded democracy in any form as 'an evil poison', was Yamagata.

At first he could rely upon a united front among his colleagues. It did not look as though the parties – notably Itagaki's *Jiyuto* and Okuma's *Kaishinto* – could have more than a minor nuisance value. After all, when the Diet met for the first time in 1890 only half a million people out of a population of nearly forty million had the vote. An uncooperative Lower House could be dissolved, and in any event it sat normally for less than a third of the year. At election time there seemed to be many weapons available to an authoritarian

government to guide the voting in the direction that it desired. In one notorious General Election, in 1892, the police
throughout the country had confidential instructions from
the Home Minister (a Choshu man) to intervene actively on
the side of the government. Using nationalist ruffians as
auxiliaries, the police turned the hustings into a bloody
battlefield, to such effect that twenty-five persons were killed
and nearly four hundred injured. Yet even under these conditions government candidates won fewer seats than their
opponents. Dissolution of the Diet, bribery on an expensive
scale, outright violence, the use of imperial rescripts – during
the nineties all were tried by various governments under
Yamagata, Ito, or Matsukata, in their efforts to suppress or
bring to heel the unruly political parties. The latter could
best irritate and embarrass the government by attacking the
annual budget. They demanded, also, that the cabinet
should be composed of party members, and they were filled
with chagrin when the government obtained an imperial
rescript stating that 'the appointment or removal of Ministers of State is absolutely at the will of the Sovereign, and no
interference whatever is allowed in this matter'.

The only time during its first ten years that the House of
Representatives showed a docile face to the oligarchy was
during the Sino-Japanese War – the Diet met at Hiroshima,
the emperor's residence for the duration of the war – when
all political differences were put aside. For the great majority of the 'liberal' party politicians were strongly nationalist,
and indeed chauvinist, in their views on the conduct of
foreign affairs. In their opinion the government, on such
questions as Korea or treaty revision, showed too little firmness, not too much. Their main quarrel with the government was that it would neither share power with them nor
protect their interests, which were those of agriculture and
rural industry.

From 1890 to 1898 the government was presided over in
turn by Yamagata (Choshu), Matsukata (Satsuma), Ito
(Choshu), Matsukata, and then, once more, by Ito. After
this, for a few months in 1898, there was actually a kind of

party cabinet headed by Okuma and Itagaki; for their parties had united in a merger that proved to be only temporary. On the formation of this cabinet the politicians in the Lower House rejoiced. But it fell apart owing to squabbles over the distribution of appointments and other spoils, this confirming no doubt Yamagata's conviction that party men were totally unfitted to govern.

A view long put forward by clan governments was that they were 'transcendental', above and impartial towards all parties. Nevertheless, before the century ended, Ito concluded that the oligarchy ought to organize a political party or ally itself with one or more of the existing parties. The idea was firmly opposed by Yamagata; and between the two outstanding holders of power, Yamagata and Ito, there opened up a rift that old associations and membership of the same clan could not heal. Ito came to an understanding with, and took command of, a new party, the *Seiyukai*, formed largely of members of the old *Jiyuto*. From Yamagata's point of view, and from the point of view of the House of Peers, Ito had betrayed his class – using this term in its official rather than social sense. But any loss of principle lay not with Ito but with the members of the *Seiyukai*. For he made it clear to them at the outset that the authoritarian, imperial, interpretation of the Constitution would have to be accepted. He told them, for example, that appointment and dismissal of cabinet ministers were the prerogative of the emperor who (so Ito declared) 'retains absolute freedom to select His advisers from whatever quarters He deems proper, be it from among the members of political parties or from circles outside those parties'.

Ito's assumption, in 1900, of the leadership of the *Seiyukai* is of historical importance for two reasons. In the first place it showed that to some extent, at least, the forms, if not the spirit, of an admittedly limited parliamentary democracy could not be ignored or completely overridden by the clan oligarchy. Secondly it was the beginning of what developed later into a civil-military rivalry within the highest reaches of government.

In Japan it has sometimes been very difficult to disentangle personal considerations from those of principle. In many important respects the principles held by Ito and Yamagata were identical. Clearly both were convinced of the unique value of an imperial house of such ancient and sacred origin. Both were single-minded in their ambition to increase the power and influence of Japan, not only in Asia but also throughout the world. Both therefore favoured a policy of national expansion. Where they and their respective successors differed was on timing and method. Yamagata, the soldier, believed first and foremost in the power of the army that he had created. As factors in the promotion of Japan's national greatness all the rest – the bureaucracy, the *zaibatsu*, the Diet politicians, even, one might add, the navy – were of secondary importance. Ito, the statesman, was aware always of the danger that what had been achieved in the nineteenth century might be thrown away in the twentieth, if military commitments were undertaken beyond the nation's strength. It would be an over-simplification to say that Yamagata was narrow-minded, whereas Ito had a broad view, based on real knowledge of the world and of its ideas. But the comment bears some crude approximation to the truth. We must remember that Ito and Yamagata, like nearly all the great Meiji leaders, were born into *samurai* households and were brought up from childhood to be warriors. It was experience of foreign travel, and of dealing with foreigners in Japan, that shaped Ito's personality, always no doubt more thoughtful and cautious than Yamagata's, into a distinctively 'civilian' mould. Thus, while Yamagata perfected a fighting force, Ito prepared a national constitution. The personalities of the two men, therefore, developed of necessity along different lines.

As these men and their colleagues grew older they were content, in time, to hand over the great offices of state, such as the premiership, to rather younger men among their own reliable followers or protégés. From 1901 to 1912, the end of the Meiji period, the premiership alternated between General Katsura, a Choshu clansman backed by Yamagata, and Marquis Saionji, a Kyoto noble who succeeded Ito as head of the *Seiyukai* and received Ito's support. But the original oligarchy abandoned only the name, not the substance, of power. For Japanese history is full of examples of men who have ruled indirectly from retirement. Even before they went into nominal retirement certain of the oligarchy were recognized, formally, by the emperor as 'elder statesmen', or *Genro*. So long as they remained alive, these *Genro*, such as Ito, Yamagata, and Matsukata, exerted very great political influence from behind the scenes; and their advice was invariably sought by the emperor when he came to choose a new prime minister. The prestige of the *Genro* increased, if anything, as the years went by. In more recent times the Japanese have looked back on them with a certain nostalgia. For as the makers of the modern state they were the giants of the Meiji era.

Chapter 6

THE GOLDEN YEARS

_____

[1]

IN 1900 Japanese troops played an important part in the rescue of the legations at Peking during the Boxer Rising. It was observed that the Japanese contingent engaged in no looting of any kind. Their behaviour fortified the growing belief in Europe – except perhaps in Germany, where the Kaiser was fond of speaking of the 'Yellow Peril' – that the Japanese were not only a force to be reckoned with but were also an admirably advanced, civilized people, who might almost be described as the British of the Far East.

It was a view on which the Koreans would have had strong reservations. Soon after the Sino-Japanese War their queen, who distrusted Japan, had been murdered with singular brutality by a gang of Korean and Japanese desperadoes who broke into the royal palace at Seoul to commit their crime. The murder took place with the connivance of the Japanese Minister, a Choshu general called Miura Goro. The government in Tokyo, so it appears, had no foreknowledge of this plot of assassination, and Miura and members of his staff were recalled to Japan and placed on trial. They were convicted of having conspired to murder the queen but were acquitted of the charge of having taken part in the actual crime. This meant that they suffered no legal penalty. The lenient treatment of those concerned in this murder was very ominous. The implication seemed to be that 'patriotic' motives could palliate the worst excesses. One of those involved in the outrage at Seoul had taken part in the bomb attack on Okuma and was to rise in later years to such heights of respectability as Home Minister of Japan.

The scandalous murder of their queen not only exacerbated the dislike that the Koreans had for the Japanese; it also diminished for a year or two Japanese influence in Korea, to the advantage of the Russians. Indeed the king of Korea took temporary refuge in the Russian Legation at Seoul.

It was to Manchuria, however, that the Russians devoted their main attention. The most direct route to Vladivostock from the Lake Baikal region lay through Manchuria; so the Russians had every reason to persuade China to agree to the construction of a railway line, linked with the Trans-Siberian, across Manchuria through Harbin to the Maritime Province. This line, known as the Chinese Eastern Railway and having a Chinese as its president, was in reality a Russian undertaking, built, stocked, maintained, and guarded by Russians. But Russian energies were not confined to the zone of this railway. In 1898 Port Arthur and the territory at the tip of the Liaotung peninsula were leased from China, and a railway line was built from Harbin to Port Arthur through Mukden and the port of Dairen, greatly developed by the Russians and renamed by them Dalny. Thus Manchuria became a territory of considerable strategic, and indeed economic, importance to Russia in the Far East. Vladivostock was ice-bound in winter. Dalny and Port Arthur were ice-free.

When the Boxer Rising occurred Russia had a pretext for moving large numbers of troops south through Manchuria and it began to look as though Russia could dominate the Gulf of Chihli from Taku Bar, at the approaches to Tientsin on the one side, to Chemulpo, at the approaches to Seoul, on the other.

All this was very galling to Japan. It was also alarming; for there was always the possibility of eventual Russian penetration of Korea south of Seoul, a region that the Japanese, having built the Pusan–Seoul railway, looked upon as ripe for control and exploitation by themselves.

The Tsar received differing counsels on the question of Korea. There were those who advised him that it was unwise for Russia to become involved, politically or commercially, in any part of Korea; and there were others who argued that Russian expansion in Korea was both necessary and desirable. Certainly the Tsar's advisers were agreed on the need for ensuring that no fortifications should be built by the Japanese on the south coast of Korea, for these would menace Russian sea communications between Vladivostock and Port Arthur. But the Japanese regarded a limitation of this kind as an affront, and it sharpened their growing belief that they would have to drive the Russians out of Korea and the Liaotung peninsula.

It was considerations of this kind that led Japan to sign the alliance with Great Britain in the early part of 1902. The possibility of an Anglo-Japanese pact had been suggested by Joseph Chamberlain to the Japanese Minister in London in 1898; but nothing had come of it. It was not until 1901 that Great Britain and Japan started negotiations for an alliance. For Great Britain it represented, of course, a departure from the policy of 'splendid isolation'; but the disadvantages of this policy had been revealed during the South African War, when Britain faced a hostile or unsympathetic world. On the Japanese side the government saw as the first purpose of an alliance with Great Britain a guarantee that Japan would be given a free hand in Korea. Hayashi Tadasu, the Minister in London, told Lord Lansdowne (the Foreign Secretary):

'My country considers as its first and last wish the protection of its interests in Korea, and the prevention of interference by any other country in Korea.'

At first the *Genro* – the elder statesmen – were not unanimous on the question of the alliance. In particular, Ito believed that Japan should try very hard to reach a firm agreement, amounting to an alliance if possible, with Russia rather than England. Ito was Premier for the fourth and last time from October 1899 to May 1901, when he handed over control of the cabinet and of the *Seiyukai* party to Saionji Kimmochi. But within a few weeks Saionji's cabinet gave way to one headed by General Katsura, nominated by Yamagata, who was strongly anti-Russian and therefore determined to secure the British alliance. Nevertheless, as a

Genro Ito still had a great deal of influence; and he was supported by his fellow-*Genro* and old friend, Inouye Kaoru. When Anglo-Japanese negotiations were already well advanced Ito paid a visit to Russia – in the autumn of 1901 he went to America, and then to St Petersburg without calling at London – but he was unable to secure an immediate agreement, although perhaps he could have negotiated an alliance with Russia had he not been opposed with great vigour by Yamagata and the Katsura cabinet at home. It must be said, too, that recognition of Russia's hegemony in south Manchuria, in return for Russian acceptance of Japan's dominant position in Korea, would have been regarded as an act of weakness by the majority of Japanese. In any case Japan was virtually committed to an alliance with Great Britain even before Ito arrived in St Petersburg.

The Anglo-Japanese Alliance was for five years in the first instance. It was revised and renewed in 1905, after the Russo-Japanese War, and renewed again, for a further ten years, in 1911. Japan, then, has had a longer political and military association with Great Britain than with any other foreign power. The alliance was valuable to Great Britain as a counterweight to Russian power in the early years of the twentieth century, and during the First World War Japanese help, especially at sea, was very useful. But it is certainly true that the alliance meant a great deal more, both politically and emotionally, to the Japanese than to the British. Politically it was of supreme importance to Japan, for two main reasons. The agreement specifically recognized that Japan was 'interested in a peculiar degree' in Korea. This meant, despite a canting phase in the agreement about Korean 'independence', that the British government quietly endorsed Japan's claim to be the only arbiter of Korea's fate. Secondly, the Treaty of Alliance ensured that in the event of war with Russia Japan could rely on benevolent neutrality on the part of Great Britain and on active British participation should another power – for example, France, Russia's ally – enter the war on Russia's side. Emotionally the conclusion of the alliance gave back to the Japanese the inner pride that they had lost half a century earlier, when Perry and his successors thrust themselves upon the country. The sense of grateful friendship towards Britain was sincere and widespread. In the minds of the people, part of the shame incurred by the Triple Intervention was now expunged. Moreover they felt better able to brace themselves for the coming struggle with Russia.

This broke out two years after the Anglo-Japanese Alliance was signed. There is no doubt that it was a most popular war. It is true that by 1904 there was an infant Socialist party (although its existence was illegal), and its members and sympathizers opposed the war. But they were very few in number. The overwhelming majority of the population felt, as many were to believe in 1941, that Japan had no choice but to take up arms. Negotiations with the Russians went on in St Petersburg through the second half of 1903. For the Katsura government, though heartened and fortified by the alliance with Great Britain, was ready to reach an understanding with Russia if this could be obtained on terms not too unfavourable to Japan. But the Russians were adamant in their insistence on their own exclusive economic control of the resources of south Manchuria, and they demanded the establishment of a neutral zone in Korea north of the thirty-ninth parallel. These were conditions that the Japanese, having regard to the state of their naval and military preparations, felt strong enough to refuse. At last, faced with an impasse, the Japanese broke off negotiations on 6 February 1904. On the same day a Russian force crossed the Yalu into Korea and a fleet of Japanese cruisers, destroyers, and transports sailed out of the naval port of Sasebo. The cruisers and transports made for Chemulpo, where, on the evening of 8 February, the troops were disembarked, took train to Seoul, and occupied the city. Meanwhile the cruisers dealt with three Russian vessels that were in Chemulpo harbour. The destroyers from Sasebo set course for Port Arthur. Here, off the port, at dead of night on 8/9 February, they found the Russian fleet at anchor with lights undimmed. The destroyers fired their torpedoes. Two battleships and a cruiser received hits. No damage was done to the Japanese. Next day Japanese battleships engaged the Russian vessels which prudently took up position within shelter of their shore batteries. Little damage was done to either side, but the Japanese could claim a moral victory. It was not until the day after – 10 February – that Japan declared war.

Of course, there was some complaint in Europe, from the Russians in particular, that Japan had broken international usage by striking before war was declared. This opinion, however, was not widely held in England. *The Times*, for example, declared: 'The Japanese Navy has opened the war by an act of daring which is destined to take a place of honour in naval annals.'

There is a certain epic quality about the Russo-Japanese War that stands out the more clearly by contrast with all the horrors that have happened since. For one thing this struggle, like the Sino-Japanese War ten years earlier, was relatively short. It lasted for less than eighteen months. The victories on land and sea were dramatic and clear-cut. Both sides fought with remarkable courage, and with some chivalry. Japanese treatment of Russian prisoners was more than correct: it was generous and humane. Two men on the Japanese side captured the imagination of the world – among the soldiers, Nogi; among the sailors, Togo. In the eyes of the public in Britain and America the issue was excitingly clear. 'Gallant Little Japan' was standing up to the Russian Bear, for whom perhaps only the French felt much affection.

On land Japanese and Russian armies fought some of the greatest battles – in terms of the numbers concerned and of the duration of the full-scale frontal clashes involved – that the world had yet seen. After the Russians were driven back into Manchuria across the Yalu the fighting broadened and was concentrated on two main fronts; before Port Arthur and astride the road and railway running north from Port Arthur and Dalny (Dairen) to Liaoyang and Mukden.

The seige of Port Arthur was the greatest ordeal that Japanese soldiers had to face until the disaster of Imphal in 1944. The fortress held out for five months against the Third Army

commanded by Nogi Maresuke, a peculiarly dedicated
general who held steadfast to all that was best in the *samurai*
tradition. Off the battlefield, no less than on it, Nogi imposed
an extremely high standard of discipline upon his troops – the
slightest misdemeanour towards civilian life or property was
very severly punished. There is a striking contrast between
the behaviour of Japanese officers and men in Manchuria in
1904–5 and their conduct in China, Malaya, the Philippines,
and other areas from 1937 to 1945.

In round figures Japanese losses in front of Port Arthur
amounted to sixty thousand; among them were Nogi's two
sons. In the capture of one vital position, 203 Metre Hill,
some ten thousand casualties were incurred. Port Arthur fell
on the last day of 1904. The Russians were treated gallantly by
their enemies, and there were many scenes of fraternization
between Japanese and Russian officers. The Russian commander, Stoessel, presented his white horse to General Nogi.

The culmination of the fighting on the other front, where
the Russians were slowly forced back beyond Liaoyang, was
the Battle of Mukden. This battle lasted from 23 February to
16 March 1905, and nearly three-quarters of a million men
were involved. The Japanese won a notable victory and
possession of Mukden, but not without cost: their casualties
were over forty thousand.

At sea the Japanese were equally victorious. True, a
Russian squadron based on Vladivostock gave them some
trouble, and they lost two battleships in two days from Russian
mines, but so effectively did they harass the Russian fleet at
Port Arthur that it was quite unable to fulfil its proper task –
the severance of sea communications between Japan and the
mainland of Asia. One bold sortie from Port Arthur – this
was in August 1904 – was brilliantly repelled and scattered
by Admiral Togo; and those Russian ships that returned
safely to the inner harbour fell into Japanese hands with the
surrender of the fortress.

Togo's outstanding achievement was the Battle of Tsushima, or (as the Japanese call it) *Nihonkai kaisen*, the Battle
of the Sea of Japan. In October 1904 a Russian fleet of some

forty vessels assembled in the Baltic and set out for the Far
East. Its progress was watched with benevolence by France,
which placed coaling stations in Madagascar and Indo-
China at its disposal ; but Great Britain, as Japan's ally, regarded the armada with hostile suspicion, more especially as
Russian ships in an excess of nerves had fired on British
trawlers in the North Sea, in the belief – not perhaps so fan-
tastic as it might sound – that they were Japanese torpedo-
boats. Not until May 1905 did the Russian fleet appear in Far
Eastern waters. It was evident that its destination was Vladivostock, and Admiral Togo forecast correctly that his opponent, Rozhdestvensky, would make for the straits between
Kyushu and Korea. The two fleets engaged on 27 May 1905,
to the east of the islands of Tsushima that lie between Japan
and Korea. Here in two days the Russian Baltic fleet was
destroyed. Only two of its vessels escaped being sunk, captured, or interned. The Japanese lost three torpedo-boats ;
and about six hundred men were killed or wounded. It was
the most dramatic and decisive sea battle for a hundred years.
The British felt almost as pleased about it as the Japanese, for
the victorious navy had been largely built and equipped at
Barrow, Elswick, and Sheffield ; and most, if not all, of the
Japanese officers had been trained or professionally advised
by Englishmen.

By this time both Russia and Japan were in a mood to seek
peace. Russia was shaken by the premonitory tremors of
revolution. Japan was strained financially and in terms of
manpower. Just after the Battle of Mukden Marshal Oyama,
the Japanese *generalissimo*, sent his chief of staff, Kodama, on
a confidential mission to Tokyo to impress upon the government the need for an early peace with Russia. And indeed,
with admirable foresight, the *Genro* and cabinet had decided,
just before the war began, to ask the United States to mediate
at a suitable moment and a special envoy had been sent to
Washington for this purpose. Thus President Theodore
Roosevelt was not taken by surprise when, within a week of
the Battle of Tsushima, he was asked by the Japanese to pro-
pose peace to the Russians.

The Treaty of Portsmouth (New Hampshire) which concluded the war was signed on 5 September 1905. The Russians agreed to recognize Japan's 'paramount political, military, and economic interests' in Korea, and to transfer to Japan the lease of the Liaotung peninsula and the railway connecting Port Arthur and Mukden as far north as Ghangchun, beyond Mukden. Russia also ceded to Japan the southern half of the island of Sakhalin together with special fishing rights.

When these terms were made public there was an immediate outburst of popular indignation in Japan. After all, the people had been fed with success stories for eighteen months. They knew that their army had defeated the Russians in three or four great battles in Manchuria and had captured a fortress and naval base so strongly defended that, like Singapore in later years, it was rumoured to be almost impregnable. They knew that their navy had swept the Russian fleet off the sea. They did not know – for nobody in authority dreamed of telling them – that their country was at the end of its tether and was therefore in no position to insist on a Russian indemnity, which most Japanese thought indispensable.* Roused by extreme nationalist groups, Tokyo crowds started to riot against the Katsura cabinet. Troops were brought in and martial law imposed before order was restored. On his return from the Peace Conference in America the Foreign Minister, Komura, had to land secretly ; for the risk of assassination was great, such was the odium heaped, undeservedly, upon his head. However, both *Genro* and government were united on the Treaty of Portsmouth, and so there was no question of the Katsura cabinet resigning in response to popular demand.

If the Japanese obtained from the war less than they felt their sacrifices warranted, they gained, none the less, some very substantial advantages. In the first place, the potential

* By the summer of 1905, Japan was near exhaustion financially and in terms of trained military manpower. The High Command in Manchuria estimated that at least a further thousand million *yen* and a quarter of a million more soldiers would be needed if the war was to be carried on.

Russian threat to Korea was now removed – the war, after all, had been fought on the Korean issue. Indeed the way was now open for a Russo-Japanese *rapprochement*, for the main consequence of Japan's military and naval victories was to turn Russian interest away from the Far East and back towards Europe, more specifically towards the Balkans, a part of the world that for ten years, much to the satisfaction of Germany and Austria, she had regarded with only passive attention. Renewed Russian concern with the Balkans was to mean war in Europe nine years later. But this was an ultimate effect of Japan's victory that few could have foreseen. Japan, back on her foothold in south Manchuria, soon made friends with her recent enemy ; and in 1907 a Russo-Japanese Convention was signed which, by its secret clauses, divided Manchuria into Russian and Japanese spheres of influence.

Manchuria, of course, was Chinese territory, so it was desirable that Chinese agreement should be obtained to the transfer from Russia to Japan of the Liaotung leasehold and the railway zone between Port Arthur and Changchun. It was only with great reluctance that China gave formal consent to this clause of the Portsmouth Treaty. But the Japanese were determined to take over from the Russians in south Manchuria, with or without Chinese agreement, and after some argument the Chinese gave way.

As for Korea, the Japanese tightened their grip on the country before the war came to an end. In 1904 Korea was forced to accept Japanese financial and diplomatic advisers ; and Japan's position in Korea began to resemble that of Great Britain in Egypt and of France in Morocco. In November 1905, a special mission headed by Ito persuaded the king of Korea to sign an agreement giving control of Korean foreign affairs to a Japanese Resident-General ; and Ito was appointed to this key position. The Korean court and government, resenting bitterly this further erosion of their dwindling independence, failed to cooperate very heartily with the Japanese advisers that were set over them ; and so in 1907 Ito presented new demands to the king. These proposed that the advisers should initiate as well as approve executive and

legislative actions. To his credit the king chose to abdicate
rather than accept such humiliating conditions. He was succeeded by the Crown Prince Yi who bowed to Japanese
pressure. Korea was now virtually a colony of Japan. Ito
however, was opposed to annexation, which was strongly advocated by Yamagata. Ito believed, in spite of all the evidence, that in modernizing the country Japan would be able
to win the good will of the Koreans, provided that firmness
was tempered with tact. But tact was a virtue ill regarded by
most of the army leaders, whose only idea was to set up a
stern Japanese military administration. Thus Ito's ultimatum
to the king in 1907 was a manoeuvre to forestall more drastic
action by the military party in Japan. But he was fighting a
losing battle. In 1908 the cabinet, headed by his friend
Saionji, gave way to General Katsura's second administration. Katsura was Yamagata's supporter and protégé. Ito's
influence was now greatly diminished, and in 1909 he resigned his appointment in Seoul. Later that year, while on a
journey in Manchuria, he was assassinated by a Korean on
the station at Harbin. So ended the career of perhaps the
greatest of the Meiji leaders. The murder gave the Tokyo
government a pretext for annexation. This took place in
August 1910, by the terms of a treaty dictated to the young
king by General Terauchi Masatake. King Yi was granted
a substantial pension ; and it was agreed that members of the
royal house of Korea, now renamed Chosen ('land of morning calm'), should be given treatment equal to that accorded
to the members of the Emperor Meiji's family.

There followed thirty-five years of Japanese rule in Korea.
It conferred a great many material benefits on the country,
and certainly it was more efficient and in some respects much
less arbitrary and harsh than that of the former royal government. But it was rigid, severe, unimaginative, and dedicated
to an almost hopeless ideal – namely the integration of the
Koreans with the Japanese. Small regard was paid to
Korean susceptibilities. Those in charge of the government
of annexed Korea were usually soldiers, alert to suppress any
signs of political disaffection. A regime of this kind merely

aggravated the demand for independence that it was at such pains to stamp out.

[II]

The Japanese would have been less than human if they had not succumbed to a wave of complacent pride after their defeat of Russia in the Far East. They were flattered now by the whole world; for such a rapid rise to international power had not been seen for centuries. In retrospect the achievements of this poor though populous group of islands seemed astonishing, for they had taken place within a mere fifty years. And by replacing Russia in south Manchuria, Japan joined the company of Western nations in their exploitation of that prostrate giant, China, whose impotence seemed assured. Who could have prophesied in 1905 that when another fifty years had passed China would be once more the armed colossus of the East, unified, totalitarian, and hard upon the road towards industrialization? Later on, when Japan bullied China, the action was often justified as having been taken for China's own good. Many times before the Pacific War Japanese propagandists claimed that Japan was merely the energetic younger brother scolding and goading into life the lazy, corrupt, and backward elder brother, China. And it is true that it was Japan's unbridled aggression against China that produced the conditions which made possible the eventual triumph of the Communists. But this particular outcome of their behaviour the Japanese did not predict.

Yet it is interesting to note that the first revolutionary movement in China in the present century owed something to Japanese support, although quite unofficially. For Sun Yat-sen and several of his revolutionary colleagues received help and, for a time, refuge in Japan.

In an earlier chapter it was remarked that the influence and example of Saigo Takamori lived on after his death in 1877. His spiritual heirs included a number of determined nationalists of the extreme kind, mostly from Kyushu, who by cajolery, propaganda, bribery, and violence sought to guide the government and people of Japan along the path that Saigo would have approved – namely the expansion of the nation's power in Asia and the thorough rejection of all foreign ideas and faiths. It was people such as these who assassinated Okubo, one of the most gifted of the early Meiji leaders, and attacked Okuma. It was they who formed the various ultra-nationalist societies, such as the famous *Kokur-yukai* (the 'Black Dragon Society' or, more correctly, the 'Society of the River Amur').* Inevitably they admired, and had close links with, the Japanese armed forces, more especially the army. As a rule they were kept in their place by the Meiji governments; but as a pressure group they could not be ignored.

These self-styled 'patriots' took full advantage of the new prestige that Japan acquired after the defeat of Russia. This prestige was especially high in Asia, where the victory of an oriental over an occidental nation was discussed in every bazaar from Hong Kong to the Persian Gulf. To Indian nationalism Japan's victory was a thunder-clap; and in the eyes of Asian revolutionaries Tokyo occupied for a time the place later held by Moscow.

Officially, of course, Japan was committed, by the terms of the renewed alliance with Great Britain, to support the preservation of British rights and interests in India and East Asia. Furthermore the government in Tokyo considered Japan's proper status to be that of a world, rather than an Asian, power. We have it on the authority of Prince Saionji, twice Premier and later *Genro*, that the Emperor Meiji disliked the use of the terms 'Orient' and 'Occident' in opposition to each other. The Japanese government, then, could hardly lend support to such ideas as 'Asia for the Asiatics'.

* This society was founded in 1901, when the nationalists were convinced that Japan would have to fight Russia. One of its activities was espionage in Manchuria and Siberia. It was fitting, therefore, that it should call itself the 'River Amur Society'. The Chinese characters for 'Amur' mean, translated literally, 'Black Dragon'. This name caught the imagination of Western journalists – brought up perhaps on Sax Rohmer – before the Pacific War.

The extreme nationalist groups, on the other hand, were deeply interested in the concept of an Asian renaissance, since they believed that it should take place under the leadership and guidance of Japan. Of these ultra-nationalists perhaps the most influential was an able and uncompromising adventurer-sage called Toyama Mitsuru. Organizer of a number of political murders he died, widely revered, in his bed at a great age towards the end of the Pacific War. After the Russo-Japanese War a procession of Chinese, Indian, Annamese, and Filippino dissidents visited Toyama at his home in Tokyo; and the most important of these were the Chinese who were plotting to overthrow the Manchu dynasty in Peking. Thus, when the Chinese Revolution occurred in 1911, Japanese nationalists felt an almost proprietorial interest in the event. This strengthened the conviction, especially among the army, that Japan had the right to shape the future course of China's development.

At the same time – that is to say during the last decade of the Meiji era – there was a modest but significant growth of Socialist feeling, some of it of an extreme kind. The authorities were not prepared to tolerate the existence of a party advocating Socialism; and so Socialist organizations and publications were suppressed by the police almost as soon as they appeared. Nevertheless, as industrialization gathered momentum, and as society took on a more decidedly capitalist flavour, both Socialism and anarchism became attractive to members of the intelligentsia, if not to any large numbers of workers. In a socialist periodical Katayama Sen had written the perilous and explosive words, now famous in Japan:

I will be the word of the people. I will be the bleeding mouth from which the gag has been snatched. I will say everything.

Katayama attended the International Congress of Socialists at Amsterdam during the Russo-Japanese War and publicy shook hands with the Russian delegate. In 1908 orthodox opinion in Japan received a further shock when there was a parade in Tokyo of Socialists and anarcho-syndicalists, carrying red banners and chanting revolutionary songs. Severe police action followed this incident ; and indeed it was during this year that the emperor was advised to issue a rescript warning the people against 'the evils of the time', although this phrase was intended to apply not only to such dangerous ideas as Socialism and anarchism but also to displays of extravagance and frivolity by the rich, whose numbers were increasing as the national economy expanded. In 1911 it was announced that the police had unearthed an anarchist plot to murder the emperor and that its alleged ringleader, Kotoku Denjiro, and eleven others had been tried and executed. The news of this plot horrified public opinion. Leftwing manifestations became anathema, and the government was able to suffocate the socialist movement for the best part of ten years. Katayama fled abroad, and so did several other Socialists. Some died in prison ; some renounced their beliefs. A few committed suicide; others lay low, biding their time.

Open and tolerated criticism of the basis of the state and of society was confined, in fact, to a few influential university professors of a liberal cast of mind. One of them, Minobe Tatsukichi of Tokyo Imperial University, advanced the theory that the emperor was one, though the highest, of several organs of the state ; and Minobe's rather liberal interpretation of the Constitution became increasingly acceptable to educated men in Tokyo at the time, although it was challenged from the outset by various nationalist scholars. But twenty-five years were to pass before Minobe was to suffer for his opinions.

At the end of July 1912 the emperor fell ill and died. During his last days the wide plaza in front of the moat and walls of the palace was filled with silent groups of people, kneeling in prayer. The funeral procession in Tokyo was perhaps the most impressive ever seen in modern times. It took place at night, along roads covered with sand, the catafalque being borne on a wagon drawn by five oxen. In the procession was a detachment of the Royal Marines from H.M.S. *Minotaur*, the British flagship in the Far East. The interment was at Momoyama near Kyoto, and buried with the coffin were four earthen effigies of warriors in full armour; for in ancient times there had been practised on such occasions the custom of *junshi*. When a ruler or great lord died certain of his retainers killed themselves so that they might escort him to the next world. It was the supreme manifestation of loyalty. The practice had been discouraged, however, long before the opening of the country.

General Nogi, the victor of Port Arthur and later Principal of the Peers' School, had decided to follow this almost forgotten custom ; and no doubt he would have done so soon after the emperor died had he not been appointed to receive Prince Arthur of Connaught, who came to Japan as King George's representative at the funeral. However, at the precise moment that the cortège left the Palace, Nogi and his wife, seated in the upper room of their house in the Azabu district of the city, committed suicide in the traditional *samurai* manner. Everybody was flabbergasted by this event. It was felt that observance of *junshi* provided only part of the reason for this act of self-immolation. Some said that Nogi wanted to take his own life much earlier, since he was oppressed by his responsibility for the death of so many thousands at Port Arthur, that the emperor had asked him to wait. . . . Others pointed out that Nogi's own testament suggested that his main motive was to remind his countrymen of the old *samurai* code, which in his view was being set aside by an increasingly hedonistic age.

The Emperor Meiji was succeeded by his son, who took as the name of his reign *Taisho*, which means 'great righteousness'. This may have been intended as an oblique admonition to his subjects, for older people were becoming very worried about the changes in the structure of society, and in popular thinking, that were taking place under the impact of industrialization. The new emperor was in weak health. Later on he showed signs of mental instability, and from 1921 to 1926, the year of his death, his eldest son was Regent.

The Taisho period had scarcely begun when there occurred a political crisis of some magnitude. The Prime Minister, Saionji, was under strong pressure from the Army General Staff, backed up of course by Yamagata, to make budgetary allotment for two new divisions. Saionji and the majority of the cabinet resisted this demand, for the financial position of the country was causing some anxiety. Finding himself outvoted in the cabinet, the Minister of War, General Uehara, submitted his resignation direct to the emperor without informing the premier. Uehara was quite entitled to do this under the Constitution, but it was a clear demonstration that in the last resort a Japanese prime minister was at the mercy of the armed services. For of course Saionji's cabinet had to resign, since no general was ready to defy his professional associates by taking Uehara's place. General Katsura, now a court official, was appointed Premier for the third time. This happened in December 1912, before the Diet assembled – this body, it will be remembered, met normally for only three months in twelve – and soon after it was convened, a good deal of trouble broke out. For Katsura was much disliked, as a rigid martinet, by most politicians. The navy, too, resented his appointment. The navy was jealous of the other service, and Satsuma–Choshu rivalry was an important factor in the situation. Furthermore, the press was on the whole very hostile to Katsura, and by this time, thanks to the spread of popular education, the press had a mass reading public ; and although they were often scurrilous, usually irresponsible, and almost always sensational, Japanese newspapers did express in a crude way the force of public opinion ; all the more so, perhaps, since in 1913 there were still only some three million people entitled to the vote. Party politicians felt that the issue of representative government was at stake, for they knew that Katsura's appointment, like Saionji's fall, had been engineered, without the least regard for the Diet, by the Choshu clan. An outstanding parliamentarian and a man of genuine principle, Ozaki Yukio, fiercely attacked Katsura and his colleagues, accusing them in a famous speech in the Lower House of using the Throne as a rampart and imperial rescripts as missiles. There was uproar in the Diet and violence outside. Rioting broke out in Tokyo, Osaka, Kyoto, Kobe, and other places. Troops were called out to help the police, and several people were killed.

All this agitation succeeded, in the sense that it brought about the resignation of the Katsura cabinet. This might have been the beginning of real party government in Japan. But it was not. The victory went, not to the House of Representatives, but to the Satsuma clan, with whom the *Seiyukai* – the majority party in the House – came to an understanding. For the new Premier was an admiral, Yamamoto Gombei ; and a cynical editor told his readers : 'Now we shall see some big naval contracts.' He was right ; but he could not have foretold that the Yamamoto cabinet would fall in little more than a year's time, thanks to a squalid bribery scandal involving naval officers and a German firm. This scandal, in which the cabinet itself was not directly involved, angered public opinion ; and further disorders occurred in Tokyo and elsewhere. Once again troops were summoned to help the police.

Yamamoto's successor was Okuma, who of late had devoted less time to politics than to Waseda University in Tokyo, which he had founded many years earlier. Okuma, who took office in the spring of 1914, had a great reputation as a tough opponent of the old clan oligarchy (to which he had originally belonged), and everyone considered him to be a champion of popular rights. But from the moment he formed his cabinet, he cooperated with Yamagata and the military party, or appeared to do so ; for in reality his Foreign Minister, Kato Takaaki, soon fell into disfavour with the now aged but still powerful Yamagata. This was on account of the so-called 'Twenty-One Demands', the ill-conceived and clumsily handled diplomatic offensive against China launched in the opening months of 1915.

[III]

The Twenty-One Demands can be summed up as an opportunist and maladroit attempt by Japan to bring China under her supervision, if not control. The European War had distracted the attention of those nations, particularly Great Britain, on whom China could depend for financial, diplomatic, and moral support in her efforts to retain some free-

dom of action against Japan, now that the latter had taken
Russia's place in south Manchuria. Great Britain's position
vis-à-vis China was rather two-sided. On the one hand, as
Japan's ally, she was prepared to accept Japanese hegemony
over south Manchuria for many years to come. On the other
hand, she was reluctant to see Japan or any other foreign
power overawe the Peking government. But by the end of
1914 Japan, having captured the German fortress of Tsingtau, was firmly established in Shantung as well as in Manchuria. Japan had entered the First World War a little more
than a fortnight after it had begun, and within a matter of
three months had seized German possessions and interests in
Shantung.* It seemed a heaven-sent opportunity to extract
important concessions from China, which as a republic appeared to be even more chaotic and powerless than in the
last years of the Manchu dynasty. But foolishly Kato, the
Foreign Minister, overplayed his hand. He might have
traded the evacuation of Shantung for solid and comprehensive Chinese concessions to Japan in both south Manchuria
and Inner Mongolia. If this had been done, the Manchurian
Incident of 1931, and all that followed in Japan and outside,
might well have been avoided. Instead, Kato accepted a plan
of action drawn up jointly by a Foreign Ministry official and
the military attaché in Peking ; and he then secured support
for it from Okuma and the rest of the cabinet.

The course adopted was to present to Yuan Shih-kai, the
Chinese President, a set of demands in five groups. These
need not be listed here. It is enough to say that not only did
they cover such matters as the transfer to Japan of German
leaseholds in Shantung and the extension of Japanese rights
in south Manchuria, but they also included demands that
the Chinese government should employ Japanese political,
financial, and military advisers, that Japanese police should
be given a share in the administration of various important
cities, that more than half of China's war material should be

* The siege of Tsingtau lasted about five weeks. A small British force
took part in the operations, and this campaign saw the first use by the
Japanese of military aviation.

purchased from Japan. It may be that the Japanese asked for much more than they expected to get, for when it came to the point of ultimatum, after weeks of negotiations in Peking, Japan saved China's face by dropping the more extreme of the demands. But the harm had been done. Virulent anti-Japanese sentiment was aroused in China, and this was harmful to Japanese trade with that country. The European nations, engrossed in the war, had little time to spare for what was going on at the other end of the world. True, the British Foreign Secretary warned the Japanese Ambassador in London that Kato should not go too far, but it was in America that there occurred the sharpest and most enduring repercussions. There was already some anti-Japanese sentiment in California, where certain politicians had played on racial prejudice to inflame public feeling against Japanese immigration; and Americans too, thanks to their considerable missionary and educational connexions with China, cherished a sentimental affection for the 'sister republic' across the Pacific. China might be weak and divided, but a new national consciousness was beginning to develop. Many Chinese nationalists had been educated in America, and those who had received help in Tokyo now became disillusioned with Japan. At all events the Twenty-One Demands became a rallying cry for patriotic Chinese and cost Japan many friends in the outside world. Under duress China was forced to sign two treaties, conceding the transfer to Japan of German interests in Shantung and giving new privileges to Japan both in south Manchuria and in the eastern part of Inner Mongolia. These concessions amounted to the bulk of four out of the five groups that comprised the original Japanese demands. It was the fifth group that was the most objectionable; and this was dropped.

The unfortunate Twenty-One Demands were a turning point in American-Japanese relations. After 1915 Japan never recovered, in the eyes of the American people, the moral prestige – so high in 1905 – that was lost at that time. From now on it was Japan that was cast in the role of the bully; and even when the Japanese behaved well towards

China, as they did at various times during the 1920s, they never got the credit for it. In terms of propaganda the Chinese, who of course often had a good case, swept the field.

It is ironic that the monumental blunder of the Twenty-One Demands should have been perpetrated, not by any swashbuckling or narrow-minded soldier, but by a civilian Foreign Minister with a good knowledge of world affairs ; for Kato Takaaki had been Japanese Ambassador in London. Indeed many of the army leaders disapproved of the way the Foreign Minister was handling Chinese affairs. Notably, Yamagata was chagrined at the ill-feeling stirred up in China by Kato's policy and he engineered his removal from office. When at last Okuma resigned, in the autumn of 1916, Yamagata made certain that one of his own henchman, Terauchi (Governor-General of Korea), should become the new Premier.

Marshal Terauchi's policy towards China was to try to control that country by means of bribes rather than threats. While Governor-General of Korea he had taken advantage of President Yuan Shih-kai's death in June 1916 to send a trusted emissary to Peking to win to Japan's side the northern warlords who were in power in Peking and who therefore represented the legal government of a very disunited China. After becoming Premier, Terauchi made use of this same emissary to negotiate numerous and substantial loans both to the central government in Peking and to various provincial administrations. When the Diet was in session these loans were the subject of a good many critical questions. Terauchi could not ignore the Diet entirely, and despite his claim that his cabinet was above, and aloof from, all party conflicts – the traditional Yamagata view of what proper government should be – he had to come to an understanding with the *Seiyukai*. But he was not deflected from his chosen policy towards China ; and certainly it was more successful than that pursued by Okuma and Kato.

The very fact that Japan was in a position to offer a number of loans to China was a testimony to the benefits that were accruing from the world war. From 1905 to 1914 Japan's financial and economic condition was neither stable nor healthy. In those years there was very considerable industrial expansion, but this had created a growing demand for imported raw materials. In one sense, it is true, Japan in 1914 was stronger than ever before. Large naval vessels could now be built in Japanese yards, and the navy would soon have over seventeen capital ships and some twenty cruisers. Yet the strain on the national finances was very severe, for in 1914, as in the preceding years, imports exceeded exports. This unfavourable balance of trade seemed particularly ominous in view of the accelerating rise in the rate of the growth of Japan's population. Between 1890 and 1900 this had risen from almost forty million to about forty-four million. Between 1900 and 1910 it rose from forty-four to close on fifty million. What was more, the land, so it seemed, was worked to capacity. From being a food-exporting country Japan was now importing a percentage of her foodstuffs, including rice. Much of this, admittedly, came from Korea ; otherwise the problem of the balance of payments would have been even more serious.

This scene was radically transformed by the world war. Japanese shipping and shipyards and the products of Japanese factories were in great demand by the Allies ; and in the markets of south-east Asia and elsewhere Japanese exports, especially textiles, were needed to meet orders that Great Britain, Germany, and France could not fulfil. It was not long, then, before Japan became a creditor instead of a debtor among the nations ; and a period of boom and business prosperity set in. War profiteers became more numerous and more noticeable as the long struggle in Europe, so favourable to Japan, continued. The *zaibatsu*, the existing financial and industrial combines, did very well of course ; but so did a host of new entrepreneurs. There was much conspicuous spending. The displays of wealth were modest no doubt by Western standards, but they seemed garish and offensive to most Japanese of that age, whose best taste was traditionally austere. The middle class, still relatively small, expanded. But, on the whole, wages by no means kept within sight of rising prices, and between the poor and those who were comfortably off there appeared a gulf wider than had been seen at any time since the Restoration. When in 1917 the Russian Revolution ran its course, those in authority had some reason to feel uneasy. For, as we have seen, the Japanese are inquisitive, alert to new ideas, as well as obedient, and there are decided limits to their famed docility.

Yet the years from 1900 to the autumn of 1918, before the shadow of the Rice Riots and of the end of the European War fell across the land, may be described aptly, in the Japanese context, as 'golden'. The last decade of the Meiji era saw a new confidence, and a new inclination towards experiment, in the world of literature and art. Borrowings from abroad became much more selective. National pride deepened, and so mellowed; it was not yet bellicose. The old leaders were still on the bridge, although as *Genro* they stood back a little, like a captain at the chartroom door, watching and, from time to time, advising the man at the helm. The massive task, undertaken after the fall of the shogunate, had been completed. Not long after the Emperor Meiji died the years were to be 'golden' in a rather literal sense; for war prosperity increased nearly a hundred-fold the gold reserves held by the government and by the Bank of Japan. Yet the satisfaction of the more thoughtful was tempered with just a touch of anxiety.

Chapter 7

THE TWENTIES

[1]

IN the summer of 1918 Japan became involved in a military undertaking that brought her little profit and no glory. This was her intervention in the Amur basin, the so-called Siberian expedition. Military planners in Tokyo became interested in a project of this kind almost as soon as the Kerensky government in Russia was overthrown by the Bolsheviks. There was plenty of support for the principle of Japanese intervention from the European allies, who were naturally fearful of the consequences of a complete breakdown on the Eastern front. In particular, the French had pressed for the dispatch of a Japanese expedition to European Russia on more than one occasion even before the Bolshevik seizure of power. Japanese leaders, both military and civilian, firmly rejected this proposal. They were interested in China and eastern Siberia. They were not prepared to do more than offer naval support in the European theatre of operations. However, the establishment of a Bolshevik regime close to Manchuria and Korea was clearly to be prevented if possible; and there were of course many elements in Siberia, as in other parts of Russia, who were prepared to resist the Bolsheviks; they ranged from die-hard right-wing monarchists to social revolutionaries. Some of them were desperately eager for Japanese help, in men as well as munitions. Moreover, there were reports – exaggerated as it turned out – of large numbers of German and Austro-Hungarian prisoners-of-war released and armed by the Bolsheviks; in the imagination of the Allies they constituted a serious menace. Then there was the question of the security of the huge dumps of war equipment at Vladivostock. The Allies feared that these might fall to the

Bolsheviks and so find their way into enemy hands. In its own eyes, the Japanese General Staff had a further motive for intervening in eastern Siberia. In the autumn of 1917 it believed, on the basis of intelligence reports, that the provisional Russian govenment had consented to open to American investment areas in the Maritime Province, Kamchatka, and Sakhalin. If the Russians were prepared to allow foreign economic exploitation of their Far Eastern territory, the Japanese, for reasons of propinquity, wanted to be the first in the field.

The General Staff in Tokyo, therefore, made fairly ambitious plans for a military expedition, and persuaded the Chinese to agree to future Japanese troop movements through northern Manchuria. However, both Yamagata and the cabinet, headed by his henchman Terauchi, moved with great caution. They were anxious to avoid giving any offence to America by precipitate, unilateral action ; and in the Diet the *Kenseikai*, one of the major parties, was opposed to intervention. In the end Japan joined, by invitation and as incomparably the biggest partner, what was officially a combined Allied expedition to rescue the Czechoslovak forces strung along the Trans-Siberian Railway from the Urals to the Pacific. But Japanese contingents remained on Russian soil long after the other nations concerned had evacuated Siberia, long after the self-reliant Czechs had saved themselves, and the Kolchak regime had collapsed. Indeed they did not leave eastern Siberia until 1922, and they remained in northern Sakhalin until 1925. The Japanese at times lent support to certain Cossack leaders who in their day-to-day administration, as well as in their operations against an admittedly unscrupulous enemy, were indistinguishable from bandits ; and the behaviour of some Japanese detachments was marked by a brutality not seen for many years. They were undoubtedly influenced by the peculiarly savage nature of the Russian Civil War ; and they received some provocation from such episodes as the massacre of their nationals, including women and children, at Nikolaevsk, at the mouth of the Amur, in the early part of 1920. The experience of the

Siberian intervention probably undermined the respect that Japanese officers and men had felt, however reluctantly, for Europeans. Undoubtedly the spectacle of Russian refugees, many of them in penury, flooding such cities as Harbin, Tientsin, and Shanghai, destroyed for ever in the eyes of the Chinese the myth of European superiority. At the same time the Siberian adventure gave some of the young officers of the Japanese forces a training in political manipulation and intrigue which they were to put to good use ten years later, after the seizure of Manchuria.

It cannot be said that the Siberian expedition was popular in Japan. Public opinion was, to say the least, apathetic towards the whole affair. With the defeat of Germany all ideas associated with militarism seemed discredited, whereas Western democracy appeared to be justified by success. Accordingly, in the bigger cities at any rate, Japanese soldiers found themselves looked at somewhat askance by the people at large; and the time came when officers in Tokyo and Osaka preferred, when off duty, to wear civilian dress rather than the emperor's uniform. In the countryside, where traditional values were dominant, they could rely on being treated with proper respect; but in the cities they were made to feel, on occasions, unpleasantly conspicuous. Mass patriotic fervour over Siberian intervention did not exist and could not be stimulated, in spite of short-lived waves of excitement about particular issues, such as the Nikolaevsk massacre.

In September 1918 the Terauchi cabinet resigned, taking responsibility for the serious rice riots that had broken out all over Japan during the previous month. The war boom had led to a continuing increase in the price of rice, the staple food. The trend was much accelerated by the forward buying of speculators, many of whom belonged to an unpopular category known as *narikin*, or 'new rich' – in other words, war profiteers. In former times a rise in the price of rice would have been a matter for almost universal satisfaction; but in the twentieth century, of course, a very large working class was growing up in the cities and towns – in Japan after 1914 the industrial revolution was fully in its stride. For urban

workers dear rice was a great hardship. By the summer of
1918 the price of rice was more than double what it had
been even in 1917, when it was already high. The patience
of the working class was strained beyond endurance, and it
snapped abruptly and spontaneously. Riots and incendiar-
ism took place in a hundred and eighty cities, towns, and
villages throughout the country and were spread over a
period of three weeks during the hot August of 1918. Troops
had to be called out, and over a hundred people lost their
lives and many thousands were arrested before these widespread disturbances were quelled.

The new government was headed by Hara Takashi,
Saionji's successor as president of the *Seiyukai* party.
(Saionji, on the emperor's invitation, had joined the charm-
ed circle of the *Genro*, or 'Elder statesmen'.) Hara was the
first commoner to be Prime Minister of Japan. It was now
thirty-five years since the cabinet system had been established, and during that time there were no less than eighteen
cabinets. But only nine men had held the premiership, and
all of them, with the exception of Okuma and Saionji, had
been members of either the Choshu or Satsuma clan. Hara
came from Iwate Prefecture, in the north-east. He had been
a journalist and a Foreign Ministry official before entering
Diet politics. One of his assets was the relationship that he
cultivated with the aged Yamagata, the senior *Genro* and
still the most powerful individual in the land. Hara handled
the old warrior with a skilful blend of deference and charm,
and made a very favourable impression on him – which was
wise, for Yamagata had not abandoned his keen dislike of
the principle of party government.

In the press at home and abroad a good deal was made of
Hara's position as the 'Great Commoner' presiding over a
cabinet all the members of which, with the exception of the
War, Navy, and Foreign Ministers, belonged to the *Seiyukai*,
the largest party in the Diet. But Hara, although in a sense a
man of the people, was by no means wedded to democratic
ideals in the contemporary Western meaning of the term.
He had some hard things to say about militarism, but on the

whole he saw eye to eye with his Minister of War, General Tanaka Giichi, who had been one of the chief planners of the Siberian expedition. He was not at all in favour of extending the franchise to the great mass of the people. He deplored the prevalence of radical thought and viewed the labour movement with hostility. He was often surrounded by a gang of *soshi*, or professional bullies, accustomed to applying physical intimidation to political opponents. In many respects he resembled the old-time ward 'boss' of American political life. Yet to a great extent he captured the imagination of a people not yet entirely disillusioned with parliamentary politics. Japanese historians agree that he was a supremely able politician, perhaps the most able in the history of the Diet. He built up his party, the *Seiyukai*, into a position of remarkable strength; and he contrived to keep on fairly level terms with such competing forces as the *Genro*, the armed services, and the higher bureaucracy. What was needed for success in Japanese politics, as elsewhere, was the right mixture of toughness and compromise. Hara had it. He was fated to meet a violent end. In November 1921 he was stabbed to death on Tokyo station by a young fanatic. The assassination occurred five weeks after that of a millionaire banker, by another fanatic (who committed suicide after the crime). Both murderers, especially the man who killed the millionaire, received a certain amount of public sympathy. For the rich were now much despised; and the prime minister had lost his early popularity, being regarded, unfairly perhaps, as sharing some responsibility for corruption scandals affecting at least three of his cabinet ministers as well as a number of members of the Diet.

By the middle of 1921 the war boom had collapsed, with consequent industrial unrest. 'Dangerous thoughts' – a phrase beloved by the police – were on the increase. Slowly, and to some extent in secret, there was growing up below the surface a contempt for the Diet and a hatred for 'Big Business'. Indeed the two were becoming identified in the eyes of the public. Thus the seeds were sown, to shoot up a decade later, of Japanese military fascism.

However, we are anticipating our chronology. We must go back to 1919, when Japan took part in the Peace Conference at Versailles. The Japanese delegation failed to get inserted in the Covenant of the League of Nations a declaration of the principle of racial equality. This setback, due largely to the intransigence of vinegary little Mr Hughes of Australia, naturally rankled in the minds of the Japanese, who felt that despite their admission to the Great Powers' Club – Japan was given a permanent seat on the League Council – they were still not regarded as full equals by the nations of the West. But they insisted on being given the former German rights in the Chinese province of Shantung, which they had taken over after the capture of Tsingtau in 1914. The Chinese had recognized Japan's succession to German rights and interests in two treaties – one signed under duress, after the ultimation of the Twenty-One Demands, and the other freely negotiated in 1918. But there were in reality two governments in China, the official administration in Peking and that of the Kuomintang in Canton, representing Chinese nationalist opinion. Both were represented in the delegation that China sent to Versailles, and it was the nationalists who were the more vocal and, from the Japanese point of view, the more tiresome at the Conference. A great deal was made of the Twenty-One Demands, and world sympathy on the whole was with the Chinese. Still, Japan had two cards to play. One was the threat to withdraw from the Conference: which was bound to impress President Wilson, as the Italians had just left Paris in high dudgeon. The other was the revelation that in 1917 Great Britain and France had agreed, in a secret undertaking, to support Japan's claims to Shantung. With great reluctance Wilson felt obliged to give way. The consequences were disastrous for him. It was thanks partly to Congressional dissatisfaction with the Shantung settlement at Versailles that the United States failed to ratify the Peace Treaty and so held aloof from the League of Nations. The benefits to Japan of this particular diplomatic victory over Shantung were offset by an anti-Japanese trade boycott in China. Less tangible, but in the long run perhaps more serious was the hardening of popular anti-Japanese sentiment in the United States. Perhaps the most solid gain for Japan at Versailles was the acquisition, under mandate from the League, of the former German islands in the Pacific north of the Equator.

Two years later, in 1921, Japan took part in the famous Washington Conference, at which a series of important agreements was concluded. There was a Naval Treaty, fixing a ratio of 5:5:3 between the capital ship tonnage of Great Britain, the United States, and Japan respectively. At first the Japanese had urged very strongly that the ratio should be 10:10:7; but as Washington had broken the wireless code in use between Tokyo and the Japanese delegation – the fact was irresponsibly revealed in a book published in the United States a few years later – the Americans were aware that the Japanese would not hold out for the higher ratio. In reality the naval settlement was very much to Japan's advantage, for it was known that if no agreement were reached the Americans were ready to build up their navy to a strength that neither Japan nor Great Britain could match. And in return for agreement on the 5:5:3 ratio America and Great Britain consented to the Japanese proposal that the *status quo* be maintained respecting naval bases and fortifications in the Pacific. Although Hawaii and Singapore were excluded from its terms, this limitation meant that the Japanese could rest assured that no first-class naval base would be constructed in the Philippines or at Hong Kong. At no cost, indeed at a very considerable saving of money, Japan obtained a measure of security that she could not have achieved in an unrestricted naval building race with the United States.

The Washington Conference also saw the end of the Anglo-Japanese Alliance, which was replaced by an empty agreement, known as the Four-Power Treaty, between the members of the British Empire, the United States, Japan, and France. It was in no sense a security pact. It was a device, which quite failed to deceive the Japanese, for winding up an alliance which, in the eyes of the British cabinet, was becoming in some ways more of an embarrassment than an asset. One of the prime aims of American policy since Versailles was to ensure that the Anglo-Japanese Alliance should not continue; and the American view was shared to some extent by the British Dominions, notably Canada. In Japan opinions varied; but on the whole the Treaty with Great Britain was still regarded as one of the recognized permanent bases of the nation's foreign policy. Great Britain's decision not to renew the Alliance – however politely swathed in face-saving references to the League Covenant and the new Four-Power Treaty – inflicted a wound received in sorrow and remembered in wrath. The termination of the Alliance removed, perhaps for ever, the possibility of friendly and effective British influence on policy-making in Tokyo, while it did nothing to strengthen the security of the United States; and of course it greatly weakened the whole strategic situation of Australia and New Zealand, to say nothing of Hong Kong and other British possessions east of the Bay of Bengal. However, in London it was hoped, and no doubt believed, that when the Singapore base was completed all would be well.

Finally, at Washington, China received the satisfaction she had failed to obtain at Versailles. Shidehara Kijuro, the principal Japanese delegate at the Conference, announced that Japan would withdraw without delay from Shantung; and a Sino-Japanese agreement was signed whereby Japan, while retaining some economic concessions in Shantung, returned to China the bulk of the interests acquired in that province under the terms of the Twenty-One Demands. Chinese security appeared to be guaranteed further by the Nine-Power Treaty, to which China herself was a signatory, whereby Japan, Great Britain, the United States, and five other nations undertook to respect Chinese sovereignty and independence together with the principle of 'equal opportunity for the commerce and industry of all nations throughout the territory of China'. The Japanese promise regarding Shantung was faithfully observed, and Sino-Japanese relations seemed to be set on a new course. Later, when he was Foreign Minister, Shidehara was always conciliatory towards China, to the fury of nationalist opinion in Japan; and his name was to become associated with what his many enemies described as 'a weak-kneed China policy'.

The Washington Conference cleared the air, and it seemed to usher in an entirely new era in the Far East. Within Japan, too, the old world, surviving from the Meiji period, was clearly coming to an end. This was symbolized in January 1922 by the death of Okuma, followed a month later by that of Yamagata. Both were in their eighties, vigorous in mind to the last. Each embodied a distinctive and contrasting aspect of the Meiji era. Although his personality was aristocratic and conservative, Okuma represented the progressive, liberal forces that opposed the clan hegemony established in the nineteenth century. He was not personally a democrat, but the people of the older generation loved him, and they turned out in thousands for his funeral. Yamagata, on the other hand, had stood rock-like for oligarchic control of policy and the political and social supremacy of the army. With his passing the traditional dominance of Choshu within the officer corps began to wane. In fact even before his death the Choshu clan had been criticized by officers who did not belong to it, and the number of such officers was increasing. They felt, with some justification, that clan favouritism often blocked their promotion. Yamagata's death left a vacuum which was filled by no individual, but rather by a succession of competing factions. As a result the strict discipline that he had enforced began to break down, if slowly at first. The consequences of this were to be extremely serious, as we shall see.

Symbolic of the new age was a photograph of the Crown Prince, now Regent, in tweed cap and plus-fours, dressed for golf (with the Prince of Wales). He visited Great Britain and France in 1921, to the alarm of many old-fashioned nationalists who feared that his young mind might be unduly influenced by the 'dangerous' ideas current in modern Europe. When the Prince of Wales returned the visit in 1922, Japanese conservatives were shocked not only by the game of golf, but also by a photograph of the English Prince

in the livery of a *jinrikisha* coolie. Some of the younger generation, in the cities at least, were heartened as well as diverted
by portents such as these. To them it seemed admirable that
the Regent showed signs of possessing a scientific bent – the
study of marine biology was to be his keenest hobby – as well
as a liberal, rather democratic outlook on affairs. It
provided, in the highest quarters, that last touch of modernity
visible already in the larger cities, where jazz, taxis, and
taxi-dancers were beginning to compete with traditional
music, *jinrikishas*, and *geisha*. In the universities – Tokyo had
perhaps the largest student population in the world – the
phenomenon of the 'Marx boy' was beginning to attract
attention. This was the left-wing student, often from an
aristocratic or wealthy home, who excited his contemporaries
and shocked his elders by his revolutionary views. There
were to be seen, in sophisticated circles at any rate, the first
signs of what was to be known as the *Moga* style. *Moga* was
the Japanese contraction of the English words, 'modern
girl'. It came to suggest, during the twenties, cloche hats
and short skirts, with the 'bob', 'shingle', or even 'Eton
crop'. Her male counterpart was the *Mobo*, the 'modern
boy' (not to be confused with the 'Marx boy') who on leaving the university adopted the latest and most flashy Western
clothes including, it might be, 'Oxford bags'. Occasionally
Mobo and *Moga* might be seen walking down the Ginza in
Tokyo hand in hand. This was very daring; but it was done.

The middle-aged, not to mention the elderly, were
genuinely worried at the seeming frivolity and individualism
of the young. The very air hummed with confusion – scandals in the Diet, 'dangerous thoughts' in the universities and
among city workers, all manner of new ideas, new fashions,
new technical inventions pouring in from abroad. Somehow
a single occurrence, widely publicized at the time, epitomized this particular age. This was the suicide, together with a
married woman many years younger than himself, of the
famous novelist Arishima Takeo. Not long before he ended
his life, in the summer of 1923, he had made over to his
tenants his landed property in Hokkaido, for he was noted

for his idealist, Tolstoyan principles. Thus he was loved as a man, while admired as a writer. The circumstances of his death created one of the greatest social sensations Japan had known since the suicide of General Nogi. Love suicides have never been uncommon in Japan; but after Arishima's death they became, for a time, so it seemed, a daily affair.

The late Taisho and early Showa periods – the twenties – are often referred to by the Japanese as the era of '*Ero, Guro, Nansensu*' – namely, eroticism, grotesquerie, and nonsense. These words applied, of course, to a minority of those who lived in the bigger cities. Perhaps our phrase, the 'Hectic Twenties', carries some equivalence of meaning. Suddenly, as though to aggravate on the material level a confusion that bewildered many souls, there took place an event of such horror that the whole world turned with sympathy to Japan.

[II]

Old superstition had it that under the surface of the land of Japan there lived a giant catfish. From time to time, so the legend went, he was irritated by the folly and wickedness of the human beings above him, and then he would heave his back in fury. Thus tremors and earthquakes have disturbed various parts of Japan from time immemorial.

One of the greatest and most terrible of these occurred at midday on 1 September 1923 in the Yokohama–Tokyo area. The day was hot, but there chanced to be a fairly strong wind blowing, and this added immeasurably to the scale of the disaster. For in many places what the shaking earth left standing, the fires, springing up everywhere and driven by the wind, consumed. Virtually the entire city of Yokohama, modern buildings and little wooden houses alike, was rocked or burnt to the ground. Well over half of Tokyo, already the third largest city in the world, was completely destroyed. Comparable ruin befell numerous towns and villages in the Kanto area. No exact statistics are available, but the death roll amounted to about one hundred thousand.

There were innumerable instances of heroism, and indeed
self-sacrifice, on the part of the people; but in Tokyo a
rumour spread, almost as fast as the raging fires, that Korean
nationalists, together with Japanese Communists, had plot-
ted to set up some kind of revolutionary government. As a
result many inoffensive Koreans were sought out and killed
by frenzied mobs or by gangs of self-styled 'patriotic' young
men. There was also a mass round-up by the police of known
anarchists, Communists, and other extreme left-wing
people, some of whom were murdered after their arrest.
This news was not revealed until many weeks later, and it
created a notable scandal. However, the punishment of
those responsible was comparatively mild.

Generously helped by gifts from abroad, especially from
America, the Japanese set about with characteristic energy
and courage to rebuild the two shattered cities. The great
earthquake and fire destroyed the last visible traces of old
Yedo, centred on Nihonbashi. The remaining walls of the
shogun's fortress, now enclosing the Imperial Palace, survived the holocaust. So did the mausolea of the *shogun* at
Ueno and Shiba. But nearly everything else redolent of
Yedo was a heap of ashes. In its place there rose a city of on
striking beauty, with wide streets and high modern buildings at its core, surrounded by a vast jumble of new wooden
houses clustered along undistinguished thoroughfares; some
of these resembled country lanes and so acquired a certain
pensive charm. Within three or four years there was little
sign that Tokyo had ever known calamity.

[III]

After Hara's assassination in November 1921, the new
Premier was Takahashi Korekiyo, who had been Finance
Minister in the Hara cabinet. He was known to be thoroughly at home in the world of business and finance and to
be decidedly anti-militarist – a year or two earlier he had
written and distributed a pamphlet advocating the abolition
of the General Staff. He lacked Hara's political skill and

was unable to dominate the *Seiyukai* or repel the attacks made on his government in both Houses of the Diet. So his administration lasted only seven months, until the summer of 1922. There followed, over the next two years, three bureaucratic cabinets that need not detain us here. Then in June 1924 a coalition party cabinet, under Kato Takaaki, was formed. This came into being after a General Election, the second since the First World War, in which the leading political parties, headed by the *Seiyukai* and *Kenseikai*, decisively defeated the nominees of the government. The party that won the most seats was Kato's *Kenseikai*.

It will be remembered that Kato Takaaki, as Foreign Minister in 1915, committed the blunder of endorsing the Twenty-One Demands. But as Premier (from June 1924 to January 1926) he left the conduct of foreign affairs to Shidehara, who did all he could, by way of conciliation, to erase from Chinese minds the recollection of past aggressiveness by Japan. Under Kato and his successor Wakatsuki – Kato died in January 1926 – Japanese politics appeared to be moving, quite firmly this time, into an era of party governments and of real, if still modified, liberalism. The trend was favoured and encouraged by Saionji, who by the end of 1924 was the last surviving *Genro*. Despite his age – he was now in his seventies – he had several more years ahead of him. In the thirties he was to become, increasingly, a civilized anachronism, a warning voice heeded by few of those who were to drive Japan to ruin. But in the days of Kato and Wakatsuki he was in tune with the time. Reactionary conservatism was still a force to be reckoned with; its twin strongholds were the House of Peers and the Privy Council, and it was not entirely absent from the Lower House, including some factions of the *Seiyukai*. But the most serious threat to the spread of liberalism could come only from the services, particularly the army, because of their entrenched powers under the practice of the Constitution. However, the power of the army seemed to be diminishing, for in 1924 an enlightened Minister of War, General Ugaki, cut down military expenditure, reducing the army's strength by no less than four divisions. The government had strong connexions, being based to some extent on ties of family relationship, with the monster Mitsubishi concern. 'Big Business' was all in favour of reduced armaments, and Mitsubishi in particular approved of Shidehara's 'good neighbour' policy towards China. Bourgeois capitalism appeared to be the operative force in Japanese inner politics; and, in the word of an American scholar, 'the carefully controlled revolution of the Meiji period was developing into a runaway liberal movement of the urban middle classes.'*

Yet liberal measures were accompanied by others that seemed to point in the opposite direction. For example, although the government saw through the Diet a manhood suffrage bill, giving all male subjects above the age of twenty-five the right to vote, it also introduced and saw enacted a bill enforcing a Peace Preservation Law. This gave the police even greater powers to deal with those who cherished 'dangerous thoughts'; and so the more radicals wing of the labour movement was considerably oppressed. The reduction in the strength of the army, too, was balanced to some extent by the posting of officers from the disbanded divisions as instructors at government higher and middle schools, to supervise a newly introduced scheme of compulsory military training.

All seemed well so far as foreign affairs were concerned. Diplomatic relations were established with Soviet Russia, a settlement being reached on the question of fisheries and on Sakhalin; the Japanese evacuated the northern part of the island in 1925. In China it was no longer the Japanese, but rather the British, who bore the brunt of nationalist ill-will. The only issue that caused real concern was the American legislation, passed by Congress in 1924, prohibiting oriental including Japanese, immigration into the United States. There was a considerable rumpus when this law was passed. The Japanese Ambassador in Washington only made matters worse by protesting while the measure was before

* Edwin O. Reischauer, *Japan Past and Present*. London (Duckworth), 1947, p. 155.

Congress. He used a phrase that spoke of 'grave consequences' if the bill was passed. Certain senators whipped up
a good deal of irrational anti-Japanese feeling when they
heard of it, and the Senate passed the exclusion bill by an
enormous majority. The hurt to Japanese pride was deep
and long lasting.

The Taisho period ended on Christmas Day 1926, with the
death of the invalid emperor, who was succeeded by his son,
the regent. The new emperor took as the title of his reign two
characters meaning 'enlightened peace', *Showa*; and it can
be said at this point that the implied aspiration was utterly
sincere. The younger emperor's chief mentor was the human-
ist, Saionji. There seemed on the face of it every reason to
believe that the new era of Showa would live up to its name.

But clouds were beginning to gather on the horizon. After
years of internal confusion China was on the eve of becoming unified under the Kuomintang regime headed by Chiang
Kai-shek. It was in 1927 that his forces, in their northward
advance, gained control of the Yangtze valley. One of his
aims was the abolition of extra-territoriality and the eventual recovery of full Chinese sovereignty over such alien en-
claves as the Chinese Eastern Railway (still under Russian
control) and the Japanese zone and leased territory in south
Manchuria. Temperamentally, if not materially, China was
at last prepared to do what Japan had done in the nineteenth
century, to modernize herself and so free herself from foreign
interference. The Nine-Power Treaty seemed to underwrite
this programme. No doubt Japan, from the Chinese point
of view, was the most intractable of all the foreign nations
having rights and interest in China. But it looked to the
Chinese, as to other outsiders, as if civilian, liberal elements
in Tokyo had now got the upper hand, as if Japanese generals would not again have a chance to influence decisions
on foreign policy. This was a gross miscalculation of the true
position, but it was quite forgivable in, say, 1927. In reality
the rising tide of armed nationalism in China, giving dynamic energy to the Kuomintang at that time, produced a
reaction of an ultra-nationalist kind in the Japanese army,

which began to feel that if the friendly, almost yielding, policy of Shidehara continued, the new China would so consolidate its unity and build up its strength that it would eventually be able to challenge the whole Japanese position in south Manchuria. In other words the government's policy towards China, in the eyes not of the army alone, began to look less like wise conciliation than time-saving weakness.

Then, in 1927, Japan experienced quite suddenly a kind of preview in miniature of the world-wide depression that was to hit the country three years later. Although the war boom had collapsed, there were many essentially unsound business undertakings, bolstered up by a top-heavy credit structure, surviving from the war period. A single bank failure led rapidly to the downfall of others; and very soon thirty-six banks, including one of the largest in the country, closed their doors. A number of medium-sized and small firms went into liquidation, to the advantage of the *zaibatsu*, the great financial and industrial empires, that took over many of these ruined firms. The sudden banking crisis of 1927 was in some respects as salutary as it was inevitable; when it was over the Japanese economy was doubtless more efficient. But it aggravated the hostility that the 'little man', lost in the economic jungle, felt towards the monster *zaibatsu* concerns. The two most powerful of these were now hand in glove with the two chief rival political parties in the Diet – Mitsubishi with the *Kenseikai* (soon to be renamed the *Minseito*), and Mitsui with the *Seiyukai*. Those ruined by the banking crisis – and its ramifications were considerable – had small reason to love the Diet. They were ready to respond to a strong nationalist appeal from some force outside the elected Diet. By virtue of the nature of Japanese state education this kind of appeal would be much more effective than that of Marxism, even if the police had permitted Marxist ideas to be disseminated. When the depression struck Japan with great force in 1930 there was of course an astronomical increase in the numbers of those who turned away, in disgust or despair, from parliamentary politics, since these were indelibly associated, in the public mind, with the power of 'Big Business'.

A further development, between the years 1927 and 1930, was the fermenting – like yeast, unseen – of extreme political and economic ideas among junior officers of the army. The most powerful of these ideas was the one that would be known in time as the concept of the 'Showa Restoration'. This, if it meant anything rational at all, was state socialism administered by a military dictatorship. In the Meiji Restoration the great lords had surrendered their fiefs to the emperor, thus nominally 'restoring' to the sovereign the lands that his family had owned and governed in ancient times. In the 'Showa Restoration' the capitalists would have to surrender, or 'restore', their riches; and the political parties, too, would be called upon to surrender their powers to the emperor. This concept owed a great deal to a remarkable book by a fanatic called Kita Ikki, who is often described as the founder of Japanese Fascism. The book, dealing with 'the Reconstruction of Japan', was published just after the First World War; and almost at once the police were at pains to discourage its circulation, for Kita, though an undoubted imperialist, was also strongly anti-capitalist. He advocated the establishment of a 'revolutionary Empire of Japan', national socialist at home and expanding territorially abroad. He believed that the best means of achieving the needed 'reconstruction' was by a military *coup d'état*, for his ideal state would give supreme power under the emperor to the armed forces alone. As time went by, Kita's book was well received by many young army officers. Not all extreme nationalists agreed with his ideas, since they smacked of revolution – a dangerous word. But among the young they gained a hearing, especially after the onset of the depression. Before 1930 the discontent of a few socially and politically dissatisfied junior officers was barely noticeable. Nevertheless beneath the outward show of strict and dedicated military discipline unrest, concealed but passionate, was beginning to simmer. One symptom was the formation in 1927 of a secret society of junior officers for the purpose of planning a future *coup d'état*. The significant thing about this clandestine group, numbering some two hundred, was that it included officers belonging to General Staff Headquarters in Tokyo, the brain-centre of the army.

It was not only in the armed services that extreme nationalist ideas were coming into vogue. Among highly educated civil servants, especially perhaps in the important Ministry of Home Affairs, there was some reappraisal, in the late twenties, of the value to the state of parliamentary forms of government. The Japanese bureaucracy, it is true, always tended to be conservative and authoritarian in its outlook. Still, several of its members entered one or other of the political parties and indeed became leading parliamentary figures. It was the phenomenon of the younger generation of officials becoming angry, as well as cynical, about parliamentary politics that was disturbing to the liberal mind.

The fact is that the main parties in the Diet dug their own graves. It would be quite unfair and misleading to suggest that the Diet politicians were invariably dishonest. There were many men of the utmost probity in both Houses. But the prevailing tone, particularly in the Lower House, was deplorable. Bribery at election time was only exceeded by the 'gifts' that large numbers of politicians received from business interests. The result was that the party in office was nearly always attacked, on various charges of corruption, by those in opposition, who in turn were often vulnerable to similar accusations. Attacks and counter-attacks of this kind were necessarily personal, and they frequently reduced Diet proceedings to a rowdy brawl. This always shocked the public beyond measure, for the Japanese paid homage to decorum, to a convincing show of harmony. The spectacle of a rather corrupt and all too often undignified Lower House might not have been serious, however greatly regretted, had Japan's economic health been sound. But while the population continued to increase, overseas markets shrank alarmingly as the depression spread. Foreign countries reacted to the Japanese export drive by raising against it the tariff barriers considered essential, in conditions of world slump, for the protection of their own industries. Japan's economic position was insecure even before 1929. After that year had ended, the deterioration was rapid, and there grew up a demand for some solution of a clear-cut, non-parliamentary kind.

[IV]

The banking crisis of 1927 brought down Wakatsuki's cabinet. His successor was a shrewd and genial soldier-politician, General Tanaka Giichi, who had taken Taka-hashi's place as president of the *Seiyukai*. This party proceeded to win by a narrow margin the General Election of 1928, the first under conditions of manhood suffrage.

The Tanaka cabinet adopted a tougher policy towards China than that of the previous government. Tanaka, who was Foreign Minister as well as Premier, was worried by the implications, for Japan's status in Manchuria, of the north-ward advance of the Kuomintang; for Chiang Kai-shek, naturally enough, had his eyes on Peking and beyond. So Tanaka sent troops to check the Kuomintang forces as they moved north. A small battle ensued, in which the Chinese were defeated. For the time being the Kuomintang advance into north China was brought to a halt.

Very soon after this another serious incident occurred. The Chinese war-lord of Manchuria, Chang Tso-lin, was assassinated near Mukden, and there was much suspicion, loudly voiced in China and whispered in Japan, that Japanese officers at Mukden had planned the whole affair, although no culprit could be readily identified since Chang Tso-lin met his death from a bomb that demolished the railway carriage in which he was travelling. An official inquiry was held, but its report was not made known. Tanaka did what he could to persuade his opponents in the Diet not to ask questions about the matter; but in this he was unsuccessful. The leading opposition party – the *Minseito* (the former *Kenseikai*, reorganized under a new name) – made the most of the government's evident em-barrassment. Eventually, in the summer of 1929, the cabinet resigned. Of all its difficulties those arising from the violent death of Chang Tso-lin were the most serious. But the full extent of these was not apparent until after the end of the Pacific War, when the inside story, or most of it, became known to the world. It was then revealed that Chang Tso-lin had indeed been killed by officers of the Kwantung Army – the Japanese garrison in south Manchuria (so called because the tip of the Liaotung peninsula, including Port Arthur and Dairen, was known as the Kwantung promontory or peninsula). The nature of the grudge that the Kwantung Army had against Chang Tso-lin does not concern us here. What is important is that it was planned that his death should be the signal for a Japanese military *coup d'état* to seize the city of Mukden and perhaps, soon afterwards, a large proportion of the southern half of Manchuria. This was in fact an attempt to carry out in 1928 what actually occurred in 1931, when the Kwantung Army took Mukden by storm. But in 1928 the conspiracy failed because the principal ringleader, a full colonel on the staff of Kwantung Army Headquarters, was not backed up by his superior officers.

When Tanaka discovered what had taken place he was eager, with the full support of the emperor, to have those concerned tried and punished, by court-martial if necessary. In fact the emperor was profoundly disturbed, and this added to Tanaka's anxieties; for he found that the Chief of the General Staff and other senior officers were stubbornly opposed to any severe disciplinary action being taken against those responsible for Chang's death, on the grounds that it would harm the prestige of the army. And so indiscipline was overlooked and another evil precedent established.

After the resignation of the Tanaka cabinet in July 1929, the *Genro* Saionji recommended the president of the *Minseito*, Hamaguchi, to the emperor as the next prime minister. Hamaguchi's cabinet, a largely *Minseito* affair, contained some excellent men. The premier himself was honest and determined, his somewhat severe countenance earning him the nickname of 'Lion'. The two service ministers, General Ugaki and Admiral Takarabe, were known to be moderate in their views, and they cooperated well with their civilian colleagues; they were certainly not prepared to be mere liaison officers between their respective general staffs and the cabinet. The Minister of Finance, Inouye Junnosuke, was a courageous anti-militarist, a great believer in retrenchment and balanced budgets. The *Minseito*-Mitsubishi connexion was symbolized by the fact that he was the son-in-law of the head of the family controlling this *zaibatsu*. Shidehara, related to the same family, was the Foreign Minister. The discordant note in this liberal administration was struck by the Home Minister, Adachi, who had a violent, ultra-nationalist past. By a change of prefectural governors he paved the way for a *Minseito* victory at the General Election of 1930.

It was unfortunate that the world depression should have come upon Japan during the lifetime of this cabinet, for the government's failure to ameliorate the situation – by returning Japan to the gold standard and cutting civil service salaries it made matters worse – lost it the public good-will that under more normal economic conditions would have been its due. The fall in exports, due to the depression, was particularly serious for those producing raw silk. When the American demand fell catastrophically in 1930, hard-pressed farmers all over Japan suffered very grievously, for silk production was a secondary employment for almost half the farmers in the land, making it just possible for most of them to avoid serious indebtedness. By far the most important overseas market for silk was the United States. This market collapsed, as was to be expected with a luxury industry at a time of profound slump; and the social and political consequences in the Japanese countryside were shocking. Northern Japan suffered more, perhaps, than other parts of the country. The small farmers there were reduced to desperate poverty, and in 1932 there was a failure of the rice crop in that region amounting to actual famine.

The core of the army came from the peasantry, and many of the officers belonged to medium and small land-owning families. Northern Japan, especially, had the reputation of supplying excellent recruits. No decent company or platoon commander could be unmoved at the distress afflicting the families of so many of his men; for in extreme privation there was only sure way for a farmer to obtain cash – namely to sell a daughter to the city brokers who toured the land on behalf of tea-houses, cafés, and brothels. Such conditions increased the exasperation of those officers who believed that parliamentary politics were ruining Japan and that only by some such drastic programme as the 'Showa Restoration' could the nation be saved. It was, of course, a breach of military discipline for regimental officers to take any part in politics. They were expressly forbidden to do so in a rescript issued many years before by the Emperor Meiji

But the emotions aroused by the agony of the countryside were in a real sense revolutionary.

The army as a whole had reason during 1930 to feel uneasy about its own future status, for it saw the rival service, the navy, forced to give way in a struggle with the government – although in truth it was not the navy as a corporate body but rather the Naval General Staff that lost this particular battle. At the London Naval Disarmament Conference of 1930 the Japanese delegation, which included the Navy Minister (Admiral Takarabe), agreed to a ratio of cruisers and other craft *vis-à-vis* America which the Naval General Staff in Tokyo regarded as below the minimum that should have been conceded. Nevertheless Hamaguchi, temporarily in charge of the Navy Ministry in Takarabe's absence, considered, together with his cabinet, that the London agreement was satisfactory, and he so advised the emperor. So in spite of the vigorous opposition of the Chief of the Naval General Staff the London Treaty was signed. There was a great outcry, in which members of the *Seiyukai* joined, against what Japanese nationalists claimed was a usurpation of power by the Prime Minister. Their view was that the emperor, in the exercise of the Supreme Command affecting naval matters, was properly advised only by the Chief of the Naval General Staff and by the Navy Minister. The fact that Hamaguchi, a civilian, was acting as Navy Minister was looked upon as irregular. In any case he ought not to have ignored the opinion of the Chief of the Naval General Staff.

When it came to the ratification of the Treaty, the Privy Council, always consulted on such matters, was very critical. But 'Lion' Hamaguchi had a will of steel. His cabinet was united on the issue. He had the emperor's backing, and he had support from at least a sizeable section of the navy. So he refused to give way, and in the end, after much argument, the Privy Council formally advised that the Treaty be ratified. But the controversy did not die down. Everybody recognized that a blow had been struck for the principle of cabinet supremacy in a debatable field where considerations of foreign policy, national defence, and strategy overlapped.

If the liberals were heartened, traditionalists were shocked. The army, in particular, saw clearly that a similar challenge might be made in future to its own exclusive right, acquired and confirmed by custom, to advise the emperor on questions relating to the military Supreme Command.

Encouraged, if not inspired, by army officers, both serving and retired, there grew up in the summer and autumn of 1930 a chorus of bitter protest, in the newspapers and from various public platforms, against the action of the cabinet. This volume of protest joined an already vocal demand, stirred up by ultra-nationalists, that Japan should take strong action in Manchuria, where Chang Tso-lin's son had declared himself ready to accept the authority of the Nanking Government established by Chiang Kai-shek.

The agitation expressed itself in an act of terrorism in November 1930, when Hamaguchi was shot and seriously injured by a right-wing 'patriot' on Tokyo station, nearly nine years to the day after Hara had been assassinated at almost the same spot. While Hamaguchi was incapacitated, the Foreign Minister, Shidehara, acted as Premier. In the spring of 1931 Hamaguchi made a very courageous effort to resume office. But he resigned in April, being succeeded by Wakatsuki. The latter made a few alterations in the cabinet, which remained a predominantly *Minseito* affair. The valiant Hamaguchi died later in the year.

Soon after the attack on Hamaguchi, members of the government heard rumours that some kind of plot was afoot among army officers in Tokyo. The police made some desultory inquiries, but nothing definite could be unearthed. In fact a *coup d'état* was being planned by a group of officers that included two or three holding fairly high rank and positions of responsibility. One of these, Major-General Koiso, was to become Prime Minister of Japan thirteen years later. The conspirators believed that the Minister of War, General Ugaki, should head the military government to be established by the armed *coup*, and they imagined at one stage that he was not unwilling to accept this position. But in March 1931 – when preparations were well in hand – Ugaki made it quite clear that he disapproved most strongly of any 'direct action', that all plans of this sort must be abandoned at once. This killed the whole conspiracy, to the great annoyance of those involved – junior officers, a few of their seniors, and a small number of civilian fanatics.

This curious affair became known as the 'March Incident', although it was not until after the Pacific War had ended that any Japanese outside a tiny circle in Tokyo was able to learn anything about it. The point of importance about the 'March Incident' is that some senior officers were implicated, besides the young hot-heads. The example they set was deplorable; and as these senior officers held key appointments in Tokyo (one of them was Vice-Chief of the General Staff) it seemed almost out of the question that they should be punished for their part in a conspiracy that was, after all, abandoned. As no action was taken against them it was impossible to reprimand their juniors, much less court-martial them. Efforts were made to hush up the entire affair; and so indiscipline of a most dangerous kind was tacitly condoned. It was to be all the more difficult in future for army leaders to restrain the younger and more politically-minded members of the officer corps.

A bare six months after Ugaki ordered the cancellation of preparations for an internal *coup d'état*, there took place another, this time outside Japan, that was to shake the world. On 18 September 1931, the Japanese Kwantung Army set about the seizure of the city of Mukden, the curtain-raiser to the occupation of all Manchuria. To some extent those who planned the Mukden *coup* had been involved in the 'March Incident' also. The tragedy for Japan was that in both cases the cabinet, left largely in the dark by the Army General Staff, was at a loss how to deal with a situation that was indeed out of its control.

Chapter 8

THE DARK VALLEY

[I]

THE Japanese often give the name, *kurai tanima* – 'dark valley' – to the period between 1931 and 1941, the decade immediately preceding the outbreak of the Pacific War. For during those years the still delicate plant of liberalism and personal freedom that had sprouted during the twenties was effectively killed. To change the metaphor again, liberal-minded men in politics, the services, education, literature, and art found themselves, after 1931, treading a path increasingly beset with dangers from the twin forces of reaction and revolution, expressed in violence none the less menacing for being intermittent and on occasions haphazard. This violence had two aspects – unchecked aggression abroad and murderous conspiracy at home.

It may be that only a minority of the nation saw the situation, at the time, in these terms. But this minority consisted of the Japanese intellectual élite, headed by the emperor himself. Why then was it unable to put up a stronger fight against the rising surge of ultra-nationalism, embracing both traditionalist and revolutionary national socialist elements, of which the army was the spear-head?

The answer lies in the nature of the structure of the Japanese state in those years. According to the Constitution, as we have seen, the emperor stood at the apex of power, vested with immense prestige of at least a semi-religious character. In theory he was the ultimate arbiter of all questions, those relating to military and naval strategy as well as to law and politics. In reality, of course, his powers were exercised only on the advice of specific persons representing such entities as the cabinet, the Army and Navy General Staffs, and the

Privy Council; and these often cherished conflicting opinions, and therefore they struggled against each other. Unhappily there was no supreme coordinating body. In the past this had been supplied, very efficiently, by the group comprising the *Genro*. After 1924, however, Saionji was the sole surviving member of this august and once most powerful body; and Saionji hoped to see Japan progress slowly but certainly towards something resembling a state under a constitutional monarchy and a parliamentary form of government. Therefore on the whole he deliberately refrained from interfering in political affairs, except to recommend a new premier after a cabinet resignation and to insist on being kept well informed as to what was going on. Saionji was not in favour of the emperor himself filling the role of coordinator of policy, in the manner of a German kaiser or a Russian tsar. On the contrary, his great concern was to keep the Throne aloof from any responsibility for making decisions of high policy. He was afraid that the emperor would become embroiled in controversy if he were to take a stand on any issue, however right and sensible it might be. Saionji feared that in the perilous context of the thirties this might endanger the prestige of the emperor or even shake the position of the imperial house. It is too facile to dismiss Saionji's view as over-timid, to point out that because the emperor's words were obeyed in 1945 they would have been obeyed with docility in 1931 or 1932 if the emperor, speaking *ex cathedra*, had called upon the army to retire in Manchuria. The risk of disobedience seemed very real. All we can claim, with the advantage of hind-sight, is that it would have been better for Japan and for the world if this risk had been taken in the thirties. Only an imperial rescript could have reversed the course of armed expansion across the Yellow Sea. One can say that the emperor's inclination was to take action of this kind, had he received firm encouragement from Saionji.

It may be asked whether in fact there was any real risk that ultra-nationalists, more especially army officers, would have ignored a specific order from the emperor. After all they claimed to be passionately loyal to the emperor, more loyal than any other group of Japanese subjects. But here we have to remember the essentially emotional, illogical psychology of such fanatics. Just as Saigo in 1877 never regarded himself as a rebel, so inevitably some right-wing 'patriots' would not necessarily have considered themselves disloyal in opposing an imperial rescript that they held to be inspired by 'evil counsellors'. In August 1945 there were to be a few who would not accept, in a sense, the evidence of their own ears, who defied the Surrender broadcast. Japanese ultra-nationalists were loyal to their conception of what the emperor ought to be. To the emperor as he was they were grossly disloyal – and a few of the more sophisticated among them were well aware of this fact.

When all this has been said, however, the balance of probability – on the showing of the overwhelming response to the Surrender broadcast of 1945 – suggests that an imperial rescript restraining the army in Manchuria or, later, in China would have been obeyed by the great majority of officers, although no doubt there would have been armed insubordination by the minority; and this would have led to short-lived confusion, even a kind of brief civil war. It was precisely this prospect that horrified senior officers and cabinet ministers, causing them to shrink from the really firm action that was required. Senior officers thus found themselves in a position of being in effect blackmailed by the threats of a lunatic fringe of 'Young Turks', very few of whom held a rank higher than that of colonel. The stage was quickly reached when senior officers in their turn could blackmail successive cabinets. A minister of war, for example, when opposing or proposing some measure in the cabinet would assert that, unless his views prevailed, it would be impossible to maintain order and discipline in the army.

We shall see in this chapter that the emperor more than once took a firm line with the army leaders; but he could do this only, as it were, on a personal level, behind the closed doors of the palace. This had at times some effect, but it was not enough. Court advisers and cabinet ministers could not agree, when it came to the point, to advise open and official action by the emperor to curb the army.

An unusually determined prime minister, of the Hamaguchi mould, might have been able, overcoming the *Genro's* hesitation, to make such action possible. Premier Inukai appears in 1932 to have planned imperial intervention of this kind; and this was the probable reason for his assassination. A few years later Konoye, as Premier, hoped to play the part of coordinator of high policy, believing that he could control the army. He deceived himself. His temperament unfitted him for the task.

On the side of the army a man of the calibre of Yamagata might well have succeeded in putting a stop to what the Japanese call *gekokujo,* or 'the overpowering of seniors by juniors'; although in fairness to the generals of the Showa period we must bear in mind that in Yamagata's heyday Choshu completely dominated the army, and *samurai* clan obligations served to strengthen Yamagata's authority. By the thirties many officers, including three or four of high rank, had no connexion with Choshu. An increasing number did not even come from families of *samurai* stock. All the same, the army leaders of the Showa period were unworthy heirs of Yamagata and Nogi. Their efforts to restore unity and discipline were spasmodic, however sincere; and there was all too often an unreadiness to accept individual responsibility. * Even collectively they took the line of least resistance. So in the end they brought their country to the critical impasse of 1941, when it was presented with three brutal

*Whatever else may be said of General Tojo it must be recognized that he accepted full responsibility for leading Japan into war. In order to coordinate policy at the highest level he was Minister of War and Home Minister as well as Premier, and in 1944 he assumed the additional office of Chief of the Army General Staff. Yet he declared after the war, and we may believe him, that he was never informed of the details of the plan to attack Pearl Harbour. This was a naval affair, and could not be entirely revealed in advance to an army officer, even if he happened to be Prime Minister. The fact remains that the *decision* to make war rested in the final analysis with General Tojo and the army. The navy leaders for their part prepared a battle plan – the attack on Pearl Harbour – for a contingency, namely war with America, that they hoped would not arise.

alternatives – massive loss of face, economic suicide, or war. This downhill course must now be described, beginning with the 'Manchurian Incident'.

[II]

For many months before September 1931, when the Mukden *coup* occurred, there was serious friction between the Japanese, in their leased territory and along the zone of the South Manchurian Railway, and the Chinese authorities in Manchuria headed by Chang Tso-lin's son, the 'Young Marshal', Chang Hsueh-liang. For the latter, having associated himself with the Kuomintang regime, had begun to wage economic warfare against the Japanese by the construction of lines competing with the Japanese-owned South Manchurian Railway system. This was a very natural course for Chang to have adopted; and in view of Shidehara's declared policy of friendship, Chang may have felt that there was little risk of the Japanese resorting to the kind of retaliation that he provoked from the Russians in 1929, when he tried to take over their controlling interests in the Chinese Eastern Railway. On that occasion Soviet forces lost no time in intervening, and Chang had to give way to Russian demands. Certainly it was Chinese policy to squeeze out, little by little, Japanese interests in Manchuria. This general Sino-Japanese quarrel in Manchuria was aggravated in the summer of 1931 by some minor incidents which confirmed certain Japanese officers on the spot in their determination to gain control of all Manchuria before it was too late. These officers had friends and supporters in Tokyo, notably in General Staff Headquarters – the same men who had planned the abortive 'March Incident' described in the previous chapter. So in the summer of 1931 a plan was worked out by these officers, in Tokyo and at Kwantung Army Headquarters, for the sudden occupation of Mukden, to be followed by the seizure of other towns in Manchuria. To what extent those in high military command were aware of this plan cannot be assessed with any certainty. What can be said is that army leaders were exasperated with Shidehara's 'weak diplomacy' and were eager for Japan to adopt a very firm stand in Manchuria. Indeed in August 1931 the Minister of War, now General Minami, called a conference of divisional commanders and other important senior officers, and in addressing them he openly attacked the China policy of his cabinet colleague, the Foreign Minister.

The Japanese generals were also perturbed by insistent pressure from the Minister of Finance, Inouye Junnosuke, for a reduction in the army budget; and there also loomed ahead the prospect of a World Disarmament Conference at Geneva early in the following year. The government was already asking the army to nominate its delegates.

Early in September, if not before, Shidehara began to receive reports from Japanese consular officers in Manchuria that some kind of 'direct action' was being planned by the Kwantung Army against the Chinese. These reports were sufficiently specific and reliable to alarm both Shidehara and the Premier, Wakatsuki. They protested vigorously to General Minami, the Minister of War. They must have underlined the ominous significance of these reports when reporting their substance to the emperor; for the latter saw Minami and told him to his face that the army in Manchuria must be restrained.

In response to those admonitions Minami adopted a curious course of action. He wrote an urgent and confidential letter to the Commander-in-Chief, Kwantung Army, advising him to cancel any plans that might have been made for military action against the Chinese. Then he gave the letter to a major-general in Tokyo and told him to take it to Manchuria. This major-general had been heavily involved in the 'March Incident', and even if he was not equally implicated in the plot to seize Mukden, he was known to favour 'direct action', and to be intimately associated with ultra-nationalist junior officers. The War Minister's letter could hardly have been entrusted to a less suitable courier; and what happened was not very surprising. The major-general, instead of flying at once to Port Arthur, travelled by train through Korea to Mukden. He arrived in the Japanese zone at Mukden in the

evening of 18 September. He met the colonel who was in
fact one of the principal architects of the *coup d'état* that was
to be carried out a few hours later and then proceeded to a
geisha-house. Later that night, while he was regaling himself – his letter still undelivered – the first shots were fired in
what became known as the 'Manchurian Incident'.

The Japanese claimed that Chinese soldiers tried to
sabotage the South Manchurian Railway just north of
Mukden. To this day the precise truth of this allegation
remains unknown. At any rate it gave to the Japanese
officers on the spot the pretext they needed for an attack on
Chinese troops in Mukden, and fighting on a noisy and
considerable scale was soon in progress. The local Japanese
Consulate remonstrated with the colonel directing operations but was told to mind its own business; and when a
member of the Consulate (in later years a Socialist representative in the Diet) visited this colonel's headquarters he
had a rough reception, one officer threatening him with a
drawn sword. Meanwhile the Commander-in-Chief, at Port
Arthur, was asked to put his seal to orders already prepared
for the movement of more troops into Mukden, and he
approved an immediate signal to the Commander-in-Chief,
Korea, appealing for reinforcements.

On 19 September, then, the cabinet in Tokyo was presented with the *fait accompli* of the Japanese military
occupation of Mukden and, later on the same day, of
Changchun many miles to the north. That night, in Mukden, General Minami's courier at last handed over the
urgent letter from Tokyo.

There now followed weeks of public embarrassment and
secret humiliation for the Wakatsuki government. While the
army in the field boldly extended the scope of its operations,
Japanese representatives at the League of Nations in
Geneva, and at London, Washington, and other capitals,
declared that these military measures were only temporary
and would soon cease. Indeed, on 30 September Japan
accepted a resolution by the Council of the League calling
for the withdrawal of Japanese troops to the South Man-

churian Railway zone. So far from any withdrawal taking place, further advances were made and Chang Hsueh-liang's provisional capital was bombed from the air.

This blatant contrast between Japanese promises and the action of Japanese troops spreading fan-like through Manchuria led the world to suppose that the cabinet in Tokyo had adopted a policy of deliberate chicanery and deceit. This was not so. What was happening was the breakdown of coordination between the civil and military wings of the Japanese structure of state power. The position of the Wakatsuki administration is best summed up in the words of Saionji's secretary, who in a private talk at the time to members of the House of Peers declared: 'From the beginning to end the government has been utterly fooled by the army.'

As military operations went forward, overcoming Chinese resistance everywhere, and as almost all Manchuria passed under Kwantung Army control – Chang Hsueh-liang retired south of the Great Wall at the end of the year – there arose in Japan a wave of nationalist emotion; and the climate of the day soon made it seem treasonable for anyone publicly to oppose what was happening. There was in any case, for the Japanese, an almost mystical significance about south Manchuria, where so many lives had been lost in the struggle against the Russians. There was now, thanks to the depression, a very practical interest in the open spaces of Manchuria, which it was thought might help to solve Japan's population problem. World disapproval, symbolized by the hardening of the attitude of the League of Nations, merely cemented instinctive patriotic feeling.

The government's anxieties were not lessened by the discovery in October of another officers' plot in Tokyo. This conspiracy, which was exposed thanks to a change of heart among some of the ringleaders, envisaged the annihilation of the cabinet, while in session, by air bombardment and the establishment of a military junta in control of affairs. A day or two under arrest, a reprimand, and posting outside Tokyo were the only punishment meted out to those involved. This so-called 'October Incident' was of course carefully hushed up, and no hint of it was allowed to leak out to the public. The Premier now began to talk of resigning; but he struggled on until December, when the refusal of the Home Minister to attend meetings of the cabinet effectively sabotaged the government.*

The Wakatsuki cabinet was followed by a *Seiyukai* administration under Inukai Tsuyoshi. It was the last party cabinet in Japan until after the Pacific War. Just as there were close affiliations between the *Minseito* cabinet of Wakatsuki and the Mitsubishi *zaibatsu*, so there existed similar contacts between the *Seiyukai* cabinet and Mitsui. Almost the first act of the new government was to reverse the financial policy of its predecessor and take Japan off the gold standard. There was much to be said for this, but the merits of the action attracted less public attention than the fact that it happened to be immensely profitable at that moment to certain segments of the Mitsui empire.

Inukai was seventy-five when he became Premier. He was something of a chauvinist; but in the past he had opposed clan oligarchy and he did not look with any favour on military usurpation of political power. He was determined, being a very loyal as well as a courageous old man, to heed the message passed to him from the emperor when he was asked to form a cabinet. The emperor's bidding included the following sentence:

The army's interference in domestic and foreign politics, and its wilfulness, is a state of affairs which, for the good of the nation, we must view with apprehension.

So, using channels of his own, Inukai tried to open negotiations with the Chinese. A trusted friend was sent on a secret mission to China, and arrangements were made for him to communicate directly with the Prime Minister in a code unknown to the army. At the same time, if we can

* The Home Minister, Adachi, advocated a coalition with the *Seiyukai*. He may have been impressed by the creation of the MacDonald 'National Government' in Great Britain. When Wakatsuki objected to his negotiations with the *Seiyukai*, Adachi refused either to attend cabinet meetings or to resign.

accept his son's evidence, Inukai set about preparing for the emperor to issue a rescript commanding the army to cease all operations in Manchuria. But the chief cabinet secretary, an ambitious *Seiyukai* politician unwisely confided in by Inukai, was on intimate terms with extreme nationalists in the army and outside. They were informed by him, so it seems, of Inukai's plans.

Meanwhile, early in 1932 fighting broke out in Shanghai between the Chinese 19th Route Army and the Japanese naval landing party stationed in the city. A world not yet entirely hardened to the spectacle of repeated air attacks on densely populated towns was shocked by the vigorous bombing, by Japanese naval airplanes, of Chinese positions in the Chapei district of Shanghai. The naval force had to be rescued from defeat by the army, which in the end committed no less than four divisions to a battle that raged with great ferocity for about six weeks before the resolute Chinese withdrew.

The Shanghai fighting was dying down when it was announced from Manchuria that an independent government had been set up there under Pu Yi, the last of the Chinese emperors. This young man had been escorted in the previous autumn from Tientsin to south Manchuria by Kwantung Army officers. He was made chief executive of the new state of Manchukuo, and later he was made emperor of this Japanese creation. Tremendous efforts were made – their disingenuous character was almost engaging – to convince world opinion that Manchukuo was a truly independent state. In particular it was hoped that the Lytton Commission, sent to the Far East on behalf of the League of Nations, would be bamboozled by the fiction of this new Manchurian nation established by the will of the inhabitants of the country with some benevolent help from the Kwantung Army.

It was during the Shanghai fighting and while the Kwantung Army was acting as midwife to the birth of Manchukuo that two notable murders took place in Japan within the space of four weeks. The victims were Inouye Junnosuke, the former Minister of Finance, and Baron Dan, chief director

of the Mitsui holding company. They were killed by members of a secret association of young ultra-nationalist fanatic
known as the 'League of Blood'. This group had made
ready a list of some twenty people, famous in politics and
business, who were to be assassinated, individually as opportunity offered. Premier Inukai was among those on the list.

However, he was to meet his death at the hands of another,
though related, gang of assassins. On 15 May 1932 his official
residence was invaded by nine young men, naval officers and
army cadets. They sought out and shot down the old man
who had received them with composure and suggested that
they talk things over before using their weapons. While this
was going on, another detachment, made up of young farmers, attempted to sabotage the Tokyo power stations.

This affair, known as the '15 May Incident' effectively put
an end to party cabinets in Japan for the next thirteen years;
henceforth the army would not supply a minister of war to a
government headed by a party leader. Furthermore, although people in Tokyo were undoubtedly shocked by the
murder of Inukai and by the two assassinations carried out
by the 'League of Blood', at their trial there was much public
sympathy with the murderers, for their motives were regarded
as purely unselfish. None received a capital sentence, and
most of them emerged from prison well before the Pacific War.

Inukai's successor was Admiral Saito. He held office until
July 1934, when his cabinet resigned in consequence of alle-
gations, totally unproven, that certain ministers had been
concerned in a notorious bribery scandal. Admiral Saito,
who had been a rather enlightened Governor-General of
Korea in the previous decade, was conservative, high-
minded, realistic, moderately liberal, but over-cautious no
doubt and inclined to be too sanguine about the way
events were shaping. 'Everything will be all right', he
remarked privately, in the summer of 1932, 'so long as we
old men are here to put on the brakes.'

But the most powerful man in the cabinet was General
Araki, the Minister of War. He and his friend General
Mazaki, soon to be made Inspector-General of Military

Training, were regarded as leaders of a faction in the army known as the *Kodo-ha*, or 'Imperial Way School'. Its great rival was a faction usually called the *Tosei-ha*, or 'Control School'. The *Koda-ha* was the more influential from about 1932 until the end of 1934, when its supremacy started to wane very rapidly. The years 1932–6 can be interpreted in terms of a struggle for power between these two dominant factions in the army. Both factions embraced ultra-nationalist elements, with civilian hangers-on. The *Kodo-ha* was the more radical of the two, for it contained most of the young officers who were active in the cause of 'the Showa Restoration'. But the leaders of the *Kodo-ha*, although they sympathized with the naïve aspirations of their juniors, were not necessarily in favour of changing the system of government by *coup d'état*. They were obsessed by the prospect of war with the Soviet Union. In their view the occupation of Manchuria was the requisite first step in the direction of a struggle with the Russians, and they were not very interested in plans for a Japanese advance south of the Great Wall into China. On the other hand, the *Tosei-ha* thought it wise to maintain friendly relations with the Soviet Union and to make China the main target of Japanese expansion once Manchuria had been secured.

These internal stresses within the Japanese army were of course hidden from the contemporary world. What was undeniable was that Japan appeared to be firmly committed to a programme of aggression on the continent of Asia; within a year of the creation of Manchukuo Japanese troops advanced into Inner Mongolia and soon compelled the Chinese to accept a very large demilitarized zone between Peking and the Manchurian border. Within this zone, and in fact in north China generally, Japanese political and commercial penetration increased at a remarkable pace.

Inevitably the Lytton Report on the Manchurian affair was a condemnation, none the less clear for being tactfully phrased, of Japan's action. It was adopted by the League of Nations. Whereupon Japan, much to the private anguish of the emperor, flounced out of the League.

Diplomatically the country was now as isolated as it had been in 1895, after the Triple Intervention. Economically it was hard pressed. In terms of armed strength alone it was undoubtedly formidable. Liberal-minded people in Europe and America began to place Japan in the same camp as Fascist Italy and the new Nazi Germany. To those who relied on the League of Nations to keep the peace Japan appeared as an outlaw among the nations; for she had defied the League with impunity.

Nationalism scored a notable triumph in Japan when, soon after the occupation of Manchuria, the barely tolerated left-wing social democratic movement split between those who adhered to the ideals of international socialism and those who succumbed to patriotic sentiment, or to the fear of intensified police surveillance, and came out in support of the army's action; and there was unquestionably a sincere conviction among many socialists who climbed on to the nationalist band-wagon that the army had a real sympathy, not very noticeable among most *Minseito* and *Seiyukai* politicians, with those oppressed by capitalism. Indeed, the Kwantung Army boasted that it would not allow the established *zaibatsu* in Japan, such as Mitsui and Mitsubishi, to exploit the wealth of Manchukuo. This country, it was said, would be run on national socialist lines, as a kind of pilot project for the later 'Showa Restoration' in Japan.*

Government action against Marxist thought was much intensified, being symbolized by the death in police custody of the young left-wing writer, Kobayashi Takiji. But life became progressively more difficult for all who were in any way out of tune with the superheated atmosphere of the day. The teaching profession from top to bottom was forced to give more time in the school curriculum to the propagation of

* None of this was put into practice; but the economic development of Manchukuo was largely kept out of the hands of the existing *zaibatsu*. At first the South Manchurian Railway Company dominated the field. After 1937, when the development of Manchukuo was accelerated following the outbreak of the Sino-Japanese war, new business groups, notably the Nissan firm, became very powerful in Manchukuo. These new groups, encouraged by the army, were known as *shinko-zaibatsu*, or 'new zaibatsu'.

Shinto mythology, to ethnocentric ideas generally, and to military training. It is then no wonder that in the years after 1945 the Japan Teachers' Union should have acquired a reputation for being very Left in its complexion. In the universities conformist pressure, though in some ways less directly overpowering, made it increasingly hazardous for academic staff to retain the self-respect that comes from intellectual integrity. Between 1933 and 1937 several scholars were forced to resign from their university posts, and some of them saw their publications banned. One professor at Kyoto, a Marxist economist with a national reputation in the academic world, was arrested and spent some years in prison. But perhaps the most publicized case was that of Professor Minobe, a very distinguished *savant* and a member of the House of Peers, to whom reference has been made in a previous chapter.* In a speech that electrified the country he was violently attacked early in 1935 by a fellow member of the House, for having dared to discuss the emperor's position in the state in terms of conventional political science rather than in those of divinity. The book in which this had been done had already been out for years, but the general fuss was exploited by extreme nationalists, the more sophisticated of whom used the agitation for ulterior ends to discredit not only the cabinet but also the emperor's personal advisers, who were considered to be disgracefully liberal in their convictions. In consequence of what was known as his 'organ theory', Minobe was driven out of public and academic life; but he was fortunate at least in escaping imprisonment or assassination – though a personal assault was made on him. The emperor's comment on the affair bears quotation:

Much is being said about Minobe; but I do not believe he is disloyal. Just how many men of Minobe's calibre are there in Japan today? It is a pity to consign such a scholar to oblivion.

Barely two years later the emperor himself was to be an object of criticism, in nationalist circles in Tokyo, for spending too much time on the scientific study, marine biology, to which

* See p. 148.

he was devoted. The shadows of *kurai tanima*, 'the dark valley', were deepening on every side.

[III]

The Saito cabinet, before it resigned in the summer of 1934, had survived a murderous conspiracy as sensational as any that had been known before. The plot, like the 'October Incident' of 1931, included preparations for the liquidation of the government at one blow by bombing from the air. The military cabinet to be established by the *coup d'état* was to be headed by a prince of the imperial house. However, on this occasion the army, in the persons of politically active junior officers, was not involved in the conspiracy. The ringleaders were civilian extremists. It was only by a lucky chance that the police were able to discover the plot in the nick of time.

No mention at all was made of the affair until 1935, two years after it had occurred. The trial of the accused did not begin until 1937 and was not completed until 1941, when a judgement was given that (in the words of the *Japan Times*) was 'a triumph of law in Japan and a brilliant piece of political adjustment'. The accused received short terms of imprisonment, with immediate remission of sentence. However, this particular plot, since it came to nothing, was a minor affair compared with the famous outbreak, or mutiny, of February 1936, which terminated the life of the next cabinet, that of Admiral Okada.

The military eruption of February 1936 was to some extent heralded by premonitory rumbles caused by that factional struggle within the army to which reference has already been made. From the end of 1934 the *Kodo-ha*, the so-called 'Imperial Way School', began to lose ground very rapidly to its rival, the *Tosei-ha* or 'Control School'. Early in that year General Araki, the Minister of War, resigned due to ill-health. This was a blow to the *Kodo-ha*, for Araki and his friend General Mazaki held two of the three supposedly most important positions in the army – Araki as Minister of War, Mazaki as Inspector-General of Military Training. The third post, that of Chief of the General Staff, was occupied by Prince Kanin, who as a member of the imperial house could not properly be identified with any faction. His Vice-Chief, however, belonged to the *Tosei-ha*; and so did an officer, Major-General Nagata, who held an appointment of great significance in the Ministry of War, that of Chief of the General Affairs Bureau, in control of military postings and promotions as well as of army administration generally. Araki's successor as Minister of War was General Hayashi Senjuro, and he soon came under the influence of his subordinate at the Ministry, Major-General Nagata, who was determined if possible to remove known members of the *Kodo-ha* from key commands and staff appointments in the army. This could not be done, of course, while Araki was Minister. From the point of view of Nagata and the *Tosei-ha* it was desirable to secure the removal of Mazaki from his post of Inspector-General. Nagata claimed that the retention of Mazaki in this appointment was bad for discipline, that Mazaki was idolized by the radical young officers whose agitation must be checked at all costs. Nagata strengthened his case in the eyes of the Minister of War and the Chief of the General Staff by uncovering, in November 1934, a good deal of dangerous political activity, aimed at securing 'the Showa Restoration', among officers at the Staff College and cadets at the Military Academy. Nagata, however, was in a vulnerable position when he talked of enforcing military discipline, for he himself had been intimately involved in the 'March Incident' of 1931. Nevertheless, he insisted on the dismissal from the service of the officers concerned in the alleged Staff College conspiracy; and he then began to make plans for the removal of Mazaki.

Eventually, after a good deal of intrigue and much debate, Mazaki's resignation was effected, greatly to his chagrin. A few weeks later, in August 1935, an obscure lieutenant-colonel, excited and angered (like many other officers) at the manner of Mazaki's virtual dismissal, travelled up to Tokyo, walked into the Ministry of War, entered Nagata's room, and cut him down with a drawn sword.

There was almost hysterical support for the murderer from the wilder elements of the *Kodo-ha*, who tried to turn his court-martial into a sounding-board for their views. The defendant, through his military lawyer, summoned a number of prominent men as witnesses. Great play was made of the evils of favouritism in army administration, and this was a veiled but unmistakable attack on the *Tosei-ha*.

While this trial continued, Tokyo was alive with rumours that there would be further violence, on a much greater scale. It was said, quite correctly, that the First Division, stationed in the city, contained some unusually determined supporters of the 'Showa Restoration', that they were in close touch with the officers whom Nagata had purged and with the fanatical writer and agitator, Kita Ikki. To prevent trouble this division was ordered to proceed to Manchukuo. The advocates of ' direct action ' realized that they would have to strike at once, albeit without sufficient preparation.

During the early hours of 26 February 1936, in a severe snowstorm, detachments from two infantry regiments of the First Division, together with some sympathizers from the Guards Division, left their barracks. They split into a number of parties. Some of these made attacks on the homes of the Prime Minister and other public men; and before daylight there were some terrible scenes as doors were forced and the victims, nearly all old men, shot down. Admiral Okada escaped death, his brother-in-law being mistaken for him. Two former Premiers, Saito and Takahashi, and Mazaki's successor as Inspector-General were killed. The Grand Chamberlain, Admiral Suzuki, was dangerously wounded and was left to die. (He recovered, and he was to become Japan's last war-time premier nine years later.) An effort was made to catch the aged Saionji at his country villa ; but he got word in advance and was not at home. Other groups occupied various important buildings near the palace. The insurgents numbered about fifteen hundred officers and men. There was no officer above the rank of captain.

Having accomplished their attacks and set up a kind of occupied zone in the centre of Tokyo, these young captains and lieutenants did nothing more, except to issue a manifesto declaring that Japan's ills were due to such persons as the *Genro*, the *zaibatsu*, and political parties, and that those responsible had to be killed. The young officers went on to say that in taking direct action they were performing their duty as subjects of the emperor.

The latter, however, did not see the affair in this light. He told the Ministry of War that this was a mutiny, and that the rebels must be crushed within an hour. If the leading figures of the *Kodo-ha* had plans for stepping in and taking over the reins of government – which was what the rebels expected and hoped would happen – the emperor's immediate and unhesitating stand gave them second thoughts. Martial law was declared ; troops were brought into Tokyo from outside ; naval ratings were put ashore in the port area of the city. There was some parley with the rebels at first, Mazaki himself making great efforts to persuade them to hand in their arms. This they refused to do. But appeals to the rank and file, couched in emotional language and dropped from aircraft or suspended from captive advertisement balloons, were more effective. After four eerie days, in which two bodies of troops gazed silently at each other from their barricades across the snow, the mutineers gave in. There was no point in further resistance, as the generals of the *Kodo-ha* on whom, misled no doubt by hints and nods and sympathetic grunts, the mutinous officers had relied did not play their part. One rebel captain shot himself. The other officers gave themselves up, in the expectation of a public trial at which they could expound their views. But in the event they were tried by secret court-martial. Thirteen of them were executed ; so were Kita Ikki (the ideological sponsor of the 'Showa Restoration') and the fanatical lieutenant-colonel who had killed Nagata.

The mutiny did great harm to the *Kodo-ha*, which was believed to be responsible, indirectly at any rate, for the whole affair. At the same time, rather paradoxically, it strengthened immensely the political power of the army as a whole, as well as that of the *Tosei-ha*. The ordinary people of

Japan were rather disgusted at the idea of their capital city becoming the focus of world attention thanks to the mutinous behaviour of regular officers and men; and one consequence was a mild but fairly general popular revulsion against the army. This made it all the more essential for the military leaders, the *Tosei-ha* generals, to tighten their grip upon the state machine; and in fact they had little difficulty in dictating policy to the new cabinet of Hirota that was formed soon after the mutiny collapsed. Hirota was a professional diplomat; as Foreign Minister in the outgoing cabinet he had done well in completing negotiations for the Japanese purchase of the Russian-controlled Chinese Eastern Railway in Manchuria. When he began forming his cabinet he found that the Minister of War, General Terauchi (son of the earlier Prime Minister), had the final say in the choice of his government colleagues.

The *Tosei-ha* was now firmly in power, the Hirota cabinet being little more than its tool. Preparations were rushed forward to make Japan fully equipped for war. The proportion of the budget devoted to the armed services rose to nearly fifty per cent, and the development of heavy industry was stimulated by increased orders for munitions. The navy had abrogated the Washington and London Disarmament Treaties at the end of 1934 and had withdrawn from the London Naval Conference of the following year. It was free, therefore, to engage on expansion limited only by the country's resources.

In the field of foreign policy Japan signed the Anti-Comintern Pact with Germany in December 1936 – the negotiations had been carried out by the army, not by the Foreign Ministry – and this agreement protected Japan's north-western flank in the event of a military advance south into China.

On the home front the Ministry of Education prepared a new book on the basic principles of the *Kokutai*, of 'national polity', for distribution to all schools and colleges. The army insisted that all aspects of policy should be subordinated to national strategic needs. By the latter half of 1936 the

Minister of Finance was using the phrase, 'quasi-wartime economy', to describe a situation in which military requirements were supreme.

In January 1937 a member of the *Seiyukai* had the temerity to attack the army in the Diet for its usurpation of power, and he became involved in an angry battle of words with Terauchi, the Minister of War. Terauchi told the Premier that the House of Representatives must be dissolved. The political parties seemed to be raising their heads again ; and this was not at all to the liking of the army. But Hirota would not agree to a dissolution, so Terauchi resigned, bringing the cabinet down with him. The venerable Saionji recommended General Ugaki as the new Premier ; but Ugaki could find no soldier to serve as Minister of War, for his rather uncertain connexion with the 'March Incident' was remembered against him.* The choice then fell on General Hayashi. He was Prime Minister for only four months. He was better fitted for the barrack square than the committee rooms of the Diet. At the General Election of April 1937 his supporters were defeated, and the *Minseito* and *Seiyukai* joined forces in opposition to his Cromwellian behaviour. For the first time since 1931 the army seemed to be almost on the defensive. But it was determined not to lose any of the power that it had seized. At the same time Hayashi could not act like Yamagata and ignore the Diet altogether. So after some weeks he recognized the decision of this Election and resigned. It was the last, rather feeble, success for the Diet parties until after the Japanese Surrender nine years later.

The new Prime Minister was Prince Konoye, of the ancient and famous Fujiwara line. He had been President of the House of Peers since 1933. Even so he was much younger than the run of Japanese premiers, being forty-six years of age when he took office. He was liked and respected by nearly everyone, and he could have been premier after the February mutiny had he wished, for the army, among whom he had many friends, thought he would make a splendid figurehead. This was not so much because the generals imagined that he

* See p. 180.

would be their complacent puppet, but rather because they perceived that his mind was somewhat in tune with the nationalist movement, in spite of the fact that his political mentor had been Saionji. It is also true that his character was uneven. The elements of weakness often seemed dominant; and this impression was enhanced by the fact that, like many very refined persons, he was something of a hypochondriac. Konoye was an excellent listener. This was part of his weakness, but it endeared him to most of those who called on him, since he usually agreed, far beyond the requirements of Japanese courtesy, with what his visitors had to say. His range of acquaintances was extremely wide, and few premiers have taken office in an atmosphere of greater goodwill. Above all, it was felt that Konoye would have an entirely impartial approach to state affairs; that therefore his appointment would have a unifying effect on the political life of the nation. For his part, Konoye was not at all eager to be premier, but he thought that he would be able in his own way to exercise some control over the army.

He lost his first and perhaps vital battle within six weeks of forming his cabinet. Early in July fighting broke out near Peking between Japanese and Chinese troops. The situation deteriorated, and the Minister of War – a tough-minded *Tosei-ha* general named Sugiyama – proposed to make it worse by the dispatch of reinforcements from Manchukuo and Korea. Konoye, backed by the Navy and Foreign Ministers, tried to resist this demand. Sugiyama was adamant; so, dreading the political crisis that would occur if the War Minister resigned, Konoye gave way.

Thus the clash near Peking was allowed to widen into what became in fact an invasion of China. Undoubtedly this accorded with the plans of the *Tosei-ha*. While there is no convincing evidence, as in the case of the Mukden *coup*, that hostilities in north China in July 1937 originated from an incident planned by Japanese officers on the spot, there is reason to believe that at General Staff Headquarters in Tokyo there was a feeling, especially among colonels and below, that the time had come to settle accounts with Chiang

Kai-shek. For it was realized that China's national unity in face of Japanese pressure had been greatly strengthened by the understanding that had been reached some months earlier between Chiang and the Chinese Communists. Konoye and the navy and, in the army, the *Kodo-ha* wanted to halt operations in north China as soon as possible. But even Araki, the paladin of the *Kodo-ha*, had accepted the consequences of Japanese penetration in the Peking–Tientsin region. A year before the Sino-Japanese hostilities of 1937 broke out he remarked that talk of Japanese non-interference in north China was 'like telling a man not to get involved with a woman when she is already pregnant by him'. Chances of localizing the fighting were made more difficult at the end of July when Chinese militia, formally under Japanese control, at Tungchow – between Peking and Tientsin – killed their Japanese officers and then massacred over two hundred Japanese and Korean civilians of both sexes. A local settlement would have been, in any case, very difficult to achieve without unprecedented moderation on the part of the Japanese forces; and there was a new spirit of patriotism among the Chinese that made them determined not to make any concessions.

In August 1937 fighting began in Shanghai. As in 1932, the navy was the first to be involved; and again the army had to come to its help. Troops were poured into Shanghai, and it was not without a severe struggle, lasting for about three months, that the Japanese prevailed. By the autumn, then, undeclared war raged on two fronts, in the north and in the region of Shanghai. China appealed to the League. The latter condemned Japan for having violated the Nine-Power Treaty signed at Washington and the Kellogg Peace Pact of 1928, and proposed a meeting of the signatories of the Nine-Power Treaty to discuss the situation. The meeting was duly held, at Brussels. Japan refused to attend; and the Brussels Conference achieved nothing.

In December, after an advance up the Yangtze valley, the Japanese captured Nanking. Excesses were committed against the inhabitants of a kind that would not have been tolerated by the generals of the Meiji era. News of the atrocities was not allowed to leak into the Japanese press; but those held responsible – the Commander-in-Chief of the forces in Central China and two divisional commanders – were recalled to Japan, as were many of the reservists, summoned to the colours in the late summer of 1937, who had been given a free hand in Nanking for some days after its capture. It was indicative of the partial breakdown of military discipline that just before the fall of Nanking Japanese naval aircraft bombed and sank the U.S.S. *Panay* in the Yangtze, and an artillery unit, commanded by a notorious ultra-nationalist firebrand, shelled the British river gunboat, H.M.S. *Ladybird*. The Chamberlain Government in London felt unready to take a strong line with Japan while its appeasement policy towards Germany had yet to show results. But the *Panay* affair seemed for a moment to bring Japan and the United States to the brink of war. Sincere and prompt apologies by Japan, together with an offer of compensation and the recall of the naval air officers concerned, eased a tense situation that, on the face of it, appeared to be critical. Isolationism was still the dominant factor in popular American thinking on foreign affairs, but this incident, followed very soon by the excesses at Nanking, did fatal harm to what remained of American goodwill towards Japan.

It was generally believed in Japan that once he had lost his capital, Nanking, Chiang Kai-shek would be willing to come to terms. Indeed during the autumn approaches had been made to Chiang by Tokyo, through the good offices of the German Ambassador in China. But Chiang refused to accept the fairly drastic conditions offered to him; and in January 1938 Japan announced that there would be no further dealings of any kind with the official Kuomintang government. Nevertheless, despite this announcement, some efforts were made in 1938 to reach an agreement with Chiang; but these failed, partly because Japan's terms were too severe, but also because the army leaders in Tokyo, under varying pressures from their subordinates, could not make up their minds on the China question. It was known that in the highest circles of the Kuomintang there was a minority, led by Wang Ching-wei, that favoured acceptance of Japanese conditions, including an indemnity. So some Japanese senior officers believed, rightly as it turned out, that Wang Ching-wei could be enticed from Chiang's side. Meanwhile the war went on. After a success in Shantung in April 1938, the Chinese extricated their forces with difficulty, and with heavy losses, from a battle of encirclement mounted on an ambitious scale by the Japanese in the area of Hsuchow on the Peking–Nanking railway.

In early summer of 1938 Konoye, who was almost wistfully eager to wind up the China war, if only to curb the political arrogance of the army, reshuffled his cabinet. Araki was brought back into public life, as Minister of Education, and the rather overbearing Sugiyama was succeeded as Minister of War by a younger man, Itagaki. There was also a new Vice-Minister of War, a lieutenant-general with a Manchurian background : Tojo. General Ugaki became Foreign Minister. Konoye hoped to be able to resuscitate the *Kodo-ha* and thus make it easier for him to exercise some control over the army. In fact he was entirely unsuccessful. It was only with great difficulty that he was persuaded to remain as Premier through 1938.

In the summer of that year Japanese and Soviet troops in some strength fought a serious battle for possession of a hill known as Changkufeng, where the borders of Korea, Manchukuo, and the Russian Far East met in a conjunction not clearly defined. Neither Moscow nor Tokyo wanted war at that moment ; but there were certainly influential officers of the Japanese Ministry of War and General Staff who were prepared to fight China and the Soviet Union simultaneously. Japanese forces seemed invincible, and the self-confidence of the army had reached an almost hysterical level. At this juncture the emperor spoke his mind, at a joint audience, to his kinsman, the Chief of the Army General Staff, and to the Minister of War, Itagaki. He told them that in the past the actions of the army had often been 'abominable'. 'From now on', he declared, 'you may not move one soldier without my command.' These angry words had some effect. The Changkufeng affair was settled fairly soon, although it was to be followed within a year by much more bloody and prolonged Soviet-Japanese hostilities at Nomonhan, in the wastes of Outer Mongolia.

In the autumn the Japanese captured Hankow ; and from a landing at Bias Bay in south China they advanced at great speed and took Canton. Once again it was believed that Chiang Kai-shek would throw in his hand. Konoye issued a declaration that Japan's 'immutable policy' was the establishment of a New Order in East Asia – meaning a political, economic, and cultural union of Japan, Manchukuo, and China ; and soon afterwards Japan's peace terms were announced. The call for a Chinese indemnity was dropped, but in other respects the terms were as onerous as those contained in the most extreme of the Twenty-One Demands. Chiang publicly rejected the offer, and from his new capital in Chungking he announced that he would carry on the struggle. On his part this was a courageous gamble. For although the Japanese did not yet control those areas that they had occupied – they held the cities and railways but not the countryside – it was not true that they were 'bogged down' in China. Provided only that Japan avoided war with the United States and Great Britain, or with the Soviet Union, there was no reason why the Japanese, given time, should fail to impose their will on China in the end. Wang Ching-wei, a powerful member of the Kuomintang, saw the situation in these terms. Having failed to persuade Chiang to consider Japan's terms he escaped to Indo-China, and in 1939, with Japanese cooperation, he made his way to Shanghai. He became the most impressive of Japan's various Chinese puppets, and in due course he set up in Nanking a regime that the Japanese claimed to be the only official government of China.

Konoye, who had wanted to resign much earlier, finally insisted on surrendering his office in the opening days of 1939. The next cabinet, under Baron Hiranuma, lasted for about seven months. It was riven by the struggle between those who advocated a full-scale military alliance with Germany and those who stubbornly resisted this proposal. In view of Germany's overwhelming diplomatic victories in Europe in 1938, Berlin's proposal for a military alliance seemed very attractive. But the Foreign Minister, Arita, and the Navy Minister, Yonai, were suspicious of commitments that might embroil Japan with Great Britain and, perhaps, with the United States also. On the whole the army strongly favoured an alliance of the kind proposed by Ribbentrop, but the opposition was sufficiently firm to delay a decision on the matter. Then came the German-Soviet Pact in August 1939. This was regarded by the Japanese as a slap in the face, for at this very moment their forces were being severely mauled by the Russians, commanded by Zhukov, at Nomonhan on the borders of Manchukuo and Outer Mongolia. The fighting at Nomonhan had begun at the end of May, and was not terminated until September. Under the terms of a secret annexe to the Anti-Comintern Pact Japan might have asked for German support against the Russians. Thus Ribbentrop's flight to Moscow and his diplomatic *coup*, the Non-Aggression Pact with the Soviet Union, were looked upon as acts of betrayal, and there was a sudden revulsion against the Germans. It was generally recognized, except by the most rabidly pro-German elements in the army, that the best policy for Japan during the forthcoming war in Europe would be one of strict neutrality. Hiranuma and his cabinet resigned, and a new administration was formed under a temperate and cautious retired general called Abe, who announced that Japan would adhere to a 'middle course', in other words non-involvement in the European struggle.

[IV]

So long as the war in Europe remained relatively static and inconclusive it was possible for Abe and his successor, Admiral Yonai, to keep Japan in the position of a disinterested spectator. Although the *Blitzkrieg* in Poland created an impression of German competence, the apparent stalemate on the

Western Front made it look as though Germany was not strong enough to challenge Great Britain and France on land.

But the situation was drastically altered once Norway, Denmark, and the Low Countries were overrun, and by the collapse of France. By mid-summer 1940 it argued either staunch pro-British feelings or remarkable prescience in even the wisest Japanese for him to imagine that Germany would lose the war.*

Hitler's success had two immediate results so far as Japan was concerned. The first was the official extinction of the existing political parties. They went into voluntary liquidation, after Prince Konoye had agreed to organize a mass national party 'to assist the Imperial Throne'. Thus a form of totalitarianism was grafted on to the Constitution. It differed greatly from the German and Italian varieties, for Japan did not have a single *Führer* or *Duce*. Konoye's so-called 'New Structure' did not in fact do much to change the *status quo*, for the political parties were already virtually impotent. The second result of Germany's victories was the conclusion of the Tripartite Axis Pact of September 1940. By this time Konoye was once again Prime Minister; he succeeded Yonai in July. Japan's alliance with Germany and Italy bound her to the fortunes of these countries. In the eyes of its supporters the great virtue of the pact was that it seemed to place an effective check on any strong action by the United States, either in the Atlantic or the Pacific; for only the United States appeared to stand between Japan and the eventual consummation of the 'New Order in East Asia'. Great Britain seemed to be in no position to resist Japan. In September 1940 Great Britain had agreed to close the Burma Road for six months, as a result of Japanese pressure. As for France, she had been forced to admit Japanese troops into northern Indo-China, nominally in order to close supply

---

* There were, however, a few thoughtful Japanese who predicted Germany's defeat. Shigemitsu, the ambassador in London, always believed that Great Britain would win. And Saionji, in his ninety-first year, remarked: 'In the end I believe Great Britain will be victorious.' He said this shortly before he died, in the autumn of 1940.

routes to Chungking. The position of the Dutch East Indies, a source of oil and many other commodities required by Japan, was obviously very critical. Only America was capable of mustering a fleet strong enough to prevent a Japanese seizure by force of the rich European colonies in south-east Asia.

Konoye's Foreign Minister was a headstrong, voluble nationalist, Matsuoka Yosuke, who seems to have been bewitched by the military might of Nazi Germany. In the early part of 1941 he visited Rome and Berlin, where Ribbentrop urged him to commit Japan to an immediate assault on Singapore. On his way back through the Soviet Union he concluded a Neutrality Pact with Stalin and he returned to Japan satisfied that he was the most dynamic Foreign Minister his country had ever known. But he had not been home long when the news arrived of Germany's attack on Russia; whereupon Matsuoka insisted that Japan should seize the chance of attacking the Russians from the east. This was too much for Konoye, who, in July 1941, got rid of him by resigning together with the cabinet, and then reconstructing the cabinet without including Matsuoka. By now Japan had spent some four years in preparing for war on a large scale. These preparations had not been greatly weakened by the campaigns in China. On the contrary, the war in China stimulated munitions production and gave the authorities an excellent reason for controlling imports and for shaping the economy of the nation generally in accordance with long-term strategic needs. Only a portion of the national resources in munitions and manpower was committed to the China war, which in any case was a valuable proving-ground or dress rehearsal for a future struggle against some more powerful country. Even the Nomonhan disaster – the defeat by the Russians in 1939 – taught the army some lessons, especially the necessity of expanding the size of its armoured forces. Stocks of oil and other strategic products had been built up. But here there was reason for great anxiety. If access to oil supplies in south-east Asia and elsewhere was denied to Japan, then, in the event of war, her own stocks would suffice for no more than two years at the most.

Yet in July 1941 the army embarked on a further territorial advance that produced in retaliation economic sanctions that could have crippled Japan. In that month Japanese forces occupied bases in southern Indo-China. This was a clear threat to Siam, Malaya, and the Dutch East Indies. There is some reason to think that Konoye agreed to this move as the least of various possible evils. Germany's attack on the Soviet Union had produced among Japanese military leaders a wave of interest and excitement. There were some who, like Matsuoka, believed that Japan ought to join her ally in attacking the Russians. There were others who advocated an immediate assault on Hong Kong and Malaya. At all events there was a demand for action of some kind. The move into the Saigon area seemed to Konoye on the whole the least dangerous. Certainly he did not foresee the almost immediate reaction of America, Great Britain, and Holland.

These countries, in response to the Japanese move south, imposed an economic embargo on Japan; at the same time they hastened their military preparations in Asia and the Pacific. Japan now faced her moment of decision. Talks had been going on in Washington for many weeks between the Japanese Ambassador, Admiral Nomura, and the American Secretary of State, Cordell Hull. They had made little progress, for the aims of the two parties were almost diametrically opposed. Japan wanted America to abandon all support of the Chinese government in Chungking, to recognize Japan's hegemony in east Asia; in return, Japan would consider withdrawing in fact, if not in name, from the Tripartite Axis Pact. America distrusted Japanese motives in Asia and wanted Japan to withdraw from both China and French Indo-China. The Japanese were prepared, in the last resort, to evacuate French Indo-China, but not China proper. When the American-British-Dutch economic embargo was imposed it became urgent for Japan to reach some agreement with America. Otherwise, unless the Japanese were content to suffer slow economic strangulation, war with

Great Britain and Holland, and probably the United States also, was inevitable.

In the Washington talks America spoke for Great Britain and Holland as well as for herself. By an act of curious diplomatic self-abnegation Churchill and his cabinet seemed quite ready to leave negotiations with Japan, in a matter affecting Australia and New Zealand as much as Malaya and Hong Kong, to the good sense of the Americans. Indeed at this time there was a tendency to underrate Japan's striking power. It was thought in London, as well as Washington, that the economic sanctions would force Japan to give ground, but that, if this were not so, then by the close of 1941 Japan would find it difficult to overcome the forces that had been built up in the Philippines and Malaya. America and Great Britain, then, faced Japan with a confidence that would have been wholly admirable if it had been based on a true evaluation of strategic realities in south-east Asia.

Among Japanese leaders, on the other hand, only the army felt confident; for it considered that the United States, though rich in material wealth, lacked the fighting spirit of Japan. Both the navy and the civilian members of the cabinet felt very uncertain of the outcome of a struggle with America. To Konoye the prospect of war in the Pacific was a nightmare. But against the intransigence of his Minister of War, Tojo, no arguments seemed to prevail. He might consent, in return for a lifting of the embargo, to an evacuation of French Indo-China; there could be no question, in Tojo's view, of any retreat from the Chinese mainland.

It may be that the Atlantic meeting between Roosevelt and Churchill gave Konoye the idea of seeking direct personal contact with the President. At any rate Konoye approached the American ambassador in Tokyo and asked as a matter of great urgency to meet Roosevelt, so that the Japanese-American deadlock might be broken before the worst occurred. Konoye said that he would take with him, to meet Roosevelt, powerful senior army and navy officers who could be guaranteed to enforce upon their juniors the terms of a settlement reached between Japan and the United

States. There seemed for a while a chance that Konoye and the President would meet, either in Hawaii or Alaska. But not without good reason Washington feared the possibility of being deceived by the Japanese army. The word 'Munich' still had power to alarm American officials when they examined the idea of a Konoye–Roosevelt meeting; so the Japanese were told that some solid preliminary agreement ought to be reached before a 'summit' meeting took place.

In September an Imperial Conference – a gathering of cabinet ministers and chiefs of staff and other important officials in the presence of the emperor – formally agreed that Japan would have to be ready to fight America and Great Britain should the talks in Washington fail to make progress by mid-October. Meanwhile exercises in preparation for the attack on Pearl Harbour had already taken place very secretly at Kagoshima. Yet even now the navy was reluctant to engage in war with the United States. In fact, if the Navy Minister and the Chief of the Naval General Staff had possessed the courage of their inner convictions and had openly resisted Tojo, the Minister of War, it is possible, even probable, that with the backing both of the emperor and of Konoye they might have saved Japan at the eleventh hour by advising acceptance of the American demands regarding China. This would have been a diplomatic defeat for Japan, a loss of face; but it would have done no fundamental harm to the nation's vital interests. The navy, however, shifted its responsibilities on to Konoye. Through its representative in the cabinet, the Navy Minister, it refused to declare openly that in its view war with America should be avoided at almost any cost. As Konoye reported to the emperor:

The navy does not want war, but cannot say so in view of the decision of the Imperial Conference.

When mid-October came Konoye felt that the Washington talks must go on. A formidable crisis developed in Tokyo, since the army believed that the moment had come for Japan to decide definitely in favour of a sudden blow at both America and Great Britain. The crisis was resolved by the resignation of Konoye and the appointment of Tojo in his place, on the understanding that the deadline for the talks would be advanced by some weeks.

The Americans had broken the code in use between Tokyo and the Japanese Embassy in Washington; and therefore they knew that the Ambassador, Nomura, was instructed to obtain some agreement by the end of November. In the middle of that month Nomura was joined by a special envoy, Kurusu, who had been Ambassador in Germany. After Pearl Harbour the world believed that Kurusu's mission was merely a device by Japan to gain time and to lull the Americans into a sense of false security. There is in fact no truth in this supposition. Admiral Nomura was a sailor, not a trained diplomatist. In the critical autumn of 1941 he felt overwhelmed by the difficulties facing him and he asked for an experienced diplomatist of ambassadorial rank to be sent to help him.

Proposals and counter proposals passed between Washington and Tokyo; but neither side would give way to the extent thought satisfactory to the other. Meanwhile naval vessels took up their war stations and at ports in the Inland Sea troopships and freighters were loaded for the south. A fleet of carriers and escorting battleships and cruisers assembled in the lonely Kuriles, and on 26 November set course for the North Pacific. The commander of this fleet was told that in response to a certain signal, although not otherwise, the plan, known to very few, to attack the American fleet must be carried out. Four days after the Japanese carriers had sailed the emperor heard that the navy still wanted to avoid war. So he summoned to audience the Navy Minister and the Chief of the Naval General Staff. Were they confident of success, he asked them. They assured him that they were.

Seven days later the Japanese attacked Hawaii, Hong Kong, Malaya, Singapore, and the Philippines. The Pacific War had begun.

Chapter 9

THE PACIFIC WAR

[I]

In the early months of the war it seemed as though the Japanese could not make a false move : the American Pacific Fleet, although its carriers were not in port, was crippled by the blow at Pearl Harbour ; MacArthur's air force in the Philippines was annihilated in three days ; and the loss of the two British capital ships, *Prince of Wales* and *Repulse*, sealed the fate of Malaya. In the first week Allied disasters were relieved by two striking examples of desperate gallantry. At Wake Island in the Pacific a small force of United States marines repelled the first strong assault, sinking two Japanese destroyers ; and on the day when war was declared the tiny British river gunboat, H.M.S. *Petrel*, lying by the Bund at Shanghai, refused a demand to surrender and was sunk by the Japanese cruiser that lay close by – an episode that deserves to be remembered, for it was noted with admiration in Tokyo at the time. But one by one, Penang, Hong Kong, Manila, Singapore, Batavia, Rangoon, Mandalay fell to the Japanese. The Japanese expected that it would take them no more than three months to overrun Malaya and capture Singapore. General Yamashita's three divisions completed the task in ten weeks. By April 1942 Admiral Nagumo's carrier and battleship squadron, which had carried out the attack on Pearl Harbour and raided Darwin, was sweeping the Bay of Bengal, sinking every vessel it encountered, including a British carrier and two cruisers. A British squadron of renovated but still rather inadequate battleships was compelled to retreat to East Africa. All along the Indian coast, from the Sundarbans to Cape Cormorin, there were lively fears of invasion, while in Australia there was serious talk of evacuating the continent north of a line drawn west from Brisbane.

In April and May, however, the Japanese suffered two setbacks that caused them to postpone any tentative plans for the invasion of India and Australia. Aircraft from Nagumo's squadron were severely handled when they attacked Colombo and Trincomalee at the Easter weekend. In the following month part of the same Japanese squadron escorted troopships from Rabaul round the eastern corner of New Guinea for a landing at Port Moresby. It was engaged by an American carrier force. In what became known as the Battle of the Coral Sea both sides suffered heavy damage, but the result was that the Japanese gave up the attempt to attack Port Moresby from the sea.

Yet the accomplishments of the first six months of the war were more than enough to hearten the most cautious Japanese. Malaya and the Dutch East Indies had been seized, with their rich supplies of oil, rubber, tin, bauxite, and other vital raw materials unimpaired, for the 'scorched earth' programme had been carried out on only a puny scale. Moreover the indigenous population of this huge area was at first if anything favourably disposed to the Japanese, who claimed, of course, to be bringing with them the blessings of freedom and independence.

In military terms Japan's initial victories were due to air and sea superiority and the use of picked and extremely well-trained troops, every one of whom was a dedicated fighting man. Except by sea and in the air – and these were the strategically decisive elements in the situation – the Japanese did not rely on overwhelming superiority in numbers. The picture, cherished in England and Australia at the time, of ant-like hordes was quite misleading. On land they committed only some eleven divisions, considerably less than 200,000 men in all, to the conquest of the Philippines, Malaya, Burma, and the Dutch East Indies. But their enemies – the American, British, Dutch, and Australians – had underestimated both their intentions and capabilities. It was known, for example, that the Japanese possessed modern aircraft in quantity, but it was believed that they had only inferior pilots to man them. The army, so it was thought, had not shown itself to great advantage in China. It was notoriously under-mechanized, and it was felt that when opposed by well-equipped American and European troops, or by troops trained and led by European officers, the Japanese would soon discover, as at Nomonhan, that they had met their match. It was not recognized, save by a few unheeded specialists, that Japanese soldiers were unsurpassed in qualities of courage, tenacity, and physical endurance.

If the strength of the Japanese lay in the martial spirit of their soldiers and sailors, their weakness revealed itself, as the war progressed, in the rigidity of their overall planning, in their failure to learn new tactical methods. The Japanese are very adaptable, but they were much slower than their enemies to solve the rapidly changing problems of modern warfare. It was in fact the Allies – for example the British in Burma – who learned from painful experience, from a succession of disasters, to master the tactics of their enemy. If the Allies underestimated the Japanese before the war began, the Japanese military leaders for their part had gravely underestimated the resilience of the British and Americans. The Japanese placed far too much confidence in their own fighting spirit, admittedly Japan's greatest asset in the struggle. They were unprepared for example, for the American submarine campaign against their shipping routes, a campaign that got into its stride much sooner than the Japanese expected. They were slow to organize a convoy system, and when they did it was poorly planned and operated. At the beginning of the war their merchant ships were not armed, and indeed guns were not available to arm more than a portion of them. The Japanese, too, were short of anti-submarine vessels. Once American airpower was thrown into the scale, Japanese shipping losses rose alarmingly, so that as early as the beginning of 1943 ten times as much tonnage was sunk as was replaced by new building. This war against shipping, in which American submarines played the leading role, was the most decisive single factor in the collapse of the Japanese economy.

A by-product of Japan's fighting spirit was the reputation for implacable ferocity that the Japanese gained on all the fronts – the Solomons, New Guinea, the Pacific Islands, the Indo-Burmese frontier, and the Aleutians – that formed the highwater mark of their conquests. For their forces were used to exhaustion point with a total disregard for the human element. Officers usually treated their men with a severity that would have been thought barbaric even in the Prussian army. Historically Japan's internecine wars were peculiarly savage. The warrior class in battle asked and gave no quarter. The *samurai* tradition at its best respected the weak and defenceless. A general like Nogi was able to enforce high standards, in this tradition, on the officers and men under his command. Thus the conduct of the Japanese during the Russo-Japanese War towards both prisoners and Chinese civilians won the respect, and indeed admiration, of the world. In the Pacific War the story was very different. Prisoners-of-war were treated with cruel harshness. The attitude of many Japanese commanders to their captives was that they were lucky to be alive, that the very fact that they were prisoners showed that they were without shame and thus entitled to little consideration. Those Japanese officers in south-east Asia and the Pacific who had heard of the Geneva Convention ignored it. Protests reached the Foreign Minister in Tokyo through the representatives of neutral countries. These were passed on to the Ministry of War, which promised investigation of the complaints. But very little was done to improve the lot of the prisoners-of-war, in spite of the fact that the Ministry of War had issued regulations stating that prisoners must be treated in accordance with the terms of the Geneva Convention. Some light, perhaps, is thrown on the issue by the testimony of Shigemitsu Mamoru, Japanese Foreign Minister during much of the Pacific War.

Although I had no actual authority in the matter, I did my best to prevail on the Army Chiefs to do their best to ensure correct treatment. Senior officers agreed with my view that it should be beyond reproach. But among the middle-ranking officers as well as the troops at the front were many who were imbued with Nazi ideology. As usual they paid little heed to the orders of their superior officers and appear to have disobeyed them frequently.*

The Germans, experts in genocide when dealing with Jews and the people of Russia and Eastern Europe, on the whole behaved correctly towards the American, British, and French prisoners-of-war in their hands. The Japanese, who never descended to the cold-hearted depths plumbed by the German S.S. in their programme of scientific extermination, embittered their enemies by the haphazard, ruthless way in which they exploited or neglected their prisoners.

Similar harshness was displayed towards the bulk of the Asian peoples who came under Japanese military control. This was foolish as well as immoral. It meant that the Japanese soon dissipated the respect and goodwill with which they were greeted in many parts of south-east Asia after their first great victories. When civilian administrators or advisers were sent from Tokyo they were made to feel inferior to military men ; and among the military in the occupied areas none were more powerful than the hated *Kempei*, or military police, who ruled by terrorism, and so earned the fear and loathing of those who had hoped that the Japanese would arrive as friends rather than conquerors. The result was that the Japanese, after overthrowing the old order, ensured by the folly of their behaviour that the people of south-east Asia would never willingly accept the kind of 'Co-Prosperity Sphere' advocated by Japan, since this meant in practice exchanging one form of colonialism for another. The movements of resistance that developed in countries such as the Philippines, Burma, and Malaya were subject, as in Europe, to pronounced Communist influence ; and indeed the growth of Communism was an important legacy of Japanese misrule in south-east Asia. Furthermore the rigours of Japanese occupation, especially in the Philippines, created a prejudice that

* Mamoru Shigemitsu, *Japan and Her Destiny*. London (Hutchinson), 1958, p. 346.

slowed down Japan's re-entry, as an exporter, into the markets of south-east Asia after the war.

This having been said, it would be none the less misleading to dismiss as entirely insincere and ineffective all Japan's wartime talk of 'Greater East Asia'. Although the military men on the spot behaved, on the whole, with scant regard for the susceptibilities of the Asian races under their control, the government in Tokyo had some understanding of Asian nationalism. Tojo himself had enough imagination to perceive that, in promising independence to the colonial and semi-colonial territories of south-east Asia, Japan had a propaganda weapon of incalculable power. Idealism was not lacking in the vision of Japan as a liberating force in Asia, as senior partner, rather than dictator, of a group of newly independent nations. This was the not ignoble dream of the best men in public life, most of whom saw their country enter the war unwillingly ; and for many of them the war was only justified if this dream became a reality. But between civilian and military elements in Japanese leadership there was no cooperation on equal terms. The armed services were supreme, and among them – more especially in the army – the narrow-minded and grossly acquisitive predominated. For example, imaginative Japanese officials realized that the leaders of the so-called 'Indian National Army' – a force made up of former Indian prisoners-of-war and Indian residents in south-east Asia – must be treated as allies, not as mere puppets. After all, the arrival from Europe of Subhas Chandra Bose to head the government of 'Free India', could be regarded as a political asset of great importance to the Japanese cause. Yet the attitude of most Japanese military men towards the 'Indian National Army' was typified by that of Terauchi, the *generalissimo* in south-east Asia, who let it be known that he rather despised Chandra Bose and his followers. In conversation with other Japanese Terauchi remarked that his father, whom he greatly respected, had no time at all, when Governor-General of Korea, for colonial independence movements. So the Conference of Greater East Asia held in Tokyo in November 1943 – convened by Premier

Tojo and attended by Wang Ching-wei, representing China, and the political leaders of Manchukuo, Siam, the Philippines, Burma, and 'Free India' – was a rather meaningless affair. To be fêted in Tokyo did not quite make up for having one's face slapped in Rangoon or Manila.

Nevertheless, the granting of even sham independence to the occupied countries of Asia – in the Dutch East Indies this did not take place until the last days of the war – meant that it would be morally impossible for the Western colonial nations to refuse them real independence once Japan was defeated. Where independence after the war was whole-heartedly demanded and refused, the Asian peoples concerned had enough confidence to fight for it successfully. Thus Japanese victories, by destroying the *mystique* of White supremacy, and Japanese policies, by according to the occupied territories at least the outward forms of independence, greatly hastened the birth after the war of the new nations in south and south-east Asia.

[II]

In June 1942 the Japanese were defeated at sea in the Pacific, at the Battle of Midway. This was reported in the press at home as a notable victory. Even Tojo was not given full details of the serious losses incurred – four aircraft carriers and two heavy cruisers to be set against the sinking of u.s.s. *Yorktown* and one destroyer. The battle regained for the Americans the initiative in the Pacific. It was perhaps the turning-point of the war.

A determined advance overland towards Port Moresby from the northern coast of New Guinea was checked by the Australians some thirty miles from its objective, and step by step the Japanese were forced back over the Owen Stanley Range to the north coast, where eventually, after most cruel and bitter fighting, their force was destroyed. This, with the single exception of Nomonhan, was the first serious disaster that Japanese troops had ever suffered. Soon afterwards, however, they gave up the struggle for Guadalcanal in the

Solomons where for months, on land and sea and in the air, they had fought desperately against the Americans. The tide was turning. In the Solomons, New Guinea, New Britain, and in the archipelagoes north of New Guinea the Japanese were outmanoeuvred and defeated. Every battle was hard fought, but Allied command of the air made it possible for considerable Japanese strongpoints to be by-passed. Cut off from all help or hope of relief, many of these garrisons remained in impotent isolation until the end of the war. Some of them saved themsleves from starvation only by living off the meagre crops they were able to plant and harvest themselves. Where landings were made, the Japanese, though subjected for days beforehand to intensive bombardment from the sea and air, resisted with fierce courage, often to the last man. Japanese prisoners were few; and most of them were only captured because they were too weak, from wounds or starvation, to kill themselves.

Eighteen months after Pearl Harbour it was already clear to thoughtful people in Tokyo in a position to know what was really happening that Japan had begun to lose the war. The best hope for the country seemed to be some kind of compromise peace. But no statesman dared to voice this opinion openly. The army regarded any talk of this kind as defeatism. As optimism and excitement, engendered by the first remarkable victories, gave way to slowly increasing but perceptible war weariness, the authorities became the more watchful for any signs of public uneasiness. The ubiquitous civil police were reinforced by the *Kempei*, on whom Tojo placed much reliance, in their campaign to whip up popular support 'behind the guns'. There being no opportunities for protest, boredom and secret resentment found expression, often half-consciously only, in a kind of spreading apathy that became, in the last weeks of the war, almost listless as the horrors of mass bombings all over Japan were added to the nagging discomforts of shortages and rationing.

On the whole little profit was derived from the alliance with Germany and Italy. It was true, of course, that Germany occupied the attention of a large portion of America's armed strength, that she diverted from Japan most of Britain's power. But Germany's war with the Soviet Union gave Tokyo much anxiety. More than once the Japanese suggested that their German allies should consider coming to terms with the Russians. But Hitler would have none of it, rejecting such proposals so brusquely that the Japanese never really pressed the issue. Japanese relations with the Germans were amicable, but never intimate. There was some exchange of persons – experts and technicians – and of vital supplies by submarine; and one or two Japanese submarines from Shonan (as Singapore was renamed) reached Brest. But anything approaching cooperation of the Anglo-American type was entirely lacking. In Tokyo the only result of Italy's surrender in September 1943 was to make the army determined that there should never be a Japanese Badoglio. But in fact there were some people, among them certain ex-premiers, who were beginning to believe in their hearts that they might have to play precisely this role. However, they were not yet reconciled to the prospect of their country having to make the drastic concessions envisaged by the Cairo Declaration (1 December 1943), which implied that Japan would have to give up all the territories she had acquired in the previous fifty years. The formula of 'unconditional surrender', first propounded at Casablanca and repeated at Cairo, was not taken very seriously. If it now seemed unlikely that Japan could win the war, the idea of complete defeat was still inconceivable, except perhaps to a very few persons who knew the true facts about such matters as shipping losses. The emperor had talked privately of the need for peace as early as the spring of 1942; but those who hoped for a compromise peace felt that the army would never agree to Japan having to make more than trivial concessions to the Allies.

In 1944 Japan still had the strength to embark on two great offensive efforts. An advance was made into south-west China to capture or neutralize airfields used by the Americans. On the whole this operation succeeded. The other, and earlier, offensive was much more ambitious in every way, being nothing less than a bid to encircle and destroy British and Indian forces in the Arakan, Chin Hills, and Manipur, and then to break through into Bengal and Assam. The ultimate aim of this offensive was to capture the airfields in Assam from which supplies for Chungking were flown over the eastern Himalayas; and it was also hoped, on the word of Subhas Chandra Bose, that there would be widespread disturbances in Bengal, completing the confusion that would follow the British defeat on the Indo-Burmese frontier. This offensive ended in catastrophe. In the Battle of Kohima-Imphal, the greatest and one of the longest of the Pacific War, the Japanese were repulsed, and through the monsoon of 1944 they were pushed back towards the plains of northern Burma. British generalship, outclassed in Malaya, had made a brilliant recovery. Its excellence was to be demonstrated further, in the following spring, by Slim's encirclement of the Japanese south of the Irrawaddy.

It was during the later phases of the Imphal battle that the Americans invaded the Marianas in the Pacific. In mid-June 1944 they landed on Saipan and in a month's savage campaign overcame Japanese resistance. For Japan the loss of Saipan was very serious. It was some 1300 miles from Tokyo. This meant that once American bombers were established on airfields in the island, the capital was within their range. A powerful fleet was sent to interrupt the American landing, but this was heavily defeated.

The fall of Saipan, together with the disaster on the Assam–Burma front, brought down the Tojo cabinet. The Premier did his best to cling to office, but he had made many enemies, some of them in his own cabinet; and in any case it was the Japanese tradition that he accept responsibility for the major defeats his country had suffered. After Tojo's resignation a new government was formed under General Koiso, now on the retired list, with Admiral Yonai as unofficial Assistant-Premier. Yonai had always held moderate views and was known to have been opposed to the Axis Pact. His appointment, therefore, gave encouragement to those who were hoping that Japan could find some way of talking peace to the Allies.

Following the subjection of the Marianas the Americans drew nearer to the Philippines; and in October this archipelago was breached by a landing on the island of Leyte. There now occurred the last great naval battle of the war. The Japanese, who attacked in three groups, worked out a plan that made the best of their serious inferiority in the air, and at one critical stage of the battle it was nearly successful. But Leyte Gulf, touch and go for a time, was turned into an overwhelming American victory. Among the Japanese losses were four carriers, three battleships – including the giant 64,000-ton *Musashi* – and ten cruisers. Damage to surviving vessels was heavy. This was the not inglorious end of the old Imperial Navy, after a history of less than eighty years. One day, after the Occupation of Japan had ended, Admiral Kurita, who commanded the main battle group at Leyte Gulf, was interviewed at a baseball match in Tokyo. 'I was the pitcher', he remarked with a bitter laugh, 'in a lost war.'

On Leyte Island organized fighting did not finish until the close of 1944, by which time MacArthur's forces had landed on Mindoro and were poised for the assault on Luzon.

Meanwhile Tokyo received an unpleasant jolt from Moscow. In a speech on the anniversary of the Bolshevik Revolution Stalin denounced Japan as an aggressor nation. Although Molotov assured the Japanese Ambassador that Stalin's reference was to Japan's past conduct only, and not to her present policy, the Soviet attitude now seemed to resemble, in the words of a Japanese diplomat, 'the sharp touch of the first frost that withers the late flowers'.* And at about the same time the first considerable raid was made on Tokyo by American bombers based on the Marianas, while in the Nagoya region a great earthquake – in normal times it would have attracted the sympathy of the civilized world – caused appalling devastation, including tremendous damage to vital war industries.

In January 1945 the struggle on the Philippines entered a new phase with the American attack on Luzon; but it was

* T. Kase, *Eclipse of the Rising Sun*. London (Jonathan Cape), 1951, p. 97.

not until March that resistance in Manila was crushed; and indeed fighting continued in the Philippines until Japan surrendered, despite MacArthur's grandiloquent pronouncement, early in July, that 'the entire Philippines have now been liberated'.

In February the small but strongly defended island of Iwojima, less than nine hundred miles from Tokyo, was invaded by American marines after five weeks of preliminary sea and air bombardment. The area of Iwojima is eight square miles. The Japanese – some 23,000 of them – fought to the last man, as they had on Attu in the Aleutians a year earlier. Thus possession of the island cost America a month's heroic fighting and over 20,000 casualties. It was the same story in April, May, and June at Okinawa in the Ryukyus – about ten weeks' fighting and 39,000 casualties. Nearly a third of these occurred in the fleet supporting the troops on the ground; for by now the Japanese had resorted to the use of suicide pilots, who dived their planes, loaded with explosives, straight on to their targets. These courageous pilots were given the name of *Kamikaze*, or 'Divine Wind' – a reference to the providential typhoon that destroyed the Mongol armada in the thirteenth century.

With the fall of Okinawa an enemy landing on Japan itself could not be long delayed; for with Germany out of the war, the nation would have to face the full power of America and Great Britain. Yet it was an article of faith with the armed services that, even so, Japan might be able to avoid defeat if only the soldiers, sailors, and airmen, and the civilian population too, fought with traditional bravery and self-sacrifice. So the populace were supplied with such weapons as could be spared, though in many cases these were no more lethal than bamboo poles sharpened to a point at one end. Equipped with these spears men and women made ready to meet the enemy.

Early in April the Koiso cabinet had given place to one headed by Admiral Suzuki, President of the Privy Council, a tough, straightforward old man, who had barely survived the attack made on him by the Tokyo mutineers nine years before. Suzuki was regarded with much affection by the emperor, and in the end he saw the inevitability of Japan's surrender; but for some time he seems to have believed that his country could obtain a modification of the 'unconditional surrender' demand if she could win just one battle, at Okinawa or on the shores of the homeland. On the same day that Premier Koiso resigned the Soviet government announced that it would not renew the Neutrality Pact with Japan; and although Molotov told Ambassador Sato that no action would be taken until the Pact expired in April 1946, the Japanese now realized that there was a strong possibility of the Soviet Union entering the war against them. Of this they could not be certain, however; for they never knew that at the Yalta Conference in February Stalin had promised to join the war against Japan two or three months after the defeat of Germany. So in May the Suzuki government started to approach the Soviet Union for a renewal of the Neutrality Pact; and to this end Tokyo was ready to give up a good deal – including southern Sakhalin, the northern Kuriles, and northern Manchuria. By early summer 1945, one of the most urgent requirements for Japan was oil. Stocks were running desperately short and replenishment from tankers was now negligible. It was hoped that, in return for the gift of some Japanese cruisers and the promise (which Japan was scarcely in the position to keep) of bauxite and other materials from the occupied lands in the south, the Soviet Union would agree to provide Japan with oil.

The Russians responded to Japanese overtures in a very off-hand manner; and no progress was made either with Malik, the Soviet Ambassador in Japan, or in Moscow. Indeed Ambassador Sato had no illusions, and he kept warning Tokyo that there was very little hope of securing any kind of Soviet cooperation. But after the defeat of Germany and the fall of Okinawa, even the Minister of War and the Chief of the Army General Staff reluctantly agreed that the Russians should be asked to act as mediators for peace; and it was agreed that a special delegation, headed by Prince Konoye, should be sent to Moscow to discuss some way of bringing the war to an end. When the proposal was put to the Russians they were frostily non-committal. It was now July, and after some delay the Japanese were told that they would have to await the return of the Russian leaders from the Potsdam Conference before being given an answer. At Potsdam Stalin told President Truman and the British Prime Minister of the Japanese request for mediation. But this was not news to the American government; for Washington had already, as in 1941, intercepted and deciphered Japanese diplomatic code messages, and was thus aware of the content of the telegrams passing between the Foreign Minister (Togo Shigenori) in Tokyo and Ambassador Sato in Moscow.

[III]

On 26 July 1945 the American President and the British Premier issued from Potsdam a proclamation, to which Chiang Kai-shek, in Chungking, added his imprimatur, calling upon Japan to order the surrender of all her armed forces. 'The alternative for Japan', said the proclamation, 'is prompt and utter destruction.'

By this time Japan was being subjected to an unprecedented ordeal from the air. Already the city of Tokyo had received, in March, what was probably the most appalling air attack, in terms of loss of life, of the whole war. Incendiary bombs raised fires that turned wood-built factories and dwellings, block by block, into raging furnaces. Aircraft from American and British carriers as well as from the Marianas, Iwojima, and Okinawa ranged over the length and breadth of Japan to such effect that just before the war ended they succeeded, by the sinking of ferry-boats, in virtually severing communications between the main island and both Hokkaido in the north and Kyushu in the west. Forty per cent of the built-up area of more than sixty cities and towns was destroyed. The devastation in Tokyo, except in the heart of the business centre, surpassed that caused by the Great Earthquake twenty-two years earlier. For mile after mile the huge urban area from Tokyo through Kawasaki to Yokohama presented the spectacle of charred wood and ashes with scarcely a building standing. It was much the same at Osaka, Nagoya, and Kobe. Among the largest cities only Kyoto was untouched – thanks, so it was said, to persistent representations in Washington by the Curator of the Boston Museum of Fine Arts.

Little more than one million tons of merchant shipping, out of some ten million, remained afloat by the beginning of August. As for the navy, it had been reduced from some two and a quarter million tons to less than two hundred thousand. *Yamato* (sister ship of *Musashi*), the last great capital ship in a position to fight, had been lost in April, sunk some fifty miles from the Kyushu coast. Such air strength as remained was being kept in reserve in Japan against the expected invasion. Here the deficiency lay rather in trained pilots and fuel than in aircraft. Very large and efficient land forces remained, of course, in Japan and overseas, notably in China; but in Manchukuo the Kwantung Army was much weaker than it had been. Some of its best formations had been moved to other areas. There were, too, considerable garrisons in Siam, Malaya, the East Indies, and in Indo-China, where in the spring of 1945 the Japanese carried out a *coup*, not without bloodshed, against the French authorities, who until then had been allowed to conduct the internal administration of the colony.

It was the knowledge of this remaining military strength in Japan that made the Allies appreciate that an invasion, on the precedent of Iwojima and Okinawa, would be a costly affair, although the outcome of course could not be in doubt. If the reduction of an island like Okinawa involved nearly forty thousand casualties what would be the losses in the invasion and conquest of Kyushu, to say nothing of a later invasion of the Kanto (Tokyo) region? For precisely the same reason Japanese army and navy leaders felt they had a chance of inflicting at least one great reverse on the enemy when invasion came.

But this prospect was not good enough to allay the apprehensions of those who believed that Japan must seek peace before the country was actually invaded. A majority in the government – Premier Suzuki's own view was unclear until the very end – realized by mid-July that perhaps the only thing that could be saved from the wreckage was the imperial Throne. The monarchy must be preserved at all costs. This was their one irreducible demand. A Japan without an emperor was inconceivable. But if the Allies had to undertake an invasion, followed by a bloody campaign in Japan itself, then surely they would insist on overthrowing the imperial house. Furthermore, it was feared that among the people at large revolutionary sentiment might spread, once foreign troops began to fight their way into Japan. In the last resort the rulers of Japan feared revolution much more than defeat. At the risk of their lives they were ready to sue for peace if only the formula of 'unconditional surrender' could be modified by an Allied pledge not to tamper with the ancient institution of the Japanese monarchy. Some of them had come to the conclusion that the right-wing fanatics, who insisted on a fight to the finish, were the agents – unconscious or otherwise, it hardly mattered – of revolutionary Communism.

All the same, the Japanese government, on 28 July announced that it would ignore the Potsdam Proclamation. This of course gave everyone the impression at home and abroad that Japan's attitude was one of unbending defiance. Nevertheless, as we have seen, Washington knew that in fact the Japanese were trying desperately to seek peace.

On the morning of 6 August a single American Superfortress dropped an atomic bomb on Hiroshima. This hideous weapon might have been dropped, with the same results politically, on open country. Instead, it was used to obliterate a city, one that had not been subjected until then to any form of air attack.

When the first reports from Hiroshima reached the emperor he declared: 'No matter what happens to my safety we must put an end to this war as quickly as possible, so that this tragedy will not be repeated.' It was not known, of course, that the Americans possessed at that time only one other practicable bomb of this type; but something not far from the truth was suspected by Admiral Toyoda, Chief of the Naval General Staff, who said that even America could not have enough radioactive material ready to make a sufficient number of bombs to carry on such attacks. But he was on weaker ground when he went on to argue that world opinion would intervene to prevent a repetition of the Hiroshima atrocity. So even now the Supreme Command – or, to be exact here, the two Chiefs of Staff and the Minister of War – were reluctant to talk peace on the basis of unconditional surrender.

In bringing the war to an end a factor as decisive as the atomic bomb was the Soviet attack on Japan on 8 August. Russia's declaration of war was Molotov's gift to Sato when the latter was able, at last, to see him. Next day, perhaps the most critical in Japanese history, the small group in Tokyo known as the Supreme Council for the Direction of the War spent the morning arguing in what form Japan should ask for peace. The Supreme Council on this occasion was limited to six men – the Premier (Suzuki), the Foreign, Navy, and War Ministers (Togo, Yonai, and Anami), and the two Chiefs of Staff (General Umezu and Admiral Toyoda). They excluded from attendance at their deliberations the section chiefs and aides who often influenced their seniors and who were themselves sometimes in touch with extremists. Suzuki, Togo, and Yonai favoured acceptance of the Potsdam Proclamation with the sole reservation that the monarchy be maintained. General Anami (the War Minister) and the two Chiefs of Staff insisted on adding three further reservations: there should be no enemy occupation of Japan; the Japanese should be allowed to disarm and demobilize their own forces; Japanese war criminals should be tried by Japanese courts. Umezu, the Army Chief of Staff, emphasized reasonably enough that it might prove extremely difficult, and perhaps impossible, to ensure that Japanese troops surrendered themselves and their weapons to the enemy. However, Togo, the Foreign Minister, carried the Premier and Admiral Yonai with him when he urged that it would be useless to attach any condition, save the proviso on the monarchy, to Japan's capitulation. Deadlock ensued; and finally the meeting was adjourned – neither side having given way – so that the question could be laid before the cabinet.

That same afternoon and evening the cabinet debated the matter for over seven hours, but could not reach agreement. Some of his colleagues thought Togo was unnecessarily defeatist – this after news had come in that morning, while the Supreme Council was sitting, that a second atomic bomb had been dropped, on Nagasaki. The cabinet meeting ended, no decision having been reached, soon after ten o'clock at night. The Premier and the Foreign Minister went straight to the palace to report to the emperor. The Premier requested the summoning of an Imperial Conference – a full-dress meeting of the Supreme Council in the emperor's presence – for that same evening.

The conference was held in an underground air-raid shelter next to the palace library. From shortly before midnight to about half past two in the morning of 10 August the arguments, already thrashed out in the Supreme Council and cabinet, were firmly restated, the emperor listening in silence. On this occasion the President of the Privy Council, Hiranuma, was present. When his turn came to speak he seemed on the whole to be on Togo's side. As he was a strong nationalist of the old school his opinion perhaps carried particular weight. But he proposed that at this grave moment the emperor's own views should be sought. The Premier did not reveal explicitly what his own convictions were, but he wound up the proceedings by turning to the emperor and asking him to give a decision on the course of action to be adopted.

It is reported that the emperor spoke with great emotion but without the slightest hesitation. He said that he could not bear to see his people suffer any longer. He had been advised by some people that the issue of national survival could be decided by a battle in Japan itself; but, he said, 'the experiences of the past show that there has always been a discrepancy between plans and performance'. He said that it was unbearable for him to see the fighting men of

Japan disarmed and others, who had served him loyally, brought to trial as instigators of the war. But the time had come when one must bear what was unbearable. He recalled the feelings of his grandfather, the Emperor Meiji, at the time of the Triple Intervention, and so he gave his sanction to the proposal to accept the Potsdam Proclamation on the basis advocated by Togo, the Foreign Minister.*

The emperor then withdrew; and the Premier declared that his decision ought to be that of the Imperial Conference also. Nobody dissented. There followed a meeting of the cabinet, at which the emperor's decision was unanimously approved. Messages were then sent immediately through the Legations at Berne and Stockholm to the governments of the United States, China, Great Britain, and the Soviet Union, announcing that Japan accepted the Potsdam Proclamation on the understanding that it did not comprise 'any demand which prejudices the prerogatives of His Majesty as a Sovereign Ruler'.

In normal times a deadlock of opinion on a vital issue would have meant the resignation of the cabinet, and the emperor would not have been faced with a division of views on which to adjudicate. However, a very abnormal situation gave the emperor the chance to take a political decision, and so tilt the scales in the direction that he personally had long favoured. But the emperor's intervention did not end with the conference of the night of 9–10 August. Within the next two days another crisis arose.

The Allied reply to Japan – drafted by Byrnes, the American Secretary of State – did not include, as Tokyo hoped, any specific pledge on the monarchy. On this matter the reply simply said that from the moment of surrender 'the authority of the emperor and the Japanese government to

* This account is based on that put forward by Dr R. J. C. Butow in his book, *Japan's Decision to Surrender*. Stanford (Stanford University Press), 1954, pp. 169–76, which should be read by anyone who wishes to study this subject in detail. No minutes, it appears, were taken at the conference. But at least six of those present wrote some account of it. It is on this and other material that Dr Butow bases his version, which can be accepted as essentially true.

rule the state shall be subject to the Supreme Commander of the Allied Powers who will take such steps as he deems proper to effectuate the surrender terms'. It stated, moreover, that the ultimate form of government of Japan would be established 'by the freely expressed will of the Japanese people'.

Once again there was a sharp difference of opinion among the leaders in Tokyo. The Chiefs of the General Staff and the War Minister felt that Japan could not possibly accept the reply as the basis for peace. For it implied that the emperor would have to obey the orders of the Allied Supreme Commander, and the prospect seemed too shameful to be borne. Their own subordinates, they felt, would never agree to peace on such terms. Hiranuma, President of the Privy Council, opposed acceptance of the Allied reply because he believed that it would mean the destruction of the *Kokutai*, the fundamental national polity of Japan. This was implicit, he argued, in the statement that the ultimate form of government would be established by the freely expressed will of the people. One cannot pretend that Hiranuma was wrong on this important point; for it was true that sovereignty in Japan had never originated in the will of the people and had never depended on any such theory. For a while he was able to persuade the Prime Minister to share his view; and in the cabinet the Home Minister, and the Minister of Justice, thought along the same lines.

But arguments such as these were truly academic in face of the reality confronting Japan. If resistance continued there would be invasion, almost certainly by the Russians before the Americans and British were ready; and many in high places believed, too, that the Japanese race might well be exterminated (there was a rumour that Tokyo would be atom-bombed on 12 August) if they went on fighting. This was the fear of Togo and the Foreign Ministry, of ex-premiers such as Konoye, and of the emperor's court advisers. Even if no further atomic attacks occurred, a Russian invasion would mean an end of the imperial house.

The Allied reply was a disappointment, but at least it did not in so many words rule out the possibility of the

monarchy's survival. Togo and his Vice-Minister, Matsumoto Shunichi, backed up by the former Foreign Minister,
Shigemitsu, undoubtedly strained the plain meaning of the
Allied message to give it an interpretation compatible with
their own hopes. They took a chance that the Allies would
not insist on overthrowing the monarchy provided Japan
surrendered without further delay. They felt that another
message to the Allies, asking for elucidation or suggesting
additional conditions, would only make matters worse.
Needless to say, even at this stage their position would have
been hopeless but for the emperor's own conviction that
Japan must capitulate immediately on the basis of the
Allied reply. Fortunately Togo was able to win over the
Prime Minister once again; and so the balance of forces in
the Supreme Council was restored.

Throughout the morning and well into the afternoon of
13 August the great debate went on in the Supreme Council; but there was no agreement. Anami, Umezu, and Toyoda could not bring themselves to bow to the Allied demands.
The cabinet then met, but again there was no unanimity.
Finally, the Premier said that once more they would have to
seek a decision from the emperor. After the cabinet meeting
was over the Foreign Minister spent hours that evening
arguing with the two Chiefs of Staff, without success.

Meanwhile the war went on. That day, 13 August,
Tokyo was raided by over fifteen hundred planes from Allied
carriers cruising at will off the coast of Honshu. The whirl-
wind advance of the Russians continued. The people of
Japan knew that the situation was critical; but they were
resigned, with varying degrees of hope and despair, to the
agony of invasion. Not a word had appeared in the press
suggesting that the government had already almost accepted the Potsdam ultimatum.

But early on 14 August American aircraft deluged Tokyo
with leaflets giving the text of the messages exchanged between the government and the Allies. This increased the
likelihood that fanatical officers might attempt some *coup*
against the government, to forestall surrender.

That morning, in the palace air-raid shelter, the Supreme Council and the cabinet met as one body in the presence of the emperor. The Chiefs of Staff and Anami, the Minister of War, restated their conviction that if further clarification of the attitude of the Allies was impossible then Japan should fight on; there was at least a chance of getting better terms. When Umezu, Toyoda, and Anami had finished speaking, the emperor gave his decision.

His opinion, he said, was still the same, for he did not find the Allied reply unreasonable. He pointed out that continuation of the war might mean the death of hundreds of thousands of people. Indeed all Japan would be reduced to ashes. He declared once again that his grandfather, at the time of the Triple Intervention, had endured the unendurable; he and his subjects must do the same. It was his wish that the government should accept the Allied message forthwith.

Meeting immediately after this Imperial Conference had ended, the cabinet unanimously endorsed the emperor's decision. The Foreign Ministry lost no time in sending news of it to the Allies through neutral channels.

It had already been arranged by court officials that in the event of capitulation the emperor would take the unprecedented step of broadcasting to the nation; and close on midnight on 14 August the emperor recorded his rescript terminating the war. It was to be broadcast at noon on the following day.

In the very early hours of 15 August an attempt was made to seize and destroy this record. It was part of a desperate revolt organized by a small group of staff officers in Tokyo. The principal ringleader visited the commander of the First Guards Division, stationed close to the palace, and urged him, not for the first time, to take part in the *coup*. When he refused he was shot dead. A forged order, with the dead man's seal impressed upon it, placed the division at the disposal of the rebels. They proceeded to surround the palace and to search anxiously for the record. This they were unable to find. Meanwhile word of what was afoot reached the main army operational headquarters in Tokyo, and the general in command very courageously went at once to the palace. By the sheer force of his personality and the eloquence of what he said – Japanese officers could usually speak well when moved or excited – he persuaded the insurgent leaders that they had behaved in a wholly wrong-headed manner. They admitted their error, and four of them committed suicide on the spot. At roughly the same time the Minister of War, General Anami, was sitting on the veranda of his house writing with a brush on two scrolls of paper his farewell messages, one of them a *tanka* (a Japanese poem). At about four o'clock in the morning he faced in the direction of the Imperial Palace and drove a dagger into his belly and then into his neck. Anami held a command in the Philippines before becoming Minister of War, and at that time he had sent a message to Shigemitsu, then Foreign Minister, saying it would be wise to seek a peace settlement as soon as possible. Personally he had recognized by the end of July that it was virtually hopeless to continue the struggle, but as Minister of War he could not admit the fact officially. Had he resigned during the last days, he could have complicated matters immensely. To his credit he remained in the cabinet and accepted the emperor's decision loyally in the end. He seems to have known something of the staff officers' plot for 'direct action', yet he took no positive steps to check it, although it met with his sad disapproval.

At midday on 15 August the emperor's voice was heard throughout the land – the remotest hamlet in Japan possessed at least one wireless set. All but the incapacitated or infirm heard the broadcast. Not all the words were intelligible to everyone, since they were in a form of language familiar only to the well-educated. In any case most people were so overcome by emotion that at first they could hardly concentrate their attention. But the gist of the message was clear enough. The war was over.

An imperial rescript, of course, is drafted by more than one hand. The approval of the Surrender rescript was perhaps the last collective act of the Suzuki cabinet. It was on

Anami's insistence that enemy victories on land and sea were summed up in the rescript in a masterpiece of under-statement – 'the war situation has developed not necessarily to Japan's advantage'. There was a reference to Hiroshima – 'the enemy has begun to employ a new and most cruel bomb, the power of which to do damage is indeed incalcula-ble, taking the toll of many innocent lives. Should we con-tinue to fight, it would not only result in an ultimate collapse and obliteration of the Japanese nation, but also it would lead to the total extinction of human civilization.' It may be that among the words spoken by the emperor the most important, in their impact on his vast audience, were the following:

We are keenly aware of the inmost feelings of all of you, Our subjects. However, it is according to the dictate of time and fate that We have resolved to pave the way for a grand peace for all the generations to come by enduring the unendurable and suffering what is insufferable.

So ended a war of peculiar savagery. Japan would never have entered it had the armed forces kept out of politics, or, failing this, if the army had been content to allow the Foreign Ministry – its quality was impressive – unimpeded control of the handling of Japan's relations with China and the West during the 1930s. Making all allowance for excep-tions, the professional army abused its power by showing itself to be on the whole cruel, arrogant, and stupid. These defects outweighed the one virtue that the army possessed in the highest degree, namely physical courage. Thoughtful, imaginative, politically gifted, and sophisticated officers were overshadowed, therefore, by narrow-minded bigots, pris-oners of their own neo-*samurai* mentality. These men, it must be said, brought the good name of Japan into disrepute throughout Asia; and they very nearly destroyed for ever the monarchy and the state they were pledged to serve.

Chapter 10

THE OCCUPATION

[I]

It was at the end of August that the vanguard of the American army of occupation landed at an airfield near Tokyo. They were driven in Japanese transport to Yokohama, which was to be the headquarters of General Eichelberger's Eighth Army. As they entered what was left of the city they observed few spectators among the ruins. At every intersection stood a Japanese soldier, rifle and bayonet at the ready, with his back to the convoy. This was a precaution against any possible attack or demonstration. On the whole it was a dismal scene, suggestive of little triumph for the victors. The desolation was heightened, if anything, by the fact that the electric trains were still running along the embankment on the main line to Tokyo.

After the emperor's broadcast all kinds of rumours about the Americans had begun to spread among the people. There was a general belief that the occupying troops, filled with vengeful hatred of the Japanese, would be virtually unrestrained in their behaviour towards life and property. Many people – women especially – thought it prudent to leave Tokyo and Yokohama before the Americans moved in. But as the troops arrived by air and sea, it was soon evident that popular fears were groundless. The Americans did not behave like demons at all. So began perhaps the most peaceful and, to outward appearance, most harmonious occupation of one great country by another that has ever been known.

Japan had never known defeat, much less occupation. The people, then, had really no idea as to how they should conduct themselves in a situation that lacked all precedent. Moreover, they were confused, dazed, weary, and a quarter starved. Most of them were too relieved that the war was over to cherish much resentment against those who had defeated them, especially when the enemy turned out to be far less vindictive than had been feared. Popular resentment, in so far as it existed at all, was directed against the national leaders, in particular the generals and admirals who had led Japan into a hopeless war. Such men, it was felt, had betrayed both the emperor and the people of Japan. Towards the Americans, once the sense of unreasoning fear had been dispelled, the dominant feeling was one of friendly curiosity.

Meanwhile, the hundreds of thousands of men overseas – in China and south-east Asia – laid down their arms. Imperial Princes were sent to each Command, officially to explain and enforce the Surrender rescript. There were very few cases of any defiance of the rescript; and those that occurred were mostly among isolated units. Indeed the most serious indications of trouble appeared in Japan itself, during the brief twilight period between the emperor's broadcast and the arrival of the Americans. Airmen flew over Tokyo, dropping leaflets which said that the fight must go on. Groups of diehards committed ceremonial suicide in front of the palace. Others seized a small hill in the city, defying the police until the latter attacked them in force, whereupon they blew themselves up with hand grenades. All this made the government – a new administration headed by Prince Higashi-Kuni, the emperor's cousin – extremely nervous. But the overwhelming majority of the Japanese, servicemen and civilians alike, faithfully obeyed the command to surrender. There could have been no more impressive example of the charismatic authority of the Japanese Throne.

The formal ceremony of surrender took place on 2 September 1945, on the deck of the American battleship *Missouri*, in the presence of the man who was to take charge of the Occupation, General MacArthur, Supreme Commander for the Allied Powers. The abbreviation of this title, SCAP, came to stand both for the man himself and for his headquarters in Tokyo, and it is so used by historians. It is perhaps too early to offer a fair assessment of MacArthur as

Supreme Commander in Japan from September 1945 to April 1951, when he was dismissed by President Truman. But some things can be said with assurance, by way of an interim judgement. MacArthur revealed himself as that rare figure, the American version of the traditional British grandee. He had Curzon's vanity and touchiness and some of Curzon's intellectual gifts, without his brilliance and his unremitting capacity for prolonged hard work. And in MacArthur's case a tendency towards complacent self-dramatization was encouraged by the adulation of a devoted wartime staff that he took with him to Japan. Some of these sycophants were given appointments at the top of the Occupation machinery, and they took almost ludicrous care that only the rosiest reports of the progress of the Occupation should reach the outside world. In their debased opinion the slightest criticism of SCAP amounted to something approaching sacrilege.

MacArthur took up residence in the United States Embassy in Tokyo. Each day at the same hour he was driven to his office in a large building facing the palace moat; at the same hour each day he was driven home again. In six and a half years this daily routine was interrupted only on rare occasions, notably when the demands of some great political or military crisis took him abroad, for example to Formosa or Korea. He never toured Japan to see things for himself. He chose, so it seemed, to live in proconsular remoteness 'above the clouds', from time to time handing down pronouncements on the achievements of his regime and on the spiritual, social, and political progress of the Japanese people. The irreverent were heard to say that if a man rose early in the morning and was very lucky he might catch a glimpse of the Supreme Commander walking on the waters of the palace moat.

There is no doubt that this aloofness impressed Japanese of the conservative type. It was a posture with which they were familiar. It was inevitable that MacArthur should have been likened to a Tokugawa *shogun*. But it may well be doubted whether this kind of awed respect on the part of the

Japanese was compatible with the healthy growth of democratic sentiment. General Headquarters, SCAP, was after all a military organization, and its hierarchy was infused with the spirit of the professional officer. It is true that this hierarchy lacked the spartan arrogance characteristic of the old imperial army. The American officers were no strutting bigots; and they were not tyrants. Nevertheless they took precedence over the civilian advisers and experts sent out to Tokyo to guide SCAP. Therefore it was natural for the Japanese to feel that in America, as in Japan up to 1945, the soldier counted for more than the civilian. The Japanese perhaps learned more about democracy from MacArthur's dismissal than from anything he himself ever did or said while he was in Tokyo.

To say all this is in no way to belittle the efficiency with which MacArthur's Headquarters carried out many of the tasks before it. Demilitarization, for example, was enforced with thoroughness and dispatch; and in a remarkably short time the battered apparatus of Japan's war machine was dismantled or destroyed. The repatriation from overseas of some three million Japanese, civilians as well as soldiers and sailors, was successfully organized and completed. When starvation seemed to be a real threat, towards the end of 1945, SCAP took action to import foodstuffs from the United States, and these imports were continued for the next few years. Retribution, in the form of trials and purges, was visited on the unjust and, so far as the purges were concerned, sometimes also on the just. SCAP was responsible for a new code covering labour relations, whereby all manner of old abuses were swept away, on paper at any rate. SCAP wrote a new Constitution for Japan and directed the Japanese government to recast the judicial and administrative structure throughout the country. An ambitious programme of land reform was introduced. The *zaibatsu* were dissolved; the Home Ministry was abolished; political prisoners, some of whom had spent seventeen years in gaol, were released. The watchwords were democracy and decentralization. There was plenty of idealism as well as energy both at

Headquarters and among the Military Government teams in the prefectures. It is easy to derive amusement from the thought of a few hundred enthusiasts – many of them, especially in the early days, keen New Dealers – interfering at almost every social and political level with the traditional practices of a much older civilization and race, of whose language, culture, and psychology they were often remarkably ignorant. Sometimes they were the prisoners, without knowing it, not only of their own naïve prejudices but also of the *Nisei* (American-born Japanese) interpreters on whom they had to rely at every turn. Occasionally, bamboozled by deceit or corrupted by flattery, they failed to supervise the operation of some measure introduced at their behest. They were apt to condemn out of hand any belief or custom they regarded as 'feudalistic'. They were not over-worried if the new broom swept away some of the good together with the evil. But the fact remains that SCAP officials not only gave technological advice of permanent value but also introduced tens of thousands of men and women to an entirely new awareness of what is meant by the freedom and dignity of the individual human being. If the Americans, as occupiers of Japan, had been generally overbearing, corrupt, or inefficient, we may be sure that we should have heard of it on every side during the years of the anti-American reaction following the Treaty of Peace. However, it has been widely recognized, except by the Communists, that American intentions were benevolent. In a word, people on the whole liked them, especially during the first two or three years of the Occupation. Anti-American sentiment in Japan became noticeable on a large scale after 1952 and was largely caused by resentment against the Security Pact, or Washington's pressure for speedier Japanese rearmament. The sentiment, where it occurs, is directed not against individual Americans but rather against them collectively. Many Japanese forget the honeymoon period of the early Occupation, when everything American was the rage, when anyone with the slightest curiosity felt that the Americans could tell or show him some new thing. No doubt the rather brash confidence of the Americans that their kind of democracy, being the best, was exportable *in toto* to Japan irritated the Japanese, particularly those who were mature and well-educated. But this is not to say that even the sophisticated minority had nothing to learn from the Americans.

From 1945 to 1952, the year in which the Occupation came to an end, the popular attitude towards SCAP, as an institution, was a compound of apprehension, admiration, disappointment, and boredom. Indeed these several emotions represent, in the order in which they have just been listed, the stages through which the Japanese, speaking in the broadest sense, passed in their reaction to the Occupation as a whole. The later stages of disappointment and boredom were partly due to the length of the Occupation. As homes were rebuilt and as economic conditions improved, thanks to the Korean War, it was inevitable that the early enthusiasm for American ways should be succeeded by some reaction. It was only natural that people should get tired of seeing foreign uniforms in the streets, that the retention by the Americans of commandeered houses, hotels and railway stock should become irritating after, say, five years; whereas at first, of course, all this, and very much worse, had been expected. But there was another cause for the change in the popular attitude as the years went by. The policy of SCAP towards Japan underwent an important alteration less than three years after the Occupation began. It is not possible to give any definite date as a turning point, but at all events in the early months of 1948 it was apparent that in future the main consideration before SCAP would be to rebuild Japan as an ally of the United States in the struggle against Communism. Naturally enough such developments as the blockade of Berlin, the Chinese Revolution, and the Korean War made it all the more obvious that a strong, robustly anti-Communist Japan must be a prime American aim. In the eyes of SCAP, then, rehabilitation and revival became much more important than reform. It was not long, for example, before SCAP began to have second thoughts about the wisdom of having ordered the dissolution of the *zaibatsu* concerns.

Strikes and labour agitation, once looked upon with benevolence by SCAP as signs of democratic vitality, were now considered to be potentially dangerous. Above all, encouragement was given to rearmament.

The new Constitution, the offspring of SCAP, included a celebrated clause (Article 9) forbidding Japan the possession of any armed forces. The clause could hardly have been phrased more specifically. It ended with the words: 'The right of belligerency of the state will not be recognized.' Article 9 soon became a great embarrassment to the Americans. But this did not prevent them, or the Japanese government, from authorizing the creation, in 1950, of a National Police Reserve of over seventy thousand men armed as infantry soldiers. Within four years this was enlarged and reorganized into a well-equipped modern army; and a navy and an air force also came into being. Rearmament, together with economic revival and the reappearance on a smaller scale of the pre-war *zaibatsu*, did not offend Japanese conservatives and businessmen generally. But there is no doubt that about half the country – women, young people, most of the journalists, most of the urban working class, teachers, and the academic world in general – felt some sense of shock and confusion as SCAP's change of front became apparent. The new Constitution had been criticized from many sides, and for many valid reasons, but almost everyone had approved of Article 9, the famous disarmament clause. For pacifist feeling was sincere and almost universal, even among many old-fashioned nationalists. The disarmament clause gave Japan a unique status among the important nations of the world; and uniqueness is above all the quality that Japanese agree their country does, or must, possess. Idealists felt – it was part of the catharsis that followed defeat – that in the new atomic age Japan, thanks to its new Constitution, had set an example to the world as the one nation that would never go to war again. Hundreds of thousands of Japanese, with little or no interest in politics, were disturbed by the new orientation of SCAP's policy. They had been willing to accept, and to learn from, Americans as occupiers guiding Japan along an entirely new road away from militarist domination and war. They looked with mistrust and some fear at America playing the part of an over-powering, if generous, ally eager to enlist their physical support in the great ideological struggle that divided the world. This does not mean that they were necessarily indifferent to the threat implied by the proximity of the Soviet Union. Most Japanese have tended to underestimate China, whether Kuo-mintang or Communist. But most Japanese feel apprehensive about the Russians. Yet, however logical the arguments for rearmament may have seemed, the sense of disillusionment was real. The blame, quite irrationally, was placed on the Americans rather than on the other side in the Cold War.

[II]

In the first phase of the Occupation, from September 1945 to about the end of 1947, Japan experienced the full force of a bloodless social and cultural revolution inspired and super-vised by General Headquarters, SCAP. It is important to bear in mind, however, that the Japanese people on the whole welcomed many of the reforms introduced by the government on instructions from SCAP. Once the war was over and the almost intolerable pressure of the police state was removed, all kinds of forces, dammed up for years, were suddenly released.

It was in October 1945 that the government was instruct-ed to set free political prisoners; and out of gaol came a small band of dedicated Communists, some of whom had been behind bars for years. Unchecked by the police, they began to organize a new Japanese Communist Party, and in the acute economic distress and social confusion of the immediate post-war period they made much headway. But the Com-munists formed only a part of a resurgent left-wing move-ment, reflecting popular dissatisfaction with almost every established institution. The army, for example, was com-pletely discredited. Repatriated soldiers found a Japan that no longer cared for them. They had left their homes as heroes. They returned as living ghosts, to be submerged in the anonymous masses struggling for a bare livelihood.

The farmers, however, were somewhat better off than in the past. For inflation wiped out debts, and the countryside swarmed with visitors from the cities and towns in search of food to supplement the inadequate basic rations authorized by the government. Every evening the trains returned to the cities bulging with foragers. These trains symbolized the misery and confusion that prevailed for many months after the Surrender. When they were overcrowded to the point of suffocation there still were some energetic people who contrived to climb into the carriages through the open windows. Others rode on the buffers of the locomotive and on the couplings between the coaches. Everyone had with him a large bundle or rucksack. On the outward journey this contained household possessions which, it was hoped, could be exchanged for rice or vegetables. On the return journey there was always the risk of a police raid, followed by confiscation of the black market food. For city dwellers the winter of 1945–6 was very grim indeed.

One by one the changes, affecting the whole life of the nation, were instituted by General Headquarters, SCAP, acting through the medium of the Japanese government. The existing structure and spirit of the state-controlled educational system received a deadly blow. Eventually the schools were not only decentralized, thus removing the greater part from the supervision of the Ministry of Education, but also a system new to Japan, modelled on that of the United States, was introduced. This was co-educational and it incorporated Junior High Schools in its structure; and at the same time various colleges in all parts of the country were renamed universities. Decentralization being one of the basic aims of the early phrase of the occupation, there was a tendency to regard Japanese prefectures as potentially autonomous in matters of police and educational administration. Each state of the Union has its university; it should be the same, so it was thought, in each prefecture of Japan. From the start, of course, the curriculum in all schools was altered in such a way that the emperor was dethroned from his semi-divine position, implied by the Rescript on Education – which itself went into oblivion. Pending the rewriting of textbooks, the teaching of Japan's national history was abandoned. Many teachers, having suffered in silence for years, emerged as full-blooded radicals, republicans even, rejoicing in the new freedom associated with democracy.

Democracy – this was the talismanic word of the post-war era; and its implications were not always grasped. To many democracy meant no more than unfettered egotism, the snapping of all burdensome family and social obligations. In an overcrowded country like Japan this philosophy could have led to almost complete social disintegration. Cohesion was maintained, however, thanks to the one institution that symbolized the continuity and homogeneous union of the race. This was the monarchy.

The *mystique* surrounding the emperor was soon dissipated, in part as a result of pressure from SCAP and in part by the emperor's own wish. He was willing to abdicate in favour of his elder son, for he felt acutely that he should accept responsibility for the war. Moreover, an entirely new era had begun with the Occupation, and it seemed fitting therefore that Japan should make a new start under a new emperor. Abdication, or retirement, had taken place on a great many occasions in the past without affecting the prestige of the imperial house. But in 1945 his advisers urged that the emperor at least defer any intention to abdicate, because they feared for the monarchy's very survival should the emperor retire, for this would imply that the fortunes of the imperial house were indissolubly linked with those of the now generally despised Supreme Command. Furthermore it would be easier for the victorious Allies to indict an ex-emperor as a war criminal than to take action against a reigning monarch. All the same, when the emperor called on General MacArthur not long after the Surrender he declared that he himself, rather than any of his generals and ministers, should be held responsible for the war. It was on this occasion that a celebrated photograph was taken – and, on SCAP instructions, given much publicity – of the emperor and MacArthur standing side by side. The former, in a morning coat and striped trousers, was shown standing stiffly beside the much taller American, who looked quite relaxed and informal in his open-necked shirt, with his hands resting in his belt straps. At the time most foreigners and some Japanese believed that this photograph would do immense damage to the personal prestige of the emperor, who at first sight looked indeed not at all impressive beside his conqueror. Nearly all previous photographs of the emperor had shown him in uniform; and the one that had made perhaps the most powerful mass impact had been the annual photograph, reproduced in newsfilms all over the country, of the New Year parade in Tokyo, showing the emperor in a field-marshal's uniform mounted on a pure white horse. But if the old respect was diminished by the photograph taken at MacArthur's headquarters in 1945, a feeling of sympathy was greatly strengthened; and on reflection many Japanese came to believe that the emperor, in this rather pathetic post-war photograph, showed a certain unassailable dignity. In January 1946 the emperor issued a rescript formally renouncing any claims to a divine or semi-divine status, and to reinforce his wish to be regarded by everyone solely as a human being he undertook a number of unprecedented informal tours of the land. As the Japanese put it, 'he came down from the clouds'. Often surrounded by foreign news cameramen, or even by coloured American M.P.s, he appeared in an altogether new role, that of a tired, middle-aged man in rather old civilian clothes. He talked, in a somewhat halting way, to people in the fields, or at the work bench, or in hospital. For all to see he was a very human, bookish, rather shy, sincere man in his forties.

In this way an old concept crumbled away; in its place however there grew up the realization that the emperor, like his subjects, was 'bearing the unbearable'; and the phrase (which was often used by nationalists in the past) 'Emperor and People are One' took on an entirely new and, in a sense, profounder meaning. Thus the monarchy, battered but retaining its vital form, survived the storm of the post-war years.

The first post-war cabinet, under Higashi-Kuni, held office for no more than some eight weeks, making way in October 1945 for a new government headed by Shidehara, a genuinely liberal statesman who had been out of official favour for the past ten years. The Higashi-Kuni cabinet had no option but to resign when it was clear that the Home Minister, to mention only one member of the government, would be included in the 'purge' that SCAP was preparing for those considered responsible for aiding and abetting Japan's armed expansion overseas. Indeed, as winter drew near various political and military leaders were required to enter Sugamo prison in Tokyo pending possible indictment as war criminals. Among those who received a summons of this sort was Prince Konoye. Being reluctant to undergo what he felt to be an intolerable humiliation he ended his life by taking poison early on the morning of the day on which he was due to report at Sugamo. He felt some burden of responsibility for the ill-fated 'China Incident', but he was convinced that he had done everything possible to avert the war with America and Great Britain.

Eventually an international tribunal, on the Nuremburg pattern, sat for some two years and at the end passed sentence of death on seven Japanese leaders, including two former Prime Ministers, Tojo and Hirota. Eighteen others were sentenced to various terms of imprisonment. The voluminous documentation accompanying the International Military Tribunal for the Far East has been of great interest to historians, but it cannot be said that the Tokyo Trial made a deep impression upon the Japanese. They accepted it as the possibly inevitable punishment meted out by the victors upon the vanquished. Tojo, whose stock was very low after a bungled attempt to kill himself, somewhat enhanced his reputation by accepting, in court, full responsibility for starting the Pacific War. People felt sorry for Tojo and the others in the dock, but they did not make martyrs or heroes of them. On the whole the Japanese reaction to the Tokyo Trial was one of boredom.

So-called minor war criminals were brought to trial not only in Japan but also in Singapore and elsewhere in southeast Asia. In all over five thousand were found guilty of gross cruelty towards prisoners-of-war or natives of the occupied areas. Of this number over nine hundred were executed.

Early in 1946 SCAP conducted the first of a series of 'purges' aimed to secure the permanent removal from all offices of responsibility, local as well as national, of those thought to have supported Japan's aggressive policy. The scope of the purge was extremely broad; for under the directive, from the Joint Chiefs of Staff, received by MacArthur in September 1945, it was to be assumed 'that any persons who have held key positions of high responsibility since 1937 in industry, finance, commerce, or agriculture, have been active exponents of militant nationalism and aggression'. The purge affected about two hundred thousand Japanese. Its influence on political life was immediate and drastic. All but forty-eight members of both Houses of the Diet found themselves excluded from political activity. But in practice the 'purgees' remained in the wilderness for only a few years. By April 1952, when the Peace Treaty came into effect, most of them were eligible once more for public office, and indeed by that date a number of 'purgees' had already re-entered politics.

Probably the most important action taken by SCAP in the first year of the Occupation was the preparation of a new Constitution for Japan. The government had been told that the existing Constitution would have to be amended very radically and that this ought to be done as quickly as possible. Accordingly the Shidehara cabinet appointed a committee to draft the necessary revisions; but its suggestions did not satisfy General Headquarters. They did not go far enough, in the opinion of SCAP, towards removing the undemocratic principles expressed and implied in the Meiji Constitution. So MacArthur's own staff produced a document, in effect an entirely new Constitution, and this was presented to the cabinet with the verbal ultimatum that if it was rejected the Supreme Commander would place the draft before the Japanese people, in advance of the first post-war general election planned for the spring of 1946.

When the members of MacArthur's Government Section set about the task of drafting the Constitution they were given, by way of guidance, three principles on which the document was to be based. In the first place the monarchy should be retained, but it must be subject to the will of the people. Secondly, war was to be foresworn for ever. Thirdly, 'all forms of feudalism' must be abolished. The resultant document was adopted by the Diet with only minor alterations and was promulgated as the new Constitution in October 1946. It stated that sovereignty rested not with the emperor but with the people of Japan; and the Diet became 'the highest organ of the state'. The emperor was defined as a symbol of the state and of the unity of the people. It was this section of the draft Constitution that attracted the most critical attention during the debates in the Diet. The cabinet minister charged with the duty of presenting the Constitution to the two Houses went to ingenious lengths to explain that the drastic change in the emperor's status did not impair Japan's *kokutai*, or basic national polity. Nevertheless, the notion of the sovereignty of the people was revolutionary in Japanese eyes; and many constitutional lawyers have argued that this principle, together with the description of the Diet as the supreme organ of the state, means that Japan is a republic in fact if not in name. Ambassadors, for example, are now appointed not by the emperor but by the cabinet. The emperor merely 'attests' such appointments. He has no prescriptive right to see state papers; and legislation passed by the Diet does not require his seal.

The abrogation of war is incorporated in Article 9 of the Constitution. As we have noted already this has not prevented Japan from rearming. In 1953 Vice-President Nixon of the United States, speaking at an official banquet in Tokyo, declared that his country had been wrong to insist that the 'no war' clause should be written into the new Constitution. This remark was not universally applauded by the Japanese, many of whom were well satisfied with Article 9. Moreover it has been the contention of MacArthur's *entourage* that this clause, though heartily endorsed by MacArthur, was in fact suggested to him by Shidehara, Prime Minister at the time.*

The abolition of 'all forms of feudalism' found expression in a number of Articles that comprise what we may call a Japanese 'Bill of Rights'. Article 11, for example, states, among other things, that 'the people shall not be prevented from enjoying any of the fundamental human rights'; and these are listed or implied in the next twenty-nine Articles of the Constitution. Where the Meiji Constitution emphasized duties its successor stresses rights – such as freedom of thought, 'the right to maintain the minimum standards of wholesome and cultured living', the right of all persons 'to receive an equal education correspondent to their ability', and the equal rights of husband and wife. Thus *Jinken* ('human rights') became a catch-phrase throughout Japan; and one cannot deny that this phrase, though often abused, captured the imagination of the mass of the people, giving them a real sense of spiritual liberation.

The bicameral legislature has been preserved; but the old House of Peers was replaced by a House of Councillors, elected by universal suffrage for six years, half the members of the House being elected every three years. The Lower House, granted much greater powers than those possessed by the House of Councillors, must meet within thirty days of a general election; and a general election must be held at least every four years if there is no dissolution of the House within that period. As for the cabinet, the premier and a majority of the ministers must be members of the Diet; and the premier and all the ministers must be civilians.

Amendments of the Constitution can only be initiated by a two-thirds vote of all the members of each House and must be ratified thereafter by a popular referendum.

* In 1958 a party of Japanese constitutional lawyers on a visit to the United States addressed a number of questions to General MacArthur regarding the exact circumstances under which the new Constitution was prepared and presented to the Japanese. Objecting, apparently, to the tone of the questions MacArthur, through a former aide, declined to answer them and indeed rejected them as 'impertinent'.

The Meiji Constitution, then, was thrown on the scrap heap. The new Constitution, though in large measure the product of American brains, was broadly acceptable to the people of Japan. No doubt revision will come, but only after a fight.

[III]

The first phase of the Occupation can be called that of retribution and reform. The second phase – reconstruction – was hastened by two considerations. One of these has already been mentioned in the early part of this chapter – namely the exigencies of the Cold War. The other was the heavy cost to the United States of giving relief to a pauperized Japan. For example, during one year (1947) the amount of American aid exceeded four hundred million dollars.

In 1947 the United States tried to obtain agreement among the Allies for a Japanese peace conference. MacArthur himself felt that the time had come for the Occupation to be ended. But the countries principally concerned – the United States, China, Great Britain, and the Soviet Union – failed to agree on the form that the peace conference should take; and finally, at the beginning of 1948, the United States dropped the proposal. This meant that the Occupation would last longer than had been anticipated; but in this event it was clear that the Japanese would have to be permitted greater autonomy, and that they must be encouraged to stand, so far as possible, on their own feet. In other words the emphasis of the Occupation must be on 'recovery'; and if, in the interests of economic efficiency, this meant that various reforms would have to be abandoned, then let it be so. Thus the programme of *zaibatsu* dissolution was quietly shelved, and the Occupation authorities watched with some complacency the reappearance in public life of various 'purged' political and business leaders. Reparations were terminated; and the Japanese were allowed to resume private trade with foreign countries.

The change in Occupation policy was made all the easier

by the fact that, except for a period of some nine months, from May 1947 to early in 1948, successive Japanese cabinets were in the hands of Conservatives. The exception was the Social Democratic government headed by Katayama;* and even this was a coalition of forces that included a wing of the Conservatives under Dr Ashida. A single Japanese politician dominated the scene during the Occupation and for two years thereafter. This was Yoshida Shigeru. Succeeding Shidehara as Premier in the spring of 1946, he held office until a year later, when what proved to be a temporary swing to the Left gave the Socialists, under Katayama, a numerical lead in the General Election of April 1947. Katayama was followed by Ashida, who was in office only eight months, until October 1948. In this month Yoshida formed his second cabinet. He won a general election in January 1949. He was to be victorious in three more elections before his resignation in November 1954. In all he was Prime Minister five times and held office for nearly seven years. A former ambassador in London, Yoshida's life had been spent in the foreign service, and he was nearly seventy when he became Premier for the first time. He was untouched by the purge – which eliminated, for some years, his chief political rival, Hatoyama – because he had been arrested by the *Kempei* in 1945 for advocating an early peace. For this reason he was *persona grata* with the Occupation authorities in their earlier, reforming, phase. Later he was equally acceptable as a staunch Conservative. At the same time the Japanese admired him as one who combined obedience to SCAP directives with a certain evident, though not readily definable, independence of manner. It was part of his *panache* to assume a rather English air, suggested by his choice of clothes and his attachment to a well-worn Rolls-Royce, reputedly the only one in Tokyo. This, it was thought, was a mild, calculated irritation to the dominant Americans. Such trivialities counted for the Japanese in the first years of the Occupation and made Yoshida popular. After the Peace Treaty came into force this popu-

* Katayama Tetsu, not to be confused with Katayama Sen, see pages 147, 148.

larity dwindled away and he seemed, in Japanese eyes, to be no more than a very obstinate, cantankerous, dictatorial old man. At all events Yoshida symbolized something indestructible in Japanese life; and as this, whatever it was, clearly excluded any sympathy with Communism, it was welcomed by the Americans. Considering what was happening in China, they regarded a moderately right-wing Japan as an international asset.

The outbreak of the Korean War in the summer of 1950 naturally confirmed the Americans in this opinion. There was a moment, early in the war, when South Korea was nearly lost. Had the Americans been faced at the same time with the problem of an unreliable, restive Japan, their difficulties would have been formidable indeed. But Japan was a firm base from which support could be given to South Korea. In fact MacArthur was able at one stage to denude Japan of troops without any real anxiety. The Japanese, for their part, did well out of the war. So-called 'special procurements' for the United Nations' forces gave a great fillip to Japan's economic revival, which had just started in a modest way, thanks to a programme of wage and price stability introduced at the beginning of 1949 in response to pressure from SCAP. By 1950 the shattered cities were almost, if not quite completely, rebuilt in a rough-and-ready sort of way. Once the Korean War was in its stride Japanese factories and workshops were busy manufacturing the multitudinous variety of supplies required by the fighting services in Korea. As the war continued for some three years, the boom was very considerable. By the end of 1951 Japanese industrial production was roughly equal to what it had been twenty years previously.

As conditions improved and national morale recovered, the Occupation, although never very frankly opposed except by the Communists, became increasingly irksome in Japanese eyes. When MacArthur was summarily dismissed by President Truman in April 1951, the Japanese received the news with genuine astonishment. Their first thought was that this might in some way adversely affect the discussions already begun between the Yoshida cabinet and the President's special adviser John Foster Dulles, on a treaty of peace. This anxiety was mingled with the real sadness felt by the Japanese when they bowed farewell to the remarkable egotist who had governed them with some success for the past five and a half years. But the President lost little time in issuing a statement saying that Dulles would shortly revisit Japan for further talks.

Indeed the preparation of the Japanese Peace Treaty – signed on 8 September 1951 at San Francisco – was very largely in the hands of the indefatigable Dulles, who made several visits to Japan and who also contrived to win the agreement of Great Britain, Australia, and other countries to the kind of settlement he envisaged, namely one that would be free of punitive and restrictive features of any kind. The position of the United States in these preparatory talks with individual governments was of course a very strong one, not only because of the obvious wealth and power at the disposal of Washington, but also because American policy on the Japanese peace settlement was bi-partisan, since Dulles, a Republican, was representing a Democratic administration. All the same the reservations and objections offered by various friendly governments, to say nothing of the hostility he encountered from the Communist bloc, made Dulles's task no light one. His eventual success in obtaining the kind of treaty that he desired was all the more striking. It was perhaps his single unqualified triumph in the field of diplomacy. Great Britain wanted to see some economic restrictions included in the treaty and suggested, furthermore, that the Peking regime, recognized by London as the legitimate government of China, should be brought into the negotiations. Dulles managed to talk the British government out of its desire for the inclusion of economic restructions. As for China, it was agreed that Japan should be left to decide, after the treaty, whether she would deal with Peking or the Formosa regime. Dulles encountered a good deal of opposition in Canberra, and the government there only fell in with his proposals after the United States consented to sign a security treaty – the Anzus Pact – with Australia and New Zealand Moreover, the Philippines, with their painful memories of

Japanese aggression, demanded a defence agreement – the Philippine–United States Mutual Security Pact – as the price of their consent to Dulles's draft. The Soviet Union made many objections and declared that Communist China should be fully consulted by the American government.

In the end, having obtained the agreement of the great majority of the governments concerned, the United States felt ready to summon what was only in name a peace conference. It was, rather, a formal gathering to endorse what had already been decided. The invitation to San Francisco was issued jointly by the United States and Great Britain to Japan and to the nations that had fought against her; but neither Communist nor Nationalist China was invited.*

Prime Minister Yoshida, as chief delegate, signed the Treaty of Peace for Japan. Forty-eight other nations signed the document. The Soviet delegate, Gromyko, made a strongly worded speech attacking the Treaty. As was expected, his country, together with Poland and Czechoslovakia, refused to sign it.

By the terms of the San Francisco Treaty Japan recognized the independence of Korea and renounced all claims to Formosa and the Pescadores, to south Sakhalin and the Kuriles, and to the former mandated islands in the Pacific. American control for the time being of the Ryukyu and Bonin Islands was accepted. Such was the formal liquidation of an empire gained and lost in the course of eighty years. The Treaty placed no limitations on Japanese economy and trade; and Japan's right to self-defence, in accordance with the principles of the United Nations' Charter, was recognized.

On the same day that the San Francisco Treaty was signed – 8 September 1951 – the United States concluded with Japan a security pact in which Japan requested the retention of American forces in and about her territory as a defence

* India, Burma, and Yugoslavia declined to attend the conference. Later, settlements were made separately between Japan and these countries. As for China, Japan came to an agreement with the Nationalist regime on Formosa, signing a separate treaty with the Nationalists in April 1952.

against attack from overseas. In the pact the United States expressed the belief that Japan would 'increasingly assume responsibility for its own defence . . . always avoiding any armament which would be an offensive threat'.

The Treaty came into force on 28 April 1952; and on that date, the eve of the emperor's birthday, the Occupation officially ceased and Japan was once again formally an independent nation.

Chapter 11

THE NEW JAPAN

[1]

No sooner had the citizens of Tokyo celebrated the official appearance of Peace and Independence than they were shocked or excited, according to their political sympathies' by what occurred a day or two later on the Imperial Palace plaza. For on May Day 1952 savage fighting broke out between the police and a section of those taking part in the annual left-wing demonstration. Both sides suffered casualties; and, in addition to battling with the police, rioters set fire to American cars parked by the palace moat.

The disturbance was provoked by the Communists as part of the tactics of violence that they happened to favour at that period. The rioters were mostly students. The great majority of Japanese deplored this outburst; and indeed it did no good to the Communist cause. All the same the Japanese Left was able to win a good deal of sympathy with its complaint that, despite the Peace Treaty, the country, to all intents and purposes, was still occupied. For American troops – not to mention those from other United Nations on leave from Korea – were still seemingly ubiquitous. A great deal of property in Tokyo and other cities was still in American hands; and in most districts of Japan there appeared to be air bases and military training areas. So long as the Occupation lasted, all this had been accepted, however grudgingly. But people had expected, if only subconsciously, that with the coming into force of the Treaty the appearance of Japan would change, somehow, almost overnight.

So there developed a niggling agitation over what was soon called the 'Bases Problem'. It was not long before every serious periodical and magazine in the country seemed to be carrying some sensational story about the demoralizing influence of the American bases. During the Occupation there had been a ban on news reports of bad behaviour by American and Commonwealth servicemen. But now, in 1952, the press did not fail to give full publicity to any account of a misdemeanour by a foreign soldier; and in books and magazines many highly coloured tales, hitherto unrelated, came to light. Month after month articles pointed out that alien bases were monopolizing far too much of the already limited farming land. According to most writers the number of American bases ran into hundreds; which was doubtless true, since the list of bases usually included such installations as petrol points and P.X. depots. Several films were made, notably in 1953, presenting the bases as centres of immorality and materialism, corrupting those, particularly children and young people, who lived in their neighbourhood. A good deal of this agitation was inspired and stirred up, of course, by the Communists. But to a large extent it was also an inevitable national psychological reaction to what was, thanks to the continuance of the Korean War, virtually a prolongation, in a mild but irritating form, of the Occupation.

Anti-American feeling reached its zenith in the spring of 1954. This was due to an accident arising out of the American hydrogen bomb test in the Bikini area at the beginning of March. In the middle of that month, just a week after the signature of a Mutual Security Aid agreement between the United States and Japan, a fishing vessel came in from the Pacific to a small port some thirty miles from Tokyo. The captain reported that he and the twenty-two members of the crew were suffering ill effects from a shower of ashes, the fall-out from the Bikini explosion. They were found to be suffering from serious radiation sickness, and their catch — such of it as had not already been sold and distributed — was condemned, after inspection, as being dangerously radioactive. The popular reaction was one of momentary panic. It was known that some of the affected fish had been sent to places as distant as Niigata and Kagoshima; and as the fish was tuna, which is cut up and sold in very small portions, many inhabitants of those cities wondered whether they would long survive. People feared that all the fish in the Pacific, through some process of chain reaction, would become radioactive and unfit to eat. From one end of the country to the other fishmongers reported a drastic slump in sales; and the Japanese are perhaps the greatest fish-eaters of any race in the world. The scare was universal and genuinely felt. The first sense of panic was followed by a wave of anger. This might have been averted, to some extent, had the American Ambassador taken the kind of independent, imaginative action that would have been almost second nature to his distinguished predecessor, Mr Grew. What was called for was a personal visit, with gifts and flowers, to the afflicted seamen in hospital. A gesture of this kind would have spared the Americans a great deal of ill-will. But although the Embassy issued a message of concern and sympathy, the American authorities both in Tokyo and Washington were obviously waiting for a full report of the affair, and for accurate information as to the fishing boat's exact position when the accident occurred, before admitting, even by implication, the slightest responsibility for the accident. For example, the Secretary of State, Dulles, declined to make any comment until all the facts were known. Perhaps this was not unreasonable, though it did nothing to soothe Japanese sentiment. But Admiral Strauss of the Atomic Energy Commission was reported as saying that the fishing boat might have been within the advertised danger area in the Bikini region for purposes of espionage. This comment, whether or not correctly reported, created general indignation in Japan. In the end it became known that the fall-out from the Bikini bomb had been on a scale and in a direction not expected by the scientists who had planned the operation; and it was admitted that the fishing boat had been outside the danger zone.

The 'Bikini Incident' deserves to be recorded in some detail here; for it has never been appreciated in the West that this affair caused resentment in Japan at least equal to that occasioned by the atomic attacks on Hiroshima and Nagasaki. These after all, so the Japanese argued, occurred towards the end of a life and death struggle; but the 'Bikini Incident' took place in time of peace, and the nation responsible claimed to be Japan's principal friend and ally. Needless to say maladroit American handling of this matter was a gift to Communist propaganda.

However, despite the storm from the Left, fanned by anti-American agitation, by opposition to rearmament, and by popular disgust at various bribery scandals in which Conservative politicians among others were alleged to have been involved, Yoshida and his successors – Hatoyama, Ishibashi, and Kishi – maintained the political supremacy of the Conservatives, although the Socialists gradually improved their position in the Diet. In 1955 the latter, who for some years had been split into two groups, of the Right and Left, reunited as a single party. This merger in its turn produced another. Anxious on the score of revived Socialist unity the two main Conservative parties came together in a coalition known as the *Jiyu-Minshuto*, or Liberal Democrats. Conservative predominance, not greatly affected by Opposition fulminations on the so-called 'Reverse Course',* was supported on the two foundations of the countryside and the business world, including not only 'Big Business' but also the medium and small manufacturers and distributors to be found all over Japan. MacArthur's land reform, having lifted the burdens of debt and rent from thousands of peasant families, made the farming population as a whole deeply Conservative, and thus peculiarly sensitive to warnings that a Socialist state might well mean the nationalization of property. As for the business world, Japan's continued economic recovery, despite the minor slump that followed the Korean Armistice in 1953 and the mild recession of 1958, provided few inducements for the majority of manufacturers and shopkeepers to transfer their support from the Conservatives to the Socialists.

* A phrase much in vogue to describe any manifestation of an alleged reactionary nature.

It was always a Socialist belief that, slowly but very surely, the Conservatives would put the clock back; and to some extent the belief has been justified by such potents as rearmament. But by the end of the 1950s, at least, Japan was still a remarkably free society, despite various abuses for which some employers of labour and, on occasions, the police were responsible. It is true that in country districts the force of custom died hard. Traditional social pressures often created unpleasant difficulties for the non-conforming individual. But nowhere was the concept of 'human rights' entirely unknown; and when it was brazenly defied, there was more than a fair chance that the matter would be exposed, sooner or later, in the press. The 'Reverse Course' proceeded, then, at an almost imperceptible pace. In the eyes of some acute critics this very fact constituted a danger. One of these critics, Professor Maruyama of Tokyo University, pointed out that the trend towards reaction was indeed a very slow process and that therefore the Japanese 'must be very careful not to become accustomed to it'. These are wise words. But an indication that the Japanese may remain jealous of their liberties was provided by the successful popular opposition to a government proposal, late in 1958, to strengthen the powers of the police. In the past the Japanese undoubtedly lacked political maturity; and to this day purely social, personal, and, indeed, monetary considerations can dictate the voting habits of large masses of the population, especially in the countryside. At the same time the Japanese are becoming more sophisticated, politically, with each year that goes by. They have long been literate and have long been interested in matters of public moment, at home and abroad; but until very recently they have tended to accept the views and interpretations presented to them by local officials and men of standing in the community. There are many signs, however, that younger people are beginning to think for themselves. This surely is one result of the reforms in education introduced during the Occupation. These reforms had many defects. Much good was destroyed with the bad when the old educational structure was pulled down. But the new emphasis

on the importance of the individual produced a certain
independence of mind, a critical and wary alertness towards
all problems, that will be reflected in politics, as in other
fields, increasingly with the rising proportion of voters who
have passed through the post-war schools.*

Quite clearly the continuance of Japanese parliamentary
democracy, and of freedom generally in Japan, depends very
largely on economic factors. Extremism, whether of the Right
or of the Left, battens on slumps and unemployment. The
basic problem is how to feed and clothe a population of some
ninety million on four fairly small mountainous islands.
Thanks to natural increase and to the repatriation of Japanese from abroad the population has risen since 1940 by
more than twenty-five per cent; and during the decade
1946–56 the natural increase amounted to a million or more
each year. By 1956, it is true, the birth-rate was beginning to
decline; and the natural increase in 1957 was rather under
one million. It is estimated that Japan will have a declining
population before the end of this century. Nevertheless it has
been predicted that before 1970 the population will exceed
one hundred million.

It is a tribute to Japanese energy and skill that the difficulties suggested by these population figures have been sur-
mounted with fair success. For example, by 1953 personal
incomes in terms of purchasing power had been restored to
the pre-war level. The standard of living has continued to
rise. But to keep pace with the growth of population until,
let us say, 1970 (after which date a decline may set in) the
rising trend in living standards must be maintained. Here the

* The growth of reading habits – and the Japanese have always been
great readers – provides one example of this trend. Before the Pacific
War new books were usually published in editions of between five hundred and a thousand copies. A book that sold ten thousand copies was
regarded as a best-seller.

In the 1950s, however, a first edition ran to at least three thousand
copies, and a best-seller was one that sold over a hundred thousand. For
example, the translation of *The Diary of Anne Frank* sold over one hundred
and thirty thousand copies in 1953 alone; and this book occupied third
place in the list of best-sellers for that year.

answer must be found in increased exports, based on a sound domestic market. Both Great Britain and the United States have shown signs of discriminating against Japanese products, and although manufacturers in these countries have reason to be fearful of Japanese competition, the two governments concerned must reflect on the probable consequences politically, to a Japan once again shut out of various important markets of the world. The revived Japan – a new nation very different from the authoritarian state that existed up to 1945 – can only prosper if exports rise. Towards the close of the century they may level off with safety. It is the next fifteen or twenty years that will count.

There is of course one country close to Japan that could provide an admirable market for her products as well as a source of much needed raw materials. This is the People's Republic of China. In the decade before the Pacific War about a quarter of Japan's total trade was with the Chinese mainland. The loss of this trade after the war was serious indeed; and on the desirability of its renewal many Japanese Conservatives, with their business interests in mind, are in full agreement with the Socialists, who for their part have been influenced by more purely ideological considerations. Certainly nothing seems more natural and, taking a long view, inevitable than a thriving commerce between such near neighbours as China and Japan. But the issue is bedevilled by politics. Early in 1953, as a result of a strictly unofficial agreement concluded in the previous year, trade between Japan and Communist China opened on a very modest scale. It was somewhat enlarged by two later unofficial agreements. In 1957 it still amounted to no more than about two per cent of all Japan's overseas trade. In the spring of 1958 a fourth agreement was negotiated between a Peking government committee and a private but influential Japanese organization for promoting trade with China. Had this agreement come into force Japan's trade with the Chinese mainland in 1958 would have been nearly double what it was the year before. However, this time the Chinese insisted that the Japanese government should give some official endorsement of the agreement. Furthermore they stipulated that the Chinese trade mission to be sent to Japan under the terms of the understanding should be allowed to display the flag of the People's Republic.

The Japanese government – a Liberal-Democrat cabinet under Kishi Nobusuke – was eager to expand the China trade, but not at the cost of good relations with the Nationalist regime on Formosa, recognized by Japan as the legitimate government of China. Japan had several good reasons for wanting to remain on close terms with Formosa. Obviously an offence given to the Chinese Nationalist government would have some adverse effect on Japanese relations with the United States, and this could not be envisaged with any comfort. Secondly, Japanese trade with Formosa was fairly brisk. A third factor was Formosan sentiment towards Japan. Among Chinese of Formosan stock there is less resentment against Japan than in any other country – with the possible exception of Siam – once ruled or occupied by the Japanese. It is probably not going too far to suggest that, if given the choice, the Chinese of Formosan descent might prefer, as a second best alternative to independence, some restoration of Japanese control to government either by the Kuomintang or by the People's Republic in Peking.

The Japanese government, therefore, made it clear to Peking that endorsement of the latest trade agreement implied no change in the policy of non-recognition of the People's Republic. This statement, together with an incident at Nagasaki involving some interference with a Communist Chinese flag, led Peking to break off trade negotiations, to cancel all outstanding contracts, and in fact to sever all relations, cultural as well as commercial, with Japan. The Japanese estimated that this action cost them about one hundred and ten million pounds' worth of trade, just at a time when European nations were redoubling their efforts to capture markets in China.

This blow was delivered in May 1958, shortly before a general election. The Peking government, aware of the romantic prestige it enjoyed in the eyes of the Japanese Left, may have calculated that its action would strengthen the hands of the Japanese Socialist Party. But in fact the Conservatives – Kishi's Liberal-Democrats – probably derived some benefit from what looked like a Chinese attempt to intervene, however indirectly, in Japanese home affairs. Everyone predicted that the Socialist Party would increase its strength by about twenty seats. The Communist Party put up over a hundred candidates and seemed confident that it would at least double its representation – two members – in the Lower House. In the event the Socialists were able to win only eight more seats, while the Communists lost one of their two. Thus Kishi could form his second cabinet with a majority only very slightly reduced.

It is not easy to assess Japanese attitudes to China. Although perhaps a majority of the intelligentsia and at least a high proportion of all young people cherish a very idealized picture of the People's Republic, interpreting the Revolution and all that has followed simply as a movement to liberate the masses, it is probably fair to say that most Japanese regard the Chinese with a certain sense of superiority. They feel that the Chinese have a long way to go before they catch up industrially with Japan. Such self-confidence, though more respectable than excessive admiration or hysterical fear, is dangerous to the extent that it is based on recollections of past superiority, in war and peace, over the Chinese. Even today there are too many Japanese who do not take China very seriously. And yet from a vantage point two centuries hence Far Eastern history may be seen broadly as a tale of Chinese supremacy, interrupted for a mere hundred years or so; and in this perspective the rise of Japan will be no more than a relatively minor, though interesting, episode.

In its Chinese robes Communism has some appeal for a significant minority of the Japanese. The Russian version attracts fewer followers. Most people in Japan know that the Russians, in addition to extending their territorial waters from three to twelve miles, have for years placed severe restrictions on Japanese fishing in the seas to the north of Hokkaido. Moreover, the Russians are in possession of all the

Kurile Islands, including two islands once administratively
part of Hokkaido, and they have also annexed south Sakhalin, from which the Japanese residents were expelled under
most barbarous conditions. Much resentment, too, was
caused by Russian delay in repatriating prisoners-of-war. As
late as March 1957, Japan claimed that there were still some
eleven thousand prisoners held in the Soviet Union. The
Soviet Union, then, is an object of fear and dislike to all but
the numerically small Japanese Communist Party and some
of its fellow travellers. All the same the Japanese are less than
eager to take an aggressively determined anti-Soviet stand
in the Cold War. The Russian colossus has been something
of a menace to them for more than a century. But until the
improbable day when the Japanese are strong enough, as in
1904, to take some effective action, they consider that they
must try to keep on fairly reasonable terms with their powerful neighbour. And in October 1956, after many months of
negotiations, Japan came to an agreement with the Soviet
Union providing for the resumption of diplomatic relations
between the two countries.

Of course as long as the American alliance is operative,
whereby air and sea forces of the United States are stationed
in or off Japan, there is always the risk that the Japanese will
be involved, despite themselves, in a future Soviet-American
war. By 1958 American ground troops had left Japan. But
even when Japan recovers the sole use of airfields and naval
ports in his own country there will remain the question of
Okinawa.

Over this island of the Ryukyus Japan is said to have
'residual sovereignty'; but for practical purposes it is ruled
by the Americans, who have developed it into one of their
principal bases overseas. As time goes by Japanese agitation
for the return of the Ryukyus can be expected to become
increasingly vocal. Yet so long as the Cold War continues the
prospect of American withdrawal from the area seems very
remote indeed.

Amour propre received a fillip with Japan's admission (as the
eightieth member) to the United Nations in December 1956.

Nevertheless, by the end of the 1950s Japan, diplomatically as well as commercially, was not yet master of her own destiny. She was compelled to walk a slippery path, trying to offend neither the United States, her necessary if sometimes embarrassing friend and ally, nor the Soviet Union, a rough suitor whom she feared but dared not too blatantly repel.

As for Great Britain and the Commonwealth, relations seemed set fair, in spite of unfavourable reactions to British hydrogen bomb tests at Christmas Island, which disturbed both the government and people of Japan, and in spite of British reluctance to grant Japan the full benefits of belonging to the General Agreement on Trade and Tariffs. The Americans forgot the bitterness of the Pacific War rather more readily than their allies in Great Britain and Australia – possibly because so many Americans came to like Japan when they were stationed there during and after the Occupation years. Indeed American sentiment towards Japan performed a somersault. With China 'lost' to them, the Americans may have felt some urgent emotional need for a new protégé in the Far East, and the regenerated Japan filled the bill. Certainly by the time of the San Francisco Treaty most Americans were decidedly pro-Japanese. The British and, more so, the Australians could not change their feelings so quickly. The change of heart, when it showed signs of coming, owed much to the character and personality of the first post-war Japanese Ambassador to Australia, Nishi Haruhiko. In Great Britain a visit in 1953 by Crown Prince Akihito (to attend the Coronation) symbolized the beginning of a new relationship.

In Malaya, India, Pakistan, and Ceylon Japanese enterprise was demonstrated by those who came to buy, sell, and build. In a few years old fears and hatreds were half forgotten, like the rusting tanks abandoned in the Chindwin jungle at Shwegyin.

[II]

We are almost back where we began, with the Saito family in their Tokyo home. Mr Saito might agree with the learned professor who wrote:

Symptoms of decadence are insistent in the social conditions of Japan today – the epidemic of old Japanese warrior tunes, like flowers blooming in full out of season; strip-shows; 'nudist' pictures; obscene magazines; lotteries; the horse-racing boom; *pachinko* (pinball) halls, of which there are more than twenty thousand in Tokyo alone; new religions, with over five million adherents; bribery scandals affecting influential people in political and business life; the great increase in crime.

Symptoms of decadence? Or of vitality? Mr Saito cannot make up his mind. On the one hand, new department stores, an entirely new underground railway, shops stocked to overflowing with Western and Japanese clothes, food, books, furniture, household goods, radio and television sets, gadgets of every kind: on the other, 'the great increase in crime'. His next-door neighbour, walking home one night along a side street through the amusement district of Ikebukuro, was set upon by five youths, robbed, and beaten unconscious. Similar cases were reported in the newspapers nearly every day. The criminal youths, the so-called *gurentai*, seemed to dominate certain quarters of the city after dark; murder as well as theft marked their trail. Saito has heard that this is a world-wide phenomenon, that even the clothes and haircut affected by the *gurentai* have their counterpart in London. But this does little to allay his disquiet.

He was taken one evening by a business friend to what is known as a 'military cabaret'. At the entrance stood a man dressed as a soldier of the former imperial army; but he was clearly far too young to have taken part in the war, and his broad childish grin was very different from the stern expression that, in Saito's experience, sentries always assumed when on duty. Inside, a noisy band played rock-an'-roll versions of the old marching songs. Saito and his friend were invited to a table by two hostesses, and their drinks were brought to them by a young man clothed as a Second Class Private of the imperial army. He saluted facetiously, clicking his heels. After a while there was a strip-tease show; and as Saito watched this against a background, dimly perceived through tobacco smoke, of regimental flags on the walls and khaki-clad waiters, he was, somewhat to his own surprise, less shocked than amused. This is the proper way, he thought to himself, to purge one's memories. Make a laughing stock of the old army. Think how ridiculous it all was.

But later, on his way to a nearby station to catch the electric train home, he encountered a spectre, a thin man in dark glasses wearing a dirty white kimono – the regulation hospital garb of the war wounded. On his head was a faded khaki cap (as worn by the waiters in the cabaret). Suspended from his neck was a collecting box. With his hands he supported his body on two walking sticks. He had no legs. The stumps rested on light metal frames.

After all, Saito asked himself, am I, like this man, chained to the past? Surely I have kept up with the times. Not long after the war (his thoughts ran) I started to walk openly in the street side by side with my wife: the general custom to-day – indeed many young married couples walk arm-in-arm – but unthinkable before the war. At election time I never try to tell my wife how she should vote. Quite often nowadays she invites her own friends into the house. She has even begun to send off a few New Year cards in her own name. Nobody can call me an old-fashioned husband.

Nevertheless he had been shocked when he heard the news of the crown prince's engagement to a commoner. In the known history of the imperial house such a thing had never been heard of. Miss Shoda was undoubtedly a person of the highest character and intelligence. Her family, of impeccable repute, belonged to the upper middle class. They had been in business for generations. You had to go back a long way to find an ancestor who was a *samurai*, let alone a member of the aristocracy. Mr Saito's mother was more astonished than he was. But his wife, like nearly everybody (or so it seemed), was delighted with the match. 'This kind of thing should have happened long ago,' she told her husband. 'Fancy crown princes having to marry into only a restricted circle of Kyoto court nobility! No wonder Emperor Taisho was a bit weak in the head.' His elder son, obsessed with Marxism, seemed indifferent to the whole affair. His daughter, on the other hand, was most excited and she was one of a large animated crowd that stood outside the Shoda house in Gotanda in the hope of seeing the future empress. Mr Saito regretted that he could not feel entirely happy about the 'tennis court romance' that delighted young Japan. The last shreds of mystery, he reflected, are now torn away from our ancient Throne. The wife of an emperor will be one of us.

He was not very surprised, early in the New Year of 1959, to read that people were saying that the Imperial Palace constituted a tiresome obstacle to the swarming motor traffic of Tokyo, that its huge grounds should be turned into a public park, with broad highways criss-crossing it from every direction, for no longer could the flow of free citizens in their cars be dammed up by this survival from the Tokugawa days.

Perhaps, for Mr Saito, the most striking material symbol of the new age was the Tokyo Tower, the television pylon higher than the Eiffel Tower which, at first glance, it much resembled. Dressed overall with lights of green, gold, and vermilion it presented at night something of the appearance of a monstrous illuminated rocket about to take off for a journey to Mars.

Of greater significance, however, was another material symbol – the Japan Atomic Research Institute at Tokaimura, Ibaragi Prefecture. Here in the early morning of 27 August 1957, the first 'atomic fire' was kindled. Not quite ninety years had passed since the last of the *shogun* formally surrendered his powers to the emperor.

Such achievements were gratifying to Mr Saito, but like most of his contemporaries he was still dissatisfied with the social confusion, the rampant egotism, that had taken the place of the corporate spirit of the past. Yet a certain optimism was beginning to temper his unrest. For Japan the worst appeared to be over. Surely the future would hold in store nothing more dire and intolerable than what had been already endured and, in the end, overcome.

In 1959 Mr Saito's quiet optimism seemed, on the whole,

to be justified. The economy flourished, achieving a rate of growth higher than that of any other country in the world, and for the fifth successive year there was a bumper harvest of rice.

Yet the year was not without its portents and calamities. Early in the spring the secretary-general of the Socialist Party, Asanuma Inejiro, led a goodwill mission to the Chinese People's Republic, and while he was in Peking he made a speech in which he declared that the United States was 'the common enemy' of Japan and of the People's Republic. This extreme attitude was to lead later in the year to a split in his party – the right wing breaking away to form the 'Democratic Socialist Party' – and his injudicious speech was to be the pretext for a horrifying event, some eighteen months later, of which he would be the victim.

When the Crown Prince and Miss Shoda were wed, this bright occasion was marred for a moment by a young hooligan who tried to assault the newly married couple as they drove in an open carriage through cheering crowds in Aoyama, Tokyo.

In 1959, too, there was a more than usually cataclysmic typhoon which wrecked and flooded the Nagoya area; and in a few hours more than five thousand people lost their lives.

The following year, 1960, was remarkable for a political eruption in the capital. For many months the Japanese and American Governments had been negotiating the revision of the Security Pact that bound the two countries in a kind of military alliance. The Pact, concluded at the time of the Treaty of Peace, was in many respects unsatisfactory to the Japanese. For example, no term was set to its validity. There was nothing in the Pact to prevent American forces in Japan being equipped with nuclear weapons – a point on which the Japanese felt peculiarly sensitive. Furthermore, the Pact included a clause saying that in the event of grave internal disorder American forces in Japan could take action if asked to do so by the Japanese Government.

Any revision, then, appeared likely to be of benefit, and therefore a matter of gratification, to the Japanese. However, when it was announced in January 1960 that agreement had been reached on a new Security Pact, the news was greeted with scant enthusiasm. In fact there was much hostile comment, not only from the Socialists but also from some Government supporters. The new Pact was to remain in force for ten years. Critics said that this was too long. It was claimed, moreover, that despite the removal of the objectionable clauses in the old Pact the new agreement made no valid provision for limitation of the use of American forces, based on Japanese harbours and airfields, in any fighting that might break out in other parts of Asia.

Lurking behind these various objections was the fear that the presence of American air and sea bases would attract rockets from Russia. This fear was suddenly reinforced in the spring of 1960 by the U-2 affair, followed by the cancellation of the Paris 'Summit' conference.

The new Pact was signed in Washington but it still had to be ratified by the Diet. Mr Kishi and his cabinet felt that it must be ratified before the middle of June, when President Eisenhower was due to pay an official visit to Japan. This state visit had been planned to take place after the President's tour of the Soviet Union. The President would call at Japan on his way home across the Pacific from Russia. But the new Pact was not yet ratified when the U-2 Incident occurred, followed by a sharp tightening of East-West tension. The Socialists accordingly demanded that the Eisenhower visit be postponed until August. But the Government decided to make no change in its preparations to welcome the President in June.

Meanwhile, inside the Diet and outside, there had grown up a good deal of vociferous opposition against the revised Security Pact and against Premier Kishi personally. The critical occasion for the Pact in the Diet was the night of 19-20 May 1960. Kishi's opponents resorted to sitting on the floor of the Diet corridors, thus blocking the entrance into the House of Representatives, so that a formal session could not be held. The Government retaliated by calling in several hundred police, who removed the human barriers by physical force. Thereupon the Speaker of the House, together with a large number of Liberal-Democratic members, rushed into the chamber. In a matter of ten minutes or so this truncated assembly ratified the Pact – the Opposition parties and some members of the Liberal-Democratic Party being absent from the scene.

This unedifying affair scandalized public opinion, which on this occasion, at least, took a more lenient view of the obstructive tactics of the Socialists than of the undignified manoeuvres resorted to by the Government. The parliamentary crisis of 19 May convulsed Japan.

But what attracted the attention of the outside world was not the brawling within the Japanese Diet on 19 May but the scale and frequency of the mass demonstrations that succeeded that event. Television and news films from Japan showed scenes of tumult – students fighting with police in the heat and dust of the Tokyo streets. (Mr Saito's son, Mamoru, became involved in an ugly scuffle with the police outside Mr Kishi's house and was lucky to escape arrest.) The most active members of the almost daily rallies always seemed to belong to the huge student population of the city. Yet those taking part in processions and demonstrations also comprised many thousands of trade unionists and ordinary citizens, including many professional people. In some cases, too, the demonstrators were deliberately provoked to violence by attacks from right-wing hoodlums.

However, students had played a leading part in the stormy events in Seoul preceding the overthrow of President Synghman Rhee; so it was perhaps only natural for observers outside Japan to wonder whether a revolutionary situation was beginning to build up in Tokyo. The American President was due to arrive in the last week of June. Would he be greeted with the kind of reception that embarrassed his press secretary, Mr Hagerty, who on 10 June was trapped, together with the United States Ambassador, in a car by a mob at Tokyo Airport?

On the evening of 15 June there was a serious and prolonged struggle between demonstrators and police (and between demonstrators and right-wing myrmidons) at the gates of the Diet Building, the site of many such noisy encounters. On this occasion a girl student of Tokyo University met her death in the general mêlée – the only fatal casualty of those disturbed summer days.

At this juncture the Government decided to ask President Eisenhower to put off his visit to Japan. This was less than a week before he was due to arrive.

Demonstrations continued; but on 21 June the Emperor's seal was placed on the documents ratifying the new Pact. Two days later Kishi announced his intention to resign. He did so three weeks later, being succeeded by Ikeda Hayato who belonged to the same political party. Kishi's opponents hailed his resignation as a victory for the popular will. Nevertheless, the new Pact had been ratified, and the Socialists were little nearer to achieving power. For in the subsequent General Election, in the autumn of 1960, the conservatives – the Liberal-Democratic Party – once again obtained a substantial majority.

A balanced view of the May and June disturbances will show that they did not amount to anything approaching an insurrection. Such rioting as there was – as distinct from processions and demonstrations – took place in the immediate neighbourhood of the Diet or outside the Prime Minister's house. A truly revolutionary movement would have concentrated attention on such targets as Police Headquarters (close to the Diet) or government offices. In the summer of 1960 there was no violence at all comparable with what happened during the Rice Riots of 1918 or during political disturbances in Tokyo earlier in the century. The demonstrations of 1960 were by no means the product of some skilfully organized Communist plot. Nothing irritated the Japanese more than the facile assumption, in the United States and elsewhere, that only Communists had been involved in the mass protests against the revised Pact and against the Kishi Government.

Playing a minor but sinister rôle at this season were the small groups of the extreme Right. They not only carried out attacks on processions of demonstrators, but also engineered physical assaults on a leading Socialist politician and on the Premier himself. But their most serious intervention occurred in October 1960. Asanuma Inejiro, the secretary-general of the Socialist Party, was stabbed to death at a public meeting by a young right-wing fanatic in full view of a large audience and a battery of television cameras. The assassin, who later killed himself in a police cell, declared that he had been disgusted by Asanuma's speech in Peking during the previous year.

By comparison with 1960, the next two years were peaceful indeed. Tactfully, the new Prime Minister, Ikeda, adopted what was known as 'a low posture'. In other words he tried to placate his opponents by eschewing any hint of aggressive or arrogant leadership. He wooed the public by declaring that it was the aim of his government to double personal incomes, in terms of real purchasing power, within ten years. It was generally held that this aim could be achieved.

Our Mr Saito was certainly of this opinion, despite intimations of a recession in 1962. The very fact that Tokyo in the sixties became the largest city in the world seemed to boost his confidence. He was much encouraged, too, by the news that the monster metropolis was to be the setting for the 1964 Olympic Games.

An influential figure in the background at this period was that of Yoshida Shigeru. This remarkable veteran, eighty-four years of age in 1962, lived in retirement at Oiso, on the coast some distance from the capital. But what politicians and journalists called 'remote control from Oiso' was a factor of importance in the shaping of Japanese state affairs. For many members of the Liberal-Democratic Party respected Yoshida's judgement and experience and were linked with him by ties of obligation. Nevertheless, the old man somewhat embarrassed the cabinet by his statement, at a gathering of the America–Japan Society in July 1962, that Japan 'as a member of the Free World should be prepared to arm itself with nuclear weapons if it is to tighten its partnership with the United States'. It was fitting that he should have represented his country at the obsequies of General MacArthur in Washington in the spring of 1964. A little more than three years later, in October 1967, Yoshida died at his Oiso home in his ninetieth year. He was given a state funeral, the first in Japan since the end of the Pacific War.

Whether or not this was thanks to advice from Oiso, the Ikeda Government made some progress in the field of foreign affairs. Trade relations with Communist China were resumed; and in November 1962 a treaty of commerce and navigation was signed with Great Britain. Ikeda, who was in London for the occasion, declared that by this agreement Japan had 'attained a stature equal to the first-rate powers of the world'.

As if to illustrate the truth of this remark, Lord Home flew to Tokyo in March 1963, becoming the first British Foreign Secretary to visit Japan. And Mr Saito was amused but also pleased to read in one newspaper that this visit symbolized, eleven years after the coming into force of the Peace Treaty, 'the second grant of independence to Japan'.

But real satisfaction, true self-assurance, came at last on 10 October 1964, a day without a cloud in the blue autumn sky, when the Emperor proclaimed the opening of the 18th Olympiad, the first to be held in Asia, in the presence of athletes from ninety-four nations. This was one occasion on which every Japanese – even Mr Saito's son – could feel proud and happy. Yet six days later, just as the Games were well into their stride, a chill wind blew across the Yellow Sea when China tested its first atomic bomb.

More tests were to follow, in 1966, the year of the Great Cultural Revolution. These developments put a strain on Japanese goodwill towards Communist China. And the issue was complicated by the increasing scale and severity of the war in Vietnam. For although the Japanese looked askance at China because of the nuclear tests and the excesses of the Cultural Revolution, they could scarcely bring themselves to admit that American 'hawks' might be right in their diagnosis of mainland China as a potential threat to Japan's own security. The nightmare haunting the Japanese was the possibility of war in Vietnam leading to direct conflict between the United States and China. On the other hand, most Japanese realized that it was very difficult for their government to dissociate itself from American policy in South-east Asia.

Certainly any serious rift with the United States seemed out of the question so long as the ruling Liberal Democratic Party continued to win elections. And in the general elections of November 1963 and January 1967 the party retained a comfortable lead over its opponents. Between these elections Premier Ikeda resigned, in November 1964 due to ill-health. He was succeeded by Sato Eisaku, Mr Kishi's younger brother, and it was he who led the conservatives to victory in the 1967 election.

The fact is that with rising affluence the people of Japan were not inclined to eject from power those who had handled the nation's economic affairs with considerable ability. A few examples will suffice to illustrate not only Japan's 'economic miracle' but also the prestige that this gave the country in the eyes of the world.

In 1964 Japan became the third greatest producer of steel, surpassed only by the United States and the Soviet Union. The very big lead in the tonnage of ships built was maintained in 1967 for the twelfth successive year. Japan also led the world in the *speed* with which ship-building was carried out. A monster oil tanker, for example, could have its keel laid down in February, and the vessel could be off on its maiden voyage in December of the same year. In Olympic Year, 1964, an entirely new railway line was constructed between Tokyo and Osaka; and over the distance of 320 miles specially built trains completed the journey in three hours and ten minutes. At world-record speeds of well above 100 m.p.h. fifty round trips are made every day on the new line, which is being extended westward through Hiroshima to the Shimonoseki Straits.

For the Saito family an excitement comparable with the Olympiad was the 1970 World Exhibition at Osaka. The prospect of Expo 70, as well as agreement with America on Okinawa (to revert to Japanese rule in 1972), may have helped Premier Sato to win the election held at the end of 1969. Moreover, Expo 70 may have diverted popular attention when the Security Pact with the United States was renewed automatically in the summer of 1970, at the end of its revised ten-year term. Public agitation against the Pact was less serious than had been anticipated; which was gratifying to conservative opinion in view of the serious student unrest that had been disrupting higher education during the previous two years. Indeed the year 1970 would have ended on a quiet note but for the bizarre Mishima Affair, of 25 November. That day the gifted, eccentric writer, forty-five-year-old Mishima Yukio, forced his way into the headquarters in Tokyo of the Self-Defence Force together with four stalwarts of his ultra-nationalist 'private army'. Having appealed in vain for support in overthrowing the Constitution, Mishima and one of his myrmidons committed *hara-kiri* on the premises, in traditional style.

Further shocks came in 1971. Without warning or notice of any kind to his Japanese allies President Nixon announced his intention to visit Peking. This slap in the face (as the Japanese saw it) was followed by another, when Nixon, to buttress the dollar, imposed a ten per cent surcharge on imports to the United States.

Perhaps it was some solace to the Saito family and an estimated ninety million other Japanese to be able to enjoy, after supper on 5 October 1971, the spectacle of their Emperor and Empress driving in state with the Queen of England in brilliant autumn sunshine through the streets of London; for the scene was televised 'live' in colour by satellite. A reigning emperor was travelling overseas for the first time. It seemed to mark a new milestone in Japanese history. There were indeed to be two more such symbolic events within the next five years. Gerald Ford, in Tokyo in November 1974, was the first American President to visit the country while in office; and in May 1975 Queen Elizabeth became the first reigning British sovereign to travel to Japan. Furthermore, later that same year the Emperor and Empress were welcomed by President Ford before proceeding on a coast to coast tour of the United States.

Such events, although they gave pleasure to millions and had a significance beyond the ephemeral, were of course overshadowed by other developments, political and economic, occurring in the world at large. For example, America's *rapprochement* with Communist China greatly impressed the Japanese, once they recovered from the shock of an American diplomatic revolution of which they had received no forewarning. Premier Sato, after nearly eight years continuously in office (a record for a Japanese prime minister), was replaced in July 1972 by Tanaka Kakuei, a cabinet colleague, who hastened to follow the American initiative. He visited Peking, and Japan moved to recognize the People's Republic of China. When this was accomplished it meant a formal break with the Nationalist Republic of China on Taiwan. Although there was still much sympathy with Taiwan, the Japanese as a whole felt a sense of relief at the turn of events; and this was doubtless a major reason for Tanaka's success in the general election held at the end of 1972. However, although the Liberal Democrats were again victorious, the Communist Party made impressive gains.

A shock more profound in many ways than any experienced in the previous twenty years occurred in the wake of the Arab–Israeli war of October 1973. The prospect of a cut in Middle East oil supplies and the sharp rise in oil prices had the double effect of aggravating inflation and undermining the confidence of Japanese big business, already under popular attack for the heavy water and air pollution created by headlong economic growth. As things turned out, Japan suffered less dislocation of economic well-being, as a result of the oil crisis, than most nations of the world. Furthermore, the rate of inflation was held at a lower level, after 1973, than had been expected. But for older people the realization of the country's extreme vulnerability to any threat to its energy supplies was a painful reminder of the situation in 1941, when the oil embargo had been imposed by America, Britain, and the Netherlands.

Mr Tanaka's honeymoon with the public did not endure. He was a self-made man, not the product, like his post-war predecessors, of higher school and university. In 1974 he came under strong criticism for having allegedly amassed his private fortune by irregular means; and in December 1974 he resigned. The deputy premier, Miki Takeo, was elected president of the Liberal Democratic Party and formed a new cabinet.

However, the event that year which made the strongest impression on Mr Saito, momentarily taking his mind off such anxieties as recession and rising prices, was the arrival at Haneda airport of Second Lieutenant Onoda, of the imperial army. For in the spring of 1974 this Japanese officer emerged from the jungle of Lubang Island in the Philippines after thirty years' defiant refusal to surrender. Watching this figure on the television screen, reading his statements in the press, men of Mr Saito's generation were filled with bitter-sweet memories. But younger people could only gaze at this austere ghost from the past with wonder and incomprehension.

Throughout the 1970s the Liberal Democratic Party never lost the reins of power, although there were changes in the leadership of the party. As a result of faction fighting, associated with a general election at the end of 1976 (the government party being once again victorious), Miki Takeo gave place to Fukuda Takeo. Premier Fukuda in his turn gave way in December 1978, to Ohira Masayoshi. A general election, in October 1979, provided a further victory for the Liberal Democrats; and when yet another election was held in June 1980, the government party increased its majority, contrary to the predictions of nearly all

Japanese and foreign political pundits. But shortly before polling day Premier Ohira suddenly died. Almost certainly a large 'sympathy vote' was the main cause of the Liberal Democrats' success. Japan entered the decade of the 1980s with Suzuki Zenko as Premier, heading the association of factions, the Liberal Democratic Party, which under one name or another had now held office and power for over thirty years.

Doubtless the country's reluctance to unseat its conservative leaders was associated with Japan's immensely impressive economic record. For it was during the 1970s that the nation became the world's second largest economic power, with the possibility of moving into the first place becoming recognized in many quarters. A single example may serve to illustrate the point. At the end of 1980 Japanese annual steel production was outstripping that of the United States by a figure in the region of one million tons.

Although Japan's export drive increasingly disturbed both the United States and the E.E.C., such friction, for all the uneasiness it caused, did not affect in any drastic way the relations between Japan and America, or between Japan and the countries of Western Europe. As for Japan's growing friendship with the People's Republic of China, this was cemented by a peace treaty and the visits of Chinese leaders to Tokyo. With her Soviet neighbour, however, Japan's relations remained extremely cool, no progress being made in the matter of the Russian-occupied 'northern territories'.

[III]

Can we attempt a summing up, even in very approximate terms, of the Japanese character? It will not be easy; for the more we know about people the less ready we are to make generalizations about them. To begin with a platitude: no two Japanese are like. As between them the dissimilarities, mental as well as physical, are those that distinguish two persons of any other race. It seems necessary to stress this point, trite though it may be, because even fairly well edu-

cated people in the West, if they lack first-hand knowledge
of the Orient, sometimes tend to imagine that the Japanese –
and the Chinese too for that matter – are more uniform in
temperament and appearance than, let us say, the English
or French.

It must be remembered, moreover, that what may be
broadly true for one age-group need not apply to another, a
generation younger. For example, the education of any
Japanese born after about 1937 has been on the whole so
different from the education that shaped his parents as to
make him in some sense a stranger to them. Where he has
been taught, in school at any rate, to attach supreme
importance to the rights and aspirations of the individual,
his elders, on the other hand, were brought up to distinguish between human feelings and civic obligations: a
distinction that exists also in Western societies but in a much
milder form, generally speaking, than was common in
Japan. Japanese literature and drama of the traditional kind
dealt almost obsessively with these two values and the conflict between them, in which civic obligations, the higher
duty – of vassal to lord, of subject to ruler – took precedence
over human feelings, however deep and legitimate. Traditional *mores*, it is true, counted for less in Meiji Japan and
thereafter than in Tokugawa times; but they were still held
in respect. It was accepted, for example, that a soldier
leaving for active service overseas must stifle human feeling
so far as to look upon himself as already dead to his own
family. Whether or not he was to return to Japan alive
should matter to him not at all.

No such indoctrination, needless to say, is given to young
recruits in the present Self-Defence Force. Many of them
would hardly understand a code of this sort even if it were
put to them. They are trained to serve not the emperor but
such concepts as 'freedom' and 'the people'.

It is worth bearing in mind the formalism often noted in
the language and demeanour of the Japanese is part of the
legacy of Tokugawa society, with its punctilious regard
for hierarchy; for this imposed a careful attention to the

niceties of speech and conduct. But Japanese politeness is no matter of mere convention. It is a highly valued social lubricant, hallowed by the sanctions of the past; and its utility is reinforced by the conditions of the present, when more people than ever have to live within a limited geographical area. When an Englishman or an American says that he is going to speak quite frankly, the statement is made with pride and received with approval. But in Japanese the phrase, 'to speak frankly', is used by way of apology for rudeness. Except among the young, frankness is not commonly regarded as a virtue. On the contrary it is often, though not invariably, considered to be a mark of boorishness or naïvety. A Japanese would think little of himself if he could not convey his meaning without being what we would call 'frank' or 'straightforward'.*

Some observers, noting that the Japanese possess an excitable and volatile temperament, have suggested that the traditional code of manners was adopted as an essential check on the socially disruptive consequences that could follow from the free exercise of this temperament. Whether or not this theory has any validity, it is undeniable that the Japanese temperament is the reverse of stable. Impassivity, where it is encountered, is usually the result of self-discipline. The very fact that calmness and harmony are among the highest ideals of the race implies that they do not come naturally to the Japanese. Here it is worth bearing in mind that in the old days there was a fundamental difference in outlook and behaviour between the shogunate officials, together with their vassals and retainers, and the common folk of Yedo. While the former were, on the whole, grave and severe the latter were in general fickle and hedonistic, life-loving and iconoclastic at the same time; and in this respect,

---

*But there are the exceptions that prove the rule. A 'great man', an extrovert of the Saigo Takamori type, is permitted some latitude in these matters. If the old-fashioned diplomatist or businessman did not like to say 'no', eschewing the direct negative as the brand of ill breeding, the same was not true for the soldier, who wanted to model himself on the rough, plain-spoken warrior of earlier days.

perhaps, they did not differ very radically from the citizens of modern Tokyo. One of the main aims of government in the latter part of the Meiji era was to mould the whole race into a single austere shape, patterned on the high-minded and somewhat forbidding *samurai* ideal.

We have noted in this book from time to time the eager curiosity that the Japanese have shown towards new ideas and techniques. This is part of their innate gusto. For all their formalism they are an exceedingly competitive people. They make loyal friends, as staunch as any in the world, tireless rivals, and determined enemies. With bouts of intense and, at times, quixotic sentimentality they combine an emotional realism that makes them resemble the French perhaps more than any other European race; and indeed France has long enjoyed a peculiarly high reputation among the Japanese. This has been the result, it must be said, of French excellence in the arts.

This brings us to the last point that can be made here about the character of the Japanese. One of the wisest experts on the subject has written of the Japanese that 'there seems to be a warmth and depth in their love of beauty which qualifies them as a race apart, or at least distinguishes them from the Greeks, as the features of a Buddhist image expressing love and mercy differ from the cold marble countenances of an Apollo or Artemis'.* Sir George Sansom is speaking here primarily of the Heian period, but his remarks seem hardly less apposite to the present day. The appreciation of beauty, both in nature and in art, is a fundamental ingredient of the Japanese character. This may seem a very bold statement to the traveller who has made the railway journey from Osaka to Tokyo and remembers not only the ugliness of those cities, as seen from the train, but also the succession of advertisement billboards that so often interfered with his view of the enchanting countryside along the route. But the love of beauty is never utterly crowded out by utilitarian and commercial con-

*G. Sansom, *A History of Japan to 1854*, London (Cresset Press), 1958, pp. 194-5.

siderations. Its expression may be in miniature, like the single fresh flower in a Tokyo taxi-cab, but it is rarely, if ever, entirely absent.

Irrepressible vitality and an instinctive love of beauty form the basic constituents of the Japanese character and are among its most admirable traits. Possessing these this race has much to give the world.

BIBLIOGRAPHICAL NOTE

In the English language alone the number of books on Japan is enormous. Here only a few of the better and more interesting works are listed as a guide for the reader who is thinking of embarking on a further study of some side of Japanese history.

The rather old-fashioned, though readable, standard history, from the earliest times to the Meiji Restoration, is James Murdoch and Isoh Yamagata, *A History of Japan*, London (Routledge & Kegan Paul), three vols., third impression, 1949. This work, completed many years ago, is corrected, if not superseded, by a history (up to 1854) written by Sir George Sansom in three volumes. These are George Sansom, *A History of Japan*, London (Cresset Press), vol. I, 1958; vol. II, 1961; vol. III, 1964. The same outstanding scholar is the author of the indispensable *Japan, A Short Cultural History*, London (Cresset Press), 1946. There is, also, an excellent outline history in a condensed form by Edwin O. Reischauer – *Japan: The Story of a Nation*, London (Duckworth), 1970. General historical accounts are A. L. Sadler, *A Short History of Japan*, Sydney (Angus & Robertson), 1963 (revised edition); Malcolm Kennedy, *A History of Japan*, London (Weidenfeld & Nicolson), 1963; and W. G. Beasley, *The Modern History of Japan*, London (Weidenfeld & Nicolson), 1963; also, John W. Hall, *Japan from Prehistory to Modern Times*, London (Weidenfeld & Nicolson), 1970. Notable for combining scholarly contributions on art, literature, political economy, and law, with a narrative history is Arthur E. Tiedemann (ed.), *An Introduction to Japanese Civilization*, New York (Columbia University Press), 1974. A luxury production for the connoisseur is Bradley Smith, *Japan, A History in Art*, London (Weidenfeld & Nicolson), 1964.

A justly acclaimed study of Heian court life is Ivan Morris, *The World of the Shining Prince*, London (Oxford University Press), 1964. Examples of admirable scholarly works, some of them recondite, dealing with Japanese feudalism, are John W. Hall, *Government and Local Power in Japan, 1500–1700*, Princeton, N.J. (Princeton University Press), 1966; Jeffrey P. Mass, *Warrior Government in Early Mediaeval Japan*, New Haven (Yale University Press), 1974; H. Paul Varley, *The Onin War*, New York (Columbia University Press), 1967. For the reactions to Japan of foreign visitors and residents in the sixteenth and seventeenth centuries the reader should see the two handsome books edited by Michael Cooper, s.j., namely, *They Came to Japan: An Anthology of European Reports on Japan 1543–1640*, London (Thames & Hudson), 1965, and *The Southern Barbarians*, Tokyo (Kodansha International), 1971. For the story of the Catholic missions in that period the outstanding work is C. R. Boxer, *The Christian Century in Japan*, London (Cambridge University Press), second, corrected, printing, 1967. The same period is covered in part by an interesting biography of Tokugawa Ieyasu – A. L. Sadler, *The Maker of Modern Japan*, London (Allen & Unwin), 1937. The tale of Will Adams is told in P. G. Rogers, *The First Englishman in Japan*, London (Harvill Press), 1956. Notable studies on some of the political thinkers of the Tokugawa age are David M. Earl, *Emperor and Nation in Japan*, Seattle (University of Washington Press), 1964, and Shigeru Matsumoto, *Motoori Norinaga 1730–1801*, Cambridge, Massachusetts (Harvard University Press), 1970. A profound work on the philosophical currents influencing that period is Masao Maruyama, *Studies in the Intellectual History of Tokugawa Japan*, Tokyo (University of Tokyo Press), 1974. A reassessment of *samurai* motives in the period is provided by Harold Bolitho, *Treasures among Men: The Fudai Daimyo in Tokugawa Japan*, New Haven (Yale University Press), 1974. Recommended as a guide to the humdrum domestic scene in that age is C. J. Dunn, *Everyday Life in Traditional Japan*, London (Batsford), 1969. On schools and schoolmasters of that era a pioneer work in the English language is the excellent R. P. Dore, *Education in Tokugawa Japan*, London (Routledge & Kegan Paul), 1965.

Two books dealing, respectively, with Perry's expedition and the first resident foreign diplomatist in Japan are Arthur Walworth, *Black Ships off Japan*, New York (Alfred Knopf), 1941, and M. E. Cosenza (ed.), *The Complete Journal of Townsend Harris*, New York (Doubleday), 1930. The best study of the general impact of European civilization on Japan up to the last years of the nineteenth century is Sir George Sansom, *The Western World and Japan*, London (Cresset Press), 1950.

On the twilight years of the Tokugawa *Bakufu* three interesting works are J. H. Gubbins, *The Progress of Japan, 1853–71*, Oxford (Clarendon Press), 1911; Sir Ernest Satow, *A Diplomat in Japan*, London (Seeley, Service), 1921; and Sir Rutherford Alcock, *The Capital of the Tycoon*, London (Longmans, Green), two vols., 1863. Two important scholarly works dealing with particular aspects of this period are Marius B. Jansen, *Sakamoto Ryoma and the Meiji*

Restoration, Princeton, N.J. (Princeton University Press), 1961, and Albert M. Craig, *Choshu in the Meiji Restoration*, Cambridge, Massachusetts (Harvard University Press), 1961. On a more popular level a very readable book about foreigners (mostly British and Americans) in Japan at the time is Pat Barr, *The Coming of the Barbarians*, London (Macmillan), 1967. She has also written *The Deer Cry Pavilion*, London (Macmillan), 1968 on the same theme.

W. G. Beasley, *The Meiji Restoration*, Stanford, California (Stanford University Press), 1972 is a *magnum opus* on its subject. Chitoshi Yanaga, *Japan Since Perry*, New York (McGraw Hill), 1949, and Hugh Borton, *Japan's Modern Century*, New York (Ronald Press), 1955, cover in some detail the three reigns of the modern age – Meiji, Taisho, and Showa – up to the immediate post-war period.

The problems, economic and political, of the Meiji era receive scholarly treatment in E. H. Norman, *Japan's Emergence as a Modern State*, New York (Institute of Pacific Relations), 1940. A work of like calibre, but offering a rather different interpretation is Johannes Hirschmeier, *The Origins of Entrepreneurship in Meiji Japan*, Cambridge, Massachusetts (Harvard University Press), 1964. Carmen Blacker, *The Japanese Enlightenment*, Cambridge (Cambridge University Press), 1964, provides an admirable analysis of some of the ideas of the pioneer modernizer, Fukuzawa Yukichi. Anyone interested in Fukuzawa should also read Eiichi Kiyooka (translation), *The Autobiography of Yukichi Fukuzawa*, London (Columbia University Press), 1966. Important works on early Meiji politics are Thomas R. Havens, *Nishi Amane and Modern Thought*, Princeton, N.J. (Princeton University Press), 1970; Nobutake Ike, *The Beginnings of Political Democracy in Japan*, Baltimore (Johns Hopkins Press), 1950; Joseph Pittau, *Political Thought in Early Meiji Japan 1868-1889*, Cambridge, Massachusetts (Harvard University Press), 1967; and George Akita, *Foundations of Constitutional Government in Modern Japan, 1868-1900*, Cambridge, Massachusetts (Harvard University Press), 1967. Authoritative biographies of two important Meiji figures are Ivan Parker Hall, *Mori Arinori*, Cambridge, Massachusetts (Harvard University Press), 1973, and Roger Hackett, *Yamagata Aritomo in the Rise of Modern Japan 1838-1922*, Cambridge, Massachusetts (Harvard University Press), 1971. Two interesting works on contrasting aspects of the Meiji scene are Irwin Scheiner, *Christian Converts and Social Protest in Meiji Japan*, Berkeley (University of California Press), 1970, and Shumpei Okamoto, *The Japanese Oligarchy* nd the

Russo-Japanese War, New York (Columbia University Press), 1970. A further instructive work is Kenneth Pyle, *The New Generation in Meiji Japan*, Stanford, California (Stanford University Press), 1969; and a scholarly biography of a radical dissenter of the Meiji era is F. G. Notelhelfer, *Kotoku Shusui*, Cambridge (Cambridge University Press), 1971. A reliable work on Meiji party politics, and those of the next two decades, is Robert A. Scalapino, *Democracy and the Party Movement in Pre-War Japan*, Berkeley (University of California Press), 1953. A shorter work on the same subject is Robert K. Reischauer, *Japan, Government and Politics*, New York (Nelson), 1939. There is also the old-fashioned but useful compilation, Shigenobu Okuma (and others), *Fifty Years of New Japan*, London (Smith, Elder), two vols., 1909. Hilary Conroy, *The Japanese Seizure of Korea*, Philadelphia (University of Pennsylvania Press), 1960, is a study in detail of Japan's relations with Korea prior to annexation. Throwing light on other important aspects of the Meiji period are the following: *Awakening Japan: The Diary of a German Doctor: Erwin Baelz*, Bloomington, Indiana (Indiana University Press), 1974; Jean-Pierre Lehmann, *The Image of Japan: From Feudal Isolation to World Power, 1850–1905*, London (Allen & Unwin), 1978; and H. J. Jones, *Live Machines: Hired Foreigners and Meiji Japan*, Tenterden, Kent (Paul Norbury), 1980.

On the interplay of foreign and domestic issues in Japanese political life, during the 1920s and after, an authoritative study is Tatsuji Takeuchi, *War and Diplomacy in the Japanese Empire*, London (Allen & Unwin), 1936. Stimulating works focussing on Japanese policy in China in the second half of the 1920s are Nobuya Bamba, *Japanese Diplomacy in a Dilemma*, Vancouver (University of British Columbia Press), 1972; and William F. Morton, *Tanaka Giichi and Japan's China Policy*, Folkestone, Kent (William Dawson), 1980. The origins and history of Japan's alliance with Great Britain are thoroughly analysed and narrated in two books by Ian H. Nish, *The Anglo-Japanese Alliance*, London (University of London, Athlone Press), 1966, and *Alliance in Decline, A Study in Anglo-Japanese Relations 1908–23*, London (Athlone Press), 1972. Covering a wider field is a later work by the same scholar; namely, Ian Nish, *Japanese Foreign Policy, 1869–1942*, London (Routledge & Kegan Paul), 1977. Two useful studies of the Taisho era (1912–26) are Peter Duus, *Party Rivalry and Political Change in Taisho Japan*, Cambridge, Massachusetts (Harvard University Press), 1968, and Bernard S. Silberman (ed.) and H. D. Harootunian (ed.), *Japan in Crisis: Essays on Taisho Democracy*, Princeton, New Jersey

(Princeton University Press), 1974. Morgan Young's books – *Japan Under Taisho Tenno, 1912–26*, London (Allen & Unwin), 1928, and *Imperial Japan, 1926–38*, London (Allen & Unwin), 1938 – are very readable. Written in a somewhat caustic vein, they are not works of academic scholarship, but they are not necessarily unreliable on that account. An interesting academic study of the diplomatic history of the period between the Washington Conference and the Manchurian Incident is Akira Iriye, *After Imperialism*, Cambridge, Massachusetts (Harvard University Press), 1965. For the stormy decade preceding Pearl Harbor the reader should see David Anson Titus, *Palace and Politics in Pre-War Japan*, New York (Columbia University Press), 1974; Mark R. Peattie, *Ishiwara Kanji and Japan's Confrontation with the West*, Princeton, N.J. (Princeton University Press), 1975; George M. Wilson, *Radical Nationalist in Japan: Kita Ikki 1883–1937*, Cambridge, Massachusetts (Harvard University Press), 1969; Ben-Ami Shillony, *Revolt in Japan*, Princeton, N.J. (Princeton University Press), 1973; Richard Storry, *The Double Patriots*, London (Chatto & Windus), 1957; Joseph C. Grew, *Ten Years in Japan*, London (Hammond), 1944; and Hugh Byas, *Government by Assassination*, London (Allen & Unwin), 1943. Y. C. Maxon, *Control of Japanese Foreign Policy*, Berkeley (University of California Press), 1957, is a detailed review of civil–military rivalry between 1930 and 1945. Takehiko Yoshihashi, *Conspiracy at Mukden*, New Haven (Yale University Press), 1963, is an authoritative examination of the opening moves in the Manchurian Incident. The same may be said of Sadako N. Ogata, *Defiance in Manchuria*, Berkeley (University of California Press), 1964. Another work on the 1930s, of a scholarly character, is James B. Crowley, *Japan's Quest for Autonomy*, Princeton, New Jersey (Princeton University Press), 1966. The persecution of a famous liberal scholar is powerfully described in Frank O. Miller, *Minobe Tatsukichi*, Berkeley (University of California Press), 1965. The eclipse of the political parties is the theme of G. M. Berger, *Parties out of Power in Japan, 1931–1941*, Princeton, New Jersey (Princeton University Press), 1977.

The events leading up to the outbreak of the Pacific War are dealt with in Herbert Feis, *The Road to Pearl Harbor*, Princeton, New Jersey (Princeton University Press), 1950. Anglo-Japanese relations, 1937–41, are the main concern of Nicholas R. Clifford, *Retreat from China*, London (Longmans), 1967. Japanese foreign relations from 1937 to 1945 are the theme of F. C. Jones, *Japan's*

New Order in East Asia, London (Oxford University Press), 1954. Key works here, however, are Robert J. C. Butow, *Tojo and the Coming of the War*, Princeton, New Jersey (Princeton University Press), 1960; D. J. Lu, *From the Marco Polo Bridge to Pearl Harbor*, Washington (Public Affairs Press), 1961; and N. Ike, *Japan's Decision for War*, Stanford, California (Stanford University Press), 1967. To that list should be added R. J. C. Butow, *The John Doe Associates*, Stanford, California (Stanford University Press), 1974; Dorothy Borg and Shumpei Okamoto (ed.), *Pearl Harbor As History*, New York (Columbia University Press), 1973; and James W. Morley (ed.), *Japan's Foreign Policy 1868–1941, A Research Guide*, New York (Columbia University Press), 1974.

The broad subject of Japanese nationalism through the ages is covered by Delmer Brown, *Nationalism in Japan*, Berkeley (University of California Press), 1955. The extreme Right since the Pacific War is discussed by Ivan Morris in *Nationalism and the Right Wing in Japan*, London (Oxford University Press), 1960. The same scholar is the author of *The Nobility of Failure*, London (Secker & Warburg), 1975, a remarkable study of Japan's tragic heroes through the ages. At the other end of the political spectrum Japanese communism is the subject of two excellent works, Roger Swearingen and Paul Langer, *Red Flag in Japan*, Cambridge, Massachusetts (Harvard University Press), 1952, and Robert A. Scalapino, *The Japanese Communist Movement, 1920–1966*, Berkeley (University of California Press), 1967. Labour relations and social democracy are discussed, historically, by Iwao F. Ayusawa, *A History of Labour in Modern Japan*, Honolulu (East-West Center Press), 1966, and George Oakley Tutton III, *The Social Democratic Movement in Pre-War Japan*, New Haven (Yale University Press), 1966. An outstanding series of essays, of the highest intellectual quality, is to be found in Masao Maruyama, *Thought and Behaviour in Modern Japanese Politics*, London (Oxford University Press), 1963. A further study of the pressures faced by pre-war intellectuals in Japan is Tatsuo Arima, *The Failure of Freedom*, Cambridge, Massachusetts (Harvard University Press), 1969.

A masterly account of the course of events in Tokyo before the Pacific War ended is provided by Robert J. C. Butow, *Japan's Decision to Surrender*, Stanford, California (Stanford University Press), 1954. The domestic scene during the war is examined by Thomas Havens, *Valley of Darkness*, New York (W. W. Norton), 1978, and by Ben-Ami Shillony, *Politics and Culture in Wartime*

Japan, Oxford (Clarendon Press), 1981. On policies and plans for Japanese-occupied south-east Asia there is Joyce Lebra (ed.), *Japan's Greater East Asia Co-Prosperity Sphere in World War II: Selected Readings and Documents*, Kuala Lumpur (Oxford University Press), 1975.

For the early period of the Occupation most of the basic political documents are to be found in SCAP Government Section, *Political Orientation of Japan, September 1945 to September 1948*, Washington (U.S. Government Printing Office), two vols., 1949. Reviews of the Occupation are Edwin M. Martin, *The Allied Occupation of Japan*, Stanford, California (Stanford University Press), 1948; Robert A. Fearey, *The Occupation of Japan, Second Phase: 1948–50*, New York (Macmillan); and Kazuo Kawai, *Japan's American Interlude*, Chicago (Chicago University Press), 1960. For critical appraisals of the period the reader can see W. MacMahon Ball, *Japan, Enemy or Ally?*, New York (John Day), 1949, and H. E. Wildes, *Typhoon in Tokyo*, London (Allen & Unwin), 1954. Here one should add a study of the Tokyo War Crimes Trial, Richard Minear, *Victors' Justice*, Princeton, N.J. (Princeton University Press), 1971.

Hugh Borton and others, *Japan Between East and West*, New York (Harper), 1957, discusses events and ideas in Japan in the years immediately following the Peace Treaty. On the modern political scene in Japan, two sound and stimulating works are John M. Maki, *Government and Politics in Japan*, London (Thames & Hudson), 1962, and Robert A. Scalapino and Junnosuke Masumi, *Parties and Politics in Contemporary Japan*, Berkeley (University of California Press), 1962. An admirably well-balanced survey in the same field is J. A. A. Stockwin, *Japan: Divided Politics in a Growth Economy*, London (Weidenfeld & Nicolson), 1975. Japanese socialism receives scholarly attention in Allan B. Cole, George O. Totten and Cecil H. Uyehara, *Socialist Parties in Postwar Japan*, New Haven (Yale University Press), 1966. Also to be recommended highly, as a concise but interpretative survey, is Theodore McNelly, *Contemporary Government of Japan*, London (Allen & Unwin), 1964. Readers interested in modern Japanese constitutional law should see John M. Maki, *Court and Constitution in Japan*, Seattle (University of Washington Press), 1964. A work devoted to the 1960 demonstrations in Japan is George R. Packard III, *Protest in Tokyo, The Security Treaty Crisis of 1960*, Princeton, New Jersey (Princeton University Press), 1966. A creditable biography of the Emperor is Leonard Mosley, *Hirohito*, London (Weidenfeld Nicolson), 1966.

In the field of economics there are four noteworthy books by G. C. Allen – *A Short Economic History of Modern Japan, 1867–1937*, London (Allen & Unwin), 1951; *Japan's Economic Recovery*, London (Oxford University Press), 1958; *Japan's Economic Expansion*, London (Oxford University Press), 1965; and *The Japanese Economy*, London (Weidenfeld & Nicolson), 1981. Also to be recommended are W. W. Lockwood, *The Economic Development of Japan*, London (Oxford University Press), 1955, and two books by Jerome B. Cohen, namely *Japan's Economy in War and Reconstruction*, Minneapolis (University of Minnesota Press), 1949, and *Japan's Postwar Economy*, Bloomington, Indiana (Indiana University Press), 1958. *Consider Japan*, London (Duckworth), 1963, by correspondents of *The Economist*, is a brief but vivid survey of the economic scene. The serious student of this scene is well advised, also, to read Robert Ballon, *Doing Business in Japan*, Tokyo (Sophia University, with Tuttle), 1967. Important works dealing with religion in Japan, are Sir Charles Eliot, *Japanese Buddhism*, London (Edward Arnold) 1935; M. Anesaki, *A History of Japanese Religion*, London (Kegan Paul), 1938; D. T. Suzuki, *Studies in Zen*, London (Rider), 1955; D. C. Holtom, *The National Faith of Japan*, London (Kegan Paul), 1938; and his *Modern Japan and Shinto Nationalism*, Chicago (Chicago University Press), 1947. Harry Thomsen, *The New Religions of Japan*, Tokyo (Tuttle), 1963, discusses some interesting post-war religious developments.

A valuable sociological study of rural life before the Pacific War is John F. Embree, *A Japanese Village*, London (Kegan Paul), 1946. An equally important and interesting book on urban life during the last year of the Occupation is R. P. Dore, *City Life in Japan*, London (Routledge & Kegan Paul), 1958. The same gifted scholar is the author of *Land Reform in Japan*, London (Oxford University Press), 1959, and translator of Tadashi Fukutake, *Japanese Rural Society*, Tokyo (Oxford University Press), 1967. Two other works of sociology, among many, are Ezra F. Vogel, *Japan's New Middle Class*, Berkeley (University of California Press), 1963, and David W. Plath, *The After Hours, Modern Japan and the Search for Enjoyment*, Berkeley (University of California Press), 1964. Perhaps the best collection of photographs of Japan and the Japanese is to be found in W. Bischof, *Japan*, London (Sylvan Press), 1954. An entertaining work, good-humoured and sophisticated, is Bernard Rudofsky,

The Kimono Mind, London (Gollancz), 1965. More serious fare is supplied by David Riesman and Evelyn Thompson Riesman, *Conversations in Japan*, London (Allen Lane The Penguin Press), 1967. Further interesting works are Ronald Dore, *British Factory – Japanese Factory*, London (Allen & Unwin), 1973; George A. De Vos, *Socialization for Achievement: Essays on the Cultural Psychology of the Japanese*, Berkeley (University of California Press), 1973; Shuichi Kato, *Form, Style, Tradition*, Berkeley (University of California Press), 1971 and Richard Storry (ed.), *Kurt Singer: Mirror, Sword and Jewel*, London (Croom Helm), 1973.

Mention must be made of Ruth Benedict, *The Chrysanthemum and the Sword*, Boston (Houghton Mifflin), 1946, an investigation of the pattern of Japanese culture; but this good book has been adversely criticized by some reliable specialists; and we must remember that its conclusions may have diminishing validity as the years go by.

The following are a small sample of a large number of admirable works dealing with Japanese art and literature: R. T. Paine and A. Soper, *The Art and Architecture of Japan*, Harmondsworth (Penguin: Pelican History of Art), 1955; Peter C. Swann, *Introduction to the Arts of Japan*, Oxford (Cassirer), 1958; J. Hillier, *The Japanese Print, A New Approach*, London (Bell), 1960; Donald Keene, *Japanese Literature*, London (Murray), 1953; Donald Keene (ed.), *Modern Japanese Literature*, London (Thames & Hudson), 1956; T. Ninomiya and D. Enright, *The Poetry of Living Japan*, London (Murray), 1955; Ernest Earle, *The Kabuki Theatre*, London (Secker & Warburg), 1956; I. Morris (ed.), *Modern Japanese Stories*, Tokyo (Tuttle), 1962; Geoffrey Bownas and Anthony Thwaite, *The Penguin Book of Japanese Verse*, Harmondsworth (Penguin), 1964; J. M. Richards, *An Architectural Journey in Japan*, London (The Architectural Press), 1963; Donald Keene, *Landscapes and Portraits; Appreciations of Japanese Culture*, London (Secker & Warburg), 1972. To these we must add Hisaaki Yamanouchi, *The Search for Authenticity in Modern Japanese Literature*, Cambridge (Cambridge University Press), 1978, and Shuichi Kato, *A History of Japanese Literature: The First Thousand Years*, London and Tenterden, Kent (Macmillan and Paul Norbury), 1979.

A useful interpretative work of a general kind is John W. Hall & Richard K. Beardsley, *Twelve Doors to Japan*, New York (McGraw Hill), 1965. Three other excellent works are R. Tsuno-da, W. T. de Bary & Donald Keene, *Sources of the Japanese Tradition*, New

York (Columbia University Press), 1958; Fosco Maraini, *Meeting with Japan*, London (Hutchinson), 1959; and Donald Keene, *Living Japan*, London (Heinemann), 1959. The flavour of daily living in urban Japan is well conveyed by James Kirkup in his *Tokyo*, London (Phoenix House), 1966, and *Japan Behind the Fan*, London (Dent), 1970.

Also to be recommended are the following: Chie Nakane, *Japanese Society*, London (Weidenfeld & Nicolson), 1970; Nathaniel Thayer, *How the Conservatives Rule Japan*, Princeton, N.J. (Princeton University Press), 1969; Robert Cole, *Japanese Blue Collar*, London (University of California Press), 1971; Lawrence Olson, *Japan in Postwar Asia*, London (Pall Mall Press), 1970; Robert Guillain, *The Japanese Challenge*, London (Hamish Hamilton), 1970; Martin Weinstein, *Japan's Postwar Defense Policy, 1947–1968*, London (Columbia University Press), 1971; Herman Kahn, *The Emerging Japanese Superstate*, London (Andre Deutsch), 1971; E. O. Reischauer, *The Japanese*, Cambridge, Mass. (Harvard University Press), 1977; Ezra Vogel, *Japan as Number One: Lessons for America*, Cambridge, Mass. (Harvard University Press), 1979; and Endymion Wilkinson, *Misunderstanding: Europe versus Japan*, Tokyo (Chuokoron-sha), 1981.

Finally, let us add to this long list the following highly commendable studies: Staff of Asahi Shimbun, *The Pacific Rivals: A Japanese View of Japanese-American Relations*, Tokyo (Weatherhill/Asahi), 1972; Kenichi Yoshida, *Japan is a Circle: A Tour round the Mind of Modern Japan*, London (Paul Norbury), 1975; Frank Gibney, *Japan, The Fragile Super Power*, New York (W. W. Norton), 1975; Fosco Maraini, *Japan, Patterns of Continuity*, Tokyo (Kodansha International), 1971; Nobuya Bamba and John Howes (eds.), *Pacifism in Japan*, Vancouver (University of British Columbia Press), 1978; Victor Koschmann, *Authority and the Individual in Japan*, Tokyo (University of Tokyo Press), 1978; Murakami Hyoe and Johannes Hirschmeier (eds.), *Politics and Economics in Contemporary Japan*, Tokyo (Japan Culture Institute), 1979; Ernest van Helvoort, *The Japanese Working Man: What Choice? What Reward?*, Tenterden, Kent (Paul Norbury), 1979; Donald Roden, *Schooldays in Imperial Japan: A Study in the Culture of a Student Elite*, Berkeley (University of California Press), 1980; and Marius Jansen, *Japan and its World: Two Centuries of Change*, Princeton, New Jersey (Princeton University Press), 1980.

INDEX